BRAZILIAN
POLITICS

For my daughter, Diana, who has made me a better teacher by making me a student once again

BRAZILIAN POLITICS

REFORMING A DEMOCRATIC STATE IN A CHANGING WORLD

ALFRED P. MONTERO

polity

First published in 2005 by Polity Press

Polity Press
65 Bridge Street
Cambridge CB2 1UR, UK

Polity Press
350 Main Street
Malden, MA 02148, USA

ISBN: 0-7456-3360-9
ISBN: 0-7456-3361-7 (pb)

A catalogue record for this book is available from the British Library.

Typeset in 10 on 12 pt Sabon
by SNP Best-set Typesetter Ltd, Hong Kong
Printed and bound in the United States by the Maple-Vail Book Manufacturing Group

For further information on Polity, visit our website: www.polity.co.uk

CONTENTS

FIGURES

TABLES

Map of Brazil

An Introduction to Brazilian Politics

Porto Alegre, Brazil, and Davos, Switzerland, are two cities divided by more than an ocean. Since 2001 Porto Alegre has been home to the World Social Forum (WSF), an annual meeting of activists, scholars, and non-governmental organizations who share core concerns about the effects of global economic integration on inequality and environmental sustainability. Davos, the traditional base of the annual World Economic Forum (WEF), serves as a place of reunion for leading financial and industrial barons, economic scholars, and rich-country policy-makers. Porto Alegre and Davos have thus come to symbolize the divide between rich and poor in the world today.

It is between these two worlds that the current president of Brazil, Luiz Inácio "Lula" da Silva, is guiding his country. Once the guest of honor at the WSF in Porto Alegre and a no-show at Davos, in January 2003 Lula addressed a crowd of 75,000 cheering activists in Porto Alegre one afternoon and then jetted to Davos to address a more sedate, but no less enthusiastic, audience of bankers and industrial leaders. Having just won the presidency in October 2002 and only a couple of weeks after being handed the presidential sash by his predecessor, Fernando Henrique Cardoso (1994–2002), the ex-labor leader turned president was sending a message to both worlds, rich and poor. To the world represented at Davos, Lula wished to reassure investors and analysts who for months had been wondering out loud if the first leftist president to be elected in Brazil would disengage the ninth largest economy of the world from global markets. Lula's words concerning his government's dedication to market-friendly reforms, stable prices, and pro-investment and growth policies had the desired calming effect. To the crowds gathered at Porto Alegre, Lula stuck to his erstwhile campaign to rid the world of hunger and to fight misery in the developing world. What was striking about each presentation was how coherent his message was – how connected Lula saw the priorities of both the WSF and the WEF. He reminded the rich-country representatives that misery and hunger exist and that reducing inequality must be the top concern of development. And he reminded the throngs gathered at the WSF that promoting greater equity without securing economic growth through more competitive integration into the world economy was an impossibility.

The transformation of Lula's message to the WSF, in particular, represented an evolution in criticism of "globalization," a term used by many to describe the growing interdependence of the world's economies. Since it started in 2001, the World Social Forum has been divided between radicals who call for a fundamental transformation of the world capitalist system along socialist lines and a reformist group of non-governmental organizations (NGOs), politicians, union leaders, and movement activists who do not oppose globalization but wish to "humanize" it by making the distribution of its benefits more equal (Petras 2002). The WSF's slogan, "Another World Is Possible," speaks mostly to the pragmatic view of the second group. It is to this vision of global change that the current president of Brazil appeals in his talks with trade partners, the multilateral agencies overseeing Brazil's economic reforms, and international financial and corporate investors.

Lula's common message in Davos and Porto Alegre reflects a pragmatic governing style that bespeaks the maturation of Brazilian democracy, its evolution from a system that strictly benefits the well positioned and economically well endowed to one that attempts to address the problems of the dispossessed. For example, Lula's Workers' Party (*Partido dos Trabalhadores*, PT) is committed to broadening participation and enhancing transparency and accountability in government. This represents a sharp break with Brazil's long history of patrimonial rule for and by the few. Unlike most of its rivals, the PT enjoys the support of an extensive network of grass-roots organizations, including Brazil's largest labor confederation, new social movements, assorted non-governmental organizations, and progressive elements of the professional and academic elite. While Lula's predecessor, Cardoso, did not have as disciplined a party as the PT in his corner, he ruled with the same pragmatic style. Like Lula, Cardoso was a former leftist turned moderate who initiated a reform agenda that Lula is now dedicated to advance. Both presidents replaced ideological purity with practical political strategies. As Lula once put it regarding his cabinet appointments: "I want ministers who can produce results, not hypotheses or conversation."[1] The two presidents favored negotiating with centrist and right-wing parties rather than excluding these as opposition forces. They both focused on reasonable and viable goals and paid less heed to the methods used to achieve these ends.

And yet, in a political system as complicated as Brazil's, in a country with immense social and economic problems that seem as big as its large territory, pragmatic reform and modest progress always seem out of step with what is needed. For example, assessments of Cardoso's two terms in office tend to emphasize the progress he made in pushing some items of his reform agenda forward, particularly some fiscal and administrative reform, and his success in consolidating Brazil's transition to a free market economy. But these evaluations are almost always qualified by acknowledgement of the country's mediocre growth rate, inability to deal with most of the causes of poverty and inequality, and the slow speed and limited depth of the reforms themselves (Lamounier 2003: 269–70). Brazil's persisting social inequality is perhaps the worst of these problems, as Fernando Henrique Cardoso himself admitted soon after his

1 *Brazil Focus*, 17–23 January 2004, p. 3.

inauguration in 1995: "Brazil is not any longer an underdeveloped country. It is an unjust country."[2]

At times Brazil seems to change only in ways that avoid the worst case scenarios, but not in ways that fundamentally alter its trajectory of growth with inequality. This makes Brazil a country of odd juxtapositions: a modern, industrial economy on one side and an impoverished, unequal society on the other. The Brazilian author Francisco de Oliveira (2003) likens these incongruities in Brazil to a duckbilled platypus, a misshapen mixture of distinct kinds and levels of economic, social, and political development. Many of these aspects are in contradiction with one another. One example that Oliveira and other authors point to is the fact that the Brazilian "platypus" currently depends on large flows of capital from abroad to fuel its modern, industrialized, and service-based economy. The growth of foreign and domestic debt has in recent years outpaced the capacity of the state to make progress on the principal. Counting interest payments and amortization on the principal, Brazil spends the equivalent of almost 10 percent of its GDP on its debt. The total debt stands at over 55 percent of GDP and it is growing at an alarming rate. Oliveira (2003: 47) argues that this financial dependency is equivalent to the dependency that limited Brazil's development before 1930, when most of the economy was still controlled by coffee exporters. Pessimistically, he concludes: "the platypus has lost the capacity to choose; therewith its evolution is truncated" (ibid.: 48).

That Brazil is at an "evolutionary dead end" may be too fatalistic an observation, but that the country has evolved in ways in which the fruits of economic development and democratization are unequally distributed is undeniable. To understand this complex country one must investigate several incongruities in Brazil's political and economic evolution. This chapter introduces five thematic areas that will be the focus of more involved examination in subsequent chapters:

1   the centrality of the state and state-formation in contemporary Brazilian politics
2   the dilemma of democratic representation in an oligarchical society
3   the weakening of democratic institutions by patterns of uneven development and social inequality
4   the challenges and possibilities of the emergence of a democratic civil society
5   Brazil's position and identity in the global economy and the world of states.

These five areas may be synthesized into five questions that reflect the key challenges to Brazilian democracy and economic development in an era of globalization: (1) Does the process of reforming the state strengthen or weaken democratic institutions? (2) How can representative institutions be changed to reflect the will of the people and not the political class, as has historically been the case in Brazil? (3) How can democratic institutions be strengthened in the context of gross social and economic inequalities? (4) Is the revitalization of civil society, particularly social movements and NGOs, necessary and sufficient for reversing the socio-structural, cultural, and institutional factors

---

2   This quotation is famous because Cardoso repeated it soon after he was inaugurated. But its origins are found in the unpublished government pamphlet *Mãos à Obra Brasil* (1994).

that have weakened democracy in Brazil's past? (5) Do international political and economic structures, now changing quickly in the context of globalization, present new opportunities for enhancing democracy and development or do they more fundamentally challenge Brazil's future prosperity?

After an overview of Brazil's geography, demography, and economy, this chapter explores each of these five themes in greater detail. Each theme addresses essential dilemmas or tradeoffs that involve to some degree the evolution of Brazilian democracy and economic development.

Geography, demography, and the economy

The most distinctive physical feature of Brazil is its sheer size. With its 8.5 million square kilometers, Brazil is, as many of its inhabitants regard it, "a country of continental size." The Amazonian border alone is some 11,200 kilometers long, making it virtually impossible to patrol. It dominates the South American continent, taking up 47 percent of the landmass, and sharing borders with every country on the continent except Ecuador and Chile. Running east to west, the country stretches across four time zones. It embraces virtually every kind of climate and topography on earth, including tropical jungle and marshland in the Amazon and the Pantanal, mountain ranges along the Atlantic coast, semi-arid scrubland, plains and badlands (the rugged *sertão*) in the center-west and north, and dense forest in the south. Brazil is also home to ten of the world's twenty largest rivers, among them the Amazon, the world's largest in volume.

Brazil has the sixth largest population of any country in the world, with 170 million inhabitants. The annual population growth rate is moderate (1.3 percent). That means that the total population will level off at 250 million by 2050 and the population density will remain at the current level of eighteen to twenty per square kilometer, a figure four times smaller than density levels in advanced societies such as the United States, France, and the United Kingdom. Regarding gender and age, the Brazilian population is skewed in favor of women and the young. Brazilian women outnumber men by 5 million. The total population is also strikingly young, with the proportion of people under the age of fifteen outnumbering those over sixty-five by a factor of six (30 percent to 5 percent, respectively). Yet, as is the case with all modernizing societies, decreasing mortality and fertility levels are increasing the average age of the population so that the number of Brazilians over sixty-five will double by the year 2020. The fertility rate has fallen in the last ten years from 2.44 children per family and is nearing 2.22, the replacement level for the population. This marks a noticeable drop from fifty years ago, when fertility rates were closer to 6.0 and family planning techniques were not as widely available as they are today. On the other end of the lifecycle, life expectancy increased from 42.7 years in 1940 to 68.5 in 2000 and it is expected to climb to rich-country levels (approximately 75.5) in 2020. The availability of improved medical care, such as regular vaccination, preventive care, and the expansion of the ranks of doctors and nurses in rural areas, has reduced infant mortality rates and adult deaths.

The national identity of Brazilians is strongly focused on their self-image as "Brazilians" and not as smaller ethnically or linguistically defined "nations" within the country. But, as in many other countries in Latin America, Brazilian society is divided by distinct social categories, including class, race, religion, and region. The class structure is analyzed more fully in chapter 5, but here we may note that social inequality is the most distinct feature of Brazilian society. One rough indicator of social disparity is the fact that the top 1 percent of the population retains 40 percent of the wealth of the country. That makes Brazil one of the most unequal societies in the world. Racial divisions, which overlap with these social class distinctions in many ways (see chapter 5), are difficult to gauge precisely because the definition of who is "black" in Brazil is the subject of much cultural, political, social, and policy debate. Brazilians actually use, and the law recognizes, many distinctions made about levels of "blackness." As many as 150 are employed formally or informally today. Since the fine distinctions of "blackness" are of secondary relevance to our purpose here, we may follow the example of many recent scholars of racial politics in Brazil and conflate all of these categories into "Afro-Brazilian" (e.g., Andrews 1991; Johnson 1998). With that assumption in mind, we note that 55 percent of the population self-reports itself as "white," while 30 percent of respondents in the census claim to be "mulatto" and 5 percent call themselves "black." Less than 1 percent of the population self-reports as Asian, indigenous, or other. These aggregate results belie what is evident to any foreign observer, that Brazil is a more racially mixed society than the US or virtually any other country with a history of African slavery. The difference between the average Brazilian's self-perception of their own race and the view from the outside suggests that racial identity is complex and not easily subject to categorization.

Brazilian society is also divided by religion, but here the categories are few and self-identity is clearer. Despite the growth of Pentecostal Protestantism and the emergence of charismatic churches throughout Brazil in recent years, over 76 percent of the population is Roman Catholic. That makes Brazil the most Catholic country in the world, with 122 million worshippers. Protestants number 28.2 million and represent the fastest growing denomination outside of Catholicism. Mixed "syncretic" traditions are another element in the religious profile of Brazilians. Afro-Brazilian cult religions, known as *umbanda*, operate alongside the Catholic liturgy. One example is the use of African names for Catholic saints and the practice of African spiritual traditions on religious holidays of significance to Catholics. The Catholic Church does not formally recognize *umbanda* in its liturgical traditions, but Brazilians practice them anyway as a meaningful spiritual experience that adds to their life as Catholics.

Brazil is a multiregional country with distinct local traditions in cuisine, art, dance, and music, but these regional identities are not based on linguistic or nationalistic differences. Despite the fact that secessionist and other kinds of local revolts and revolutions have occurred throughout Brazilian history (see chapter 2), the regional identities some of these movements retained were not due to distinct linguistic or national identities. The dominance of one language – Portuguese – and one national identity around which most Brazilians appeal makes Brazil a *multicultural* but not a *multinational* state. This is especially apparent during moments of great unity such as the annual *Carnaval* celebrations and the World Soccer Championships when the members of the national team – white, black, and mulatto, Catholic and Protestant – operate as one for the honor of the country. Of course, indigenous peoples, who number only about 300,000, speak native languages and see themselves as having unique cultures. But their influence on the national Brazilian identity has been nominal. Immigrants, especially Italian, Spanish, Portuguese, Japanese, Chinese, and Korean groups, have added a dynamic cultural and linguistic mixture to Brazil's major cities. As in the other great immigrant societies of the Americas – the United States and Argentina – these groups have tended to assimilate, at least as members of the Brazilian "nation."

The Brazilian economy today is a "post-industrial" one much like the economies of all of the advanced capitalist countries and the most advanced developing or "middle-income" countries around the world. Services compose 57 percent of the Brazilian economy while industry represents 35 percent. The manufacturing sector, which grew exponentially following World War II, shrunk during the economic crises of the 1980s and 1990s, but much of this change was also a result of the relative growth and importance of services (e.g., banking, administration, commercial and retail services). As in the rich countries, a Brazilian employed in the formal labor market is more likely to work in an office than behind the control panel of a machine in a factory. Even so, manufacturing remains an important part of the Brazilian economy. The range of industrial goods Brazil manufactures is also broad, including high-tech products such as airplanes, ships, satellites, automobiles, and computer software, consumer durables such as refrigerators and television sets, and lower-tech consumer non-durables such as textiles and footwear. Commodity products such as iron ore, processed steel alloys and steel plates, paper, fertilizer, industrial chemicals, and petroleum extraction and refining form other major components of the modern economy. Taken together, services and industry represent a gross GDP in excess of $500 billion.

The importance of the Brazilian economy can also be measured in terms of its agricultural sector. Presently, Brazil has the largest herd of beef cattle in the world, and it provides just over 80 percent of the world's supply of orange juice concentrate, cotton, butter, corn, cocoa, and tobacco. Brazil is the second largest exporter of soya and the first in sugar and coffee. Its arable landmass of 112.5 million acres is massive, and it could be doubled through deforestation to satisfy future agricultural demand. Agricultural exports compose 35 percent of the country's total export bundle and they have been responsible for a large share of the recent increase in the export surplus. Most impressively, Brazil has been able to achieve a high level of international competitiveness in agriculture without the price supports and subsidies seen in the European Union and the United States (see chapter 7). Its position in the global marketplace will also expand into other areas in which it could clearly dominate. Presently, Brazil is the world's largest potential supplier of "biomass," pulp waste and other organic products that can be processed into fuel. As the result of many years of subsidizing ethanol (sugar cane and alcohol) production, all gasoline in Brazil contains 20 to 25 percent anhydrous alcohol, making all of its cars bi-fuel. Brazil thus serves a growing market in rich countries for biodiesel fuels used to reduce emissions in the face of stricter standards.

The economic development of Brazil contrasts with its social underdevelopment. Brazil has one of the most unequal distributions of wealth in the world. According to the UN's Human Development Index, an aggregate measure of human quality of life, seventy-two countries in the world have superior indices to Brazil although it is the ninth largest economy in the world (Monclaire 2004: 84). These figures point to what is the single greatest problem of Brazilian political, economic, and social development. Indeed, the issue of inequality could be thought of as a common thread in the narrative of Brazilian development, one that reflects and helps to explain imbalances in power, representation, development, and citizenship.

FIVE ANALYTICAL THEMES

Study of a complex country like Brazil is a challenge, particularly because it offers for the student of politics examples of virtually every major area of potential concern. Brazilian history is rich in distinct political traditions, experiences with different regime types (democratic and authoritarian), the function of a diverse array of political institutions, and the organization of civil society into movements and organizations, as well as classes and identities. Students of diverse topics such as the environment, violence, education, health care, industrialization, women's issues, and racial politics will find Brazil is replete with time periods, ideas, and empirical experiences that supply a treasure trove for comparative analysis. It is therefore not surprising that so many scholars of Brazil, no matter their discipline (e.g., anthropology, political science, sociology, or economics), dedicate their entire careers to the investigation of their topics of interest in the Brazilian context. These "Brazilianists" (*brasilianistas*) have broadened our understanding of topics of universal importance simply through their work on this one country (Barbosa 2002).

For the uninitiated student of Brazil, this complexity must be managed so that a more comprehensive understanding of the country, its people, and its politics is possible. After an overview of the main periods of modern Brazilian history in chapter 2, this book will examine the five themes listed earlier. As mentioned above, these are key points in the evolution of Brazilian politics, economy, and society. They are not mere descriptive snapshots of one period of time, but analytical evaluations of where the country is now on certain core questions, where it came from, and where these issues may be taking it. The five themes can be organized around the constantly evolving question of democracy. We leave this term undefined so as to allow the reader to make their own judgment about what democratic rule actually means in Brazil. While we do not offer a standard definition of democracy or an operational example to use as a comparative benchmark (e.g., the United States, Great Britain, etc.), we offer for analysis certain dimensions of democracy that are present in Brazil, but to varying degrees, and sometimes in contradiction with one another. These concepts are the strength of the state, representation, social equity, citizenship and political participation, and the role of the state in a global community of states. What is distinctive about these analytical dimensions of democracy is that Brazil presently can be and is called a "democracy," but it is a "democracy without ..." – that is, a democracy that lacks to some degree some of these essential ingredients of democratic rule.

Chapter 3 addresses the problem of "democracy without a strong state." Much of the political history of Brazil can be told through the travails of the evolving role of the central state. The pinnacle of the Brazilian state's capacity occurred during the post-World War II era, when bureaucratic agencies, national development banks, public firms in sectors such as steel and mining, and the armed forces used vast sums of money, other resources, and productive capacity to engineer one of the most remarkable periods of industrialization ever seen in a developing country. The crisis of this

"state-led development" experience during (especially) the 1980s and the reorganization of the state during the 1990s coincided with a transition to democratic rule that
has been the most sustained in the country's history. This presents several dilemmas,
not least of which is the fact that many of Brazil's problems, and particularly social
inequality, require strong state involvement in welfare distribution, health-care provision, and economic reform. Arguably democracy cannot function well without solutions to these fundamental problems. Hence the struggles of rebuilding a strong state
in Brazil will determine how strong democracy will be.

Chapter 4 concerns the problem of "democracy without representation." Oligarchical rule – the tendency of the elite few to exert decisive power over the many – is a
pillar of Brazilian history. Even when Brazil enjoyed relatively free and fair elections,
between the end of the empire in 1889 and the 1930 revolution and then again between
1946 and 1964, powerful economic and political interests have dominated the Brazilian political class. The transition to democracy in 1985 was "old wine in new bottles"
in the sense that many of the traditional elites who benefited from military rule in the
1964–85 period were elected to positions of power in the new democracy. Politicians
serve their constituents in all democracies lest they find themselves turned out at the
next election, but in Brazil, especially before the rise of mass politics after World War
II, the political class served the interests of the economic elites who supported them.
As the franchise expanded and industrialization mobilized urban workers and the
middle class, populist politicians co-opted these classes by using the state to protect
and reward these voters in return for sustained political support. The ideal of representation in which accountability and power run from the bottom up was reversed in
practice in Brazil by populism. Even in democratic Brazil today, elites tend to create
the constituencies that keep them in power and maintain their access to patronage
resources. Clientelism – the practice of exchanging favors to support a particular set
of interests – replaced representation of classes and mass groups. Thus one of the
central tasks for deepening democracy in Brazil is the creation of institutions and
organizations of representation – legislatures, political parties, and electoral rules – that
shift power to voters and enhance the interests of politicians in addressing issues of
more universal and national concern rather than personal or particular interest.

Chapter 5 addresses the problem of "democracy without equity." Political inequality and the priorities given to state intervention in the economy have historically
reflected social inequalities in Brazil. The urban poor and the rural peasantry struggle
every day to survive against the ravages of disease, unemployment, eroding wage
values, illiteracy, and violence. Democracy for these individuals cannot be divorced
from these daily experiences. For the poor, imagining a deepened democracy without
an improved social distribution of wealth and opportunity makes democracy itself a
meaningless concept. Democracy must mean enhanced education for poor children,
improved health care for remote towns, affordable food and housing, and a measure
of dignified work. Yet in many ways Brazil has democratized without making substantial improvements in equity. This has undermined the trust that most Brazilians have
in their political leaders. Without this trust, Brazilians will not engage their political
system on behalf of their own interests, thus deepening the prevalence of political
practices such as clientelistic exchange that strengthen traditional elites. The continuation of democracy without equity, then, threatens to dissolve the real meaning of
democracy for most Brazilians.

Chapter 6 turns to the challenge of "democracy without citizenship." The transition to democracy in 1985 was the result as well as a cause of a groundswell of popular mobilization. Environmental non-governmental organizations, women's and Afro-Brazilian groups, urban social and religious movements gathered on behalf of democracy and of deepening it in the years following the transition. This resurgence of democratic civil society represented a new hope for democracy in Brazil because, unlike previous experiences with democratic politics, these groups were autonomous of the central state, independent to pursue a broadened social and political agenda. By representing the weak and poor, many of these movements and organizations broadened democratic citizenship by expanding it beyond the basic political right to vote. Average Brazilians could, through the help of non-governmental organizations, exert pressure on their elected officials, mobilize information campaigns, and lobby directly their municipal, state, and federal officials for change. But the travails of these civil societal groups produced many distinct experiences, some more hopeful than others. Some contributed more to raising expectations than to generating fundamental change. Yet the work of so many groups cannot go unnoticed in a polity so used to a narrow concept of citizenship. Movements and non-governmental organizations continue to challenge oligarchical and clientelistic politics in democratic Brazil.

Chapter 7 evaluates the issue of "democracy without an international identity." More than ever before, states such as Brazil are dependent on a larger community of states. The basic rules of interstate trade, financial regulations, industrial policy, property rights, human rights, the management of common resources such as the sea and clean air, and international security are the subjects primarily of interactions among states, not the designs of a particular state or empire. Given its size, its level of development, and the professionalism of its diplomatic corps, Brazil is well placed to play a key role in world politics. Yet it must overcome its tendency, partly a product of its distinct Portuguese heritage in a largely Hispanic Latin America, to look inward. Brazil must construct an identity for itself in the world that is based on core values that it is willing to defend on the global stage, even against the interests of other powerful states such as the United States and the supranational European Union. Brazil's heavy involvement in regional trade groups and international organizations and the geostrategic and environmental importance of the vast Amazon present important opportunities for the country's leaders to forge a distinctive role in the world. What and who Brazil wishes to be in the world of states will very much affect its domestic priorities and vice versa. Its own democracy cannot prosper without a concerted and conscious effort to link these two dimensions of Brazilian politics.

The Lula da Silva presidency

No study of contemporary Brazilian politics can be complete without a thorough consideration of the remarkable rise to the presidency of Lula da Silva. As the activists of the World Social Forum know only too well, Lula is a complicated figure. The cross-pressures his presidency faces, from the need to address Brazil's social disparities to the practicalities of dispensing patronage to conservative politicians in return for their votes on reform legislation in the congress, send mixed signals about what Lula will do next. There is no doubt that Lula remains at heart a leader dedicated to improving the lives of most Brazilians, but he is also tenacious about not becoming a failure because of an inability to navigate the rough waters of his country's politics. He wishes to produce fundamental change, but he is realistic about the limits of what he can do.

Chapter 8 focuses on the main achievements and agenda items of the Lula presidency through 2004. These first two years of Lula's first term illustrated many of the challenges to democratic consolidation in Brazil. Yet Lula was successful in moving the reform agenda forward, however slowly. The hope he inspired in many Brazilians during the 2002 presidential campaign remained high as presidential approval rates of over 60 percent continued to keep him well above his political rivals in the public's regard. Yet things changed dramatically in the spring and summer of 2005. A corruption scandal involving payoffs to legislators by some key leaders of the ruling Workers' Party (PT) threatened to up-end Lula's reform agenda and tarnish his popularity. These events made the remainder of Lula's presidency more arduous than it might otherwise have been, and they put in jeopardy the hope that the former labor leader would be returned to office in October 2006.

2

HISTORICAL PATTERNS IN BRAZILIAN POLITICS

Any survey of the political history of Brazil will show that the country has weathered tremendous changes since it was colonized, beginning in the sixteenth century, by the Portuguese. Several key transitions transformed the political and economic trajectory of Brazil: independence, the replacement of the empire by the Old Republic, the revolution of 1930, the collapse of populist democracy and the rise of a bureaucratic-authoritarian regime headed by the armed forces in 1964, and, finally, the transition to democracy in 1985 and the consolidation of a democratic regime. These are the mileposts in Brazilian history that shaped the political and economic development of the country.

The historical analysis in this chapter will also attempt to highlight important continuities across these different time periods. The major ones coincide with the thematic overview given in the last chapter. The centrality of the state, the persistence of oligarchical political institutions, socio-economic inequality, the organization and mobilization of civil society, and Brazil's interaction with other states and the global economy form the analytical points of departure for these chapters. The historical survey in this chapter illustrates some of the origins and factors that sustain these enduring characteristics in Brazil. The key historical lessons are summarized in **box 2.1**. Following a conventional chronological account, this chapter will briefly examine the colonial and post-independence histories of Brazil through 1930, the 1930–64 modern period, the bureaucratic-authoritarian regime (1964–85), and the post-1985 democracy.

EARLY HISTORY: THE COLONIAL PAST, INDEPENDENCE, THE EMPIRE AND THE OLD REPUBLIC

Brazil's early history is a testament to its distinctiveness within Latin America. While most of the rest of Latin America was liberated after sustained wars of independence with Spain, Brazil's transition from its colonial past to independence was peaceful. It did not rupture its connection with the motherland as brusquely as did the Hispanic

Box 2.1   The historical origins of key characteristics of Brazilian politics

- Racial and class inequality have endured from colonial to modern times.
- The Brazilian central state was well formed as a bureaucratic entity, partially independent from prominent societal and economic elites, early in the post-independence history of the country.
- Political authority was shaped by periodic conflicts between centralizing forces (the empire, the *Estado Nôvo*, the bureaucratic-authoritarian regime) and decentralizing forces (the Old Republic and the populist period of 1945–64).
- Representation and participation tended to concentrate on the interests of the economic and political elite from the establishment of the Old Republic.
- Political parties were shaped by economic elites and/or the state but not by popular movements, such as workers' movements, until the contemporary democratic period.
- Personality and populism, not ideology or loyalty to political programs, were the bases for much of the appeal of political leaders through the contemporary democratic period.
- Industrial development in the *Estado Nôvo* was shaped fundamentally by the state through planning and other forms of state intervention. Economic reform during the contemporary period has focused on promoting industrial growth but also on the reduction of strong state intervention in the market.
- Clientelism – the involvement of private interests in the design of public policy – fundamentally shaped the intervention of the state in the market and the reform of the development model.
- Democratization during the 1980s and 1990s empowered civil society and weakened corporatism, but democratization also strengthened clientelistic networks in electoral, legislative, and constitutional politics.

colonies. Independence came when the Portuguese crown prince declared Brazil's separation from Portugal and himself emperor in 1822. The Brazilian Empire would last until 1889, when another peaceful break led to the rise of a constitutional republic based on the powers of landowners and bureaucrats.

Some of the institutions of the colonial period clearly shaped the kind of society Brazil was to have after independence and even after the empire. Racial divisions based on concepts such as the "purity of blood" justified discrimination against blacks, indigenous peoples, and people of mixed heritage (*mestizos* and mulattos). Brazilians born in Brazil, the *crioulos*, were further differentiated from Brazilians born in Portugal, who were regarded as having the purest blood of all. Ethnic and racial divisions were juxtaposed to social and economic hierarchies. Landowners, merchants, and bureaucrats of the colonial state tended to be white, while laborers, including freed slaves, artisans, and peasants, were of mixed, African, or indigenous descent and on the lower rungs of colonial society. The dominance of the plantation economy during the eighteenth and most of the nineteenth century consolidated the considerable power of large landowners with access to capital. The coffee and cattle-raising interests during the second half of the nineteenth century represented the wealthiest and most powerful of these members of the upper classes. Profits from coffee and ranching financed the early stages of industrialization, especially in the south-central states of São Paulo and Minas Gerais. These agricultural products replaced sugar and mining (gold and silver), the primary products of the colonial period, and they became the major export goods that earned foreign currency receipts at the turn of the twentieth century.

The political transitions that led to the end of the colonial period and its successor, the Brazilian Empire, were predicated on a mixture of international and domestic transformations. The Portuguese crown lost control of its largest colony after suffering from many of the crises that were afflicting absolutist kings elsewhere in Europe. British efforts to break into foreign markets by undermining the mercantilist practices of powers such as Portugal and Spain, the French Revolution, which overturned the *ancien régime* completely, and the Napoleonic Wars on the European mainland, which forced the Portuguese crown to find refuge in Brazil, catalyzed the crisis in the Portuguese colonial system. In November 1807, the Portuguese court, headed by Dom João VI, and between 10,000 and 15,000 bureaucrats, jurists, clergy, and other officials set sail for Rio de Janeiro. The royal treasury, the archives, and the contents of several libraries went along as well.

The presence of the crown in Rio produced two contradictory forces. The first was a deepening of divisions between the Portuguese and the *crioulo* elite, who now had to live in closer proximity. The second was a conflict between the reinforcement of central authority over a sprawling, continent-size colony, and the tendency of local elites to seek greater autonomy from the central state. The presence of the crown in Brazil infuriated *crioulo* northeastern interests, who saw the colonial state and its practices favoring Portuguese nobles as an impediment to their own social and political advancement. Meanwhile, revolutions and revolts beginning in 1817 in Pernambuco, the principal northeastern state, signaled the decline of the crown's hold on Brazil and the homeland. Even so, the royal army was able to keep the colony under control, as it put down these insurrections repeatedly. Events back in Portugal, however, were outside of the army's control. The Portuguese Revolution in 1820, which was caused by a combination of factors, not least of which was the continued absence of the king from Lisbon, forced Dom João VI to return. He left his son, Dom Pedro, behind as the prince regent.

Crioulos by this time had displaced Portuguese-born ministers and bureaucrats from the ranks of the colonial state. Their intent was to keep Dom Pedro in Brazil and to push for independence from the crown. As Portuguese troops loyal to the king were sent back to the homeland and as authorities in Lisbon curtailed the prince regent's powers, Dom Pedro had no choice but to embrace the independentist movement. On 7 September 1822, Dom Pedro declared Brazil independent, and three months later the prince regent was crowned emperor. He would rule until 1831 when, in the wake of his father's death in 1826, he was forced to return to Lisbon to rule Portugal as king, leaving behind his son, Dom Pedro II, to rule Brazil as emperor. Although Dom Pedro II was five years old when his father abdicated, he was Brazilian-born, and that helped to resolve lingering tensions between Portuguese and *crioulo* interests. Brazil would be for the Brazilians, to be ruled by a Brazilian emperor.

The empire (1822–89) represented a significant period for the building of central authority, but this process was also subject to international and domestic forces that conspired to undermine imperial rule. The expulsion of Portuguese troops initiated the essential process of building an independent, national army, one of the pillars of the emperor's role as a "moderating power" (*poder moderador*) within the Brazilian political order. But the emperor used his powers not just to moderate but to determine who else could participate in decision-making. Dom Pedro II appointed senators and provincial governors and he was free to call new elections after dissolving the lower house, the Chamber of Deputies (*Câmara dos Diputados*). Local elites resisted this centralization of power, and in some cases through open rebellion. Uprisings during the regency (1831–40), when governors acting in the young emperor's name held sway over the emerging national army, were common and repeatedly put down by central powers. Revolts in Pernambuco and in the south, in the modern-day country of Uruguay, led to war and the latter's independence from Brazil.

Ranching elites and coffee plantation owners in the southern states resented central authority for economic reasons. They bristled at taxation and the transfer of capital from the rich states to the poor ones. Many of these elites divided into opposing ideological camps and parties. The Liberals, who were most powerful in the south, supported an expansion of individual freedom and a decentralization of power. The Conservatives, who had their power base in the northeast, embraced many of the same ideas and, like the Liberals, supported the emperor but decried the extensive powers of the executive Council of State that served him. On the issue of slavery, these groups initially supported the institution, but, with continued British opposition to the slave trade and the British Royal Navy's apprehension of slave ships on the high seas, the commerce in slave labor became onerous. The end of the slave trade in 1850, coupled with the modernization of agriculture, and particularly the coffee sector, made the larger institution of slavery unnecessary as well as unsustainable. Large-scale immigration later in the century deepened these tendencies.

Without slavery, one of the essential reasons for landed elites to maintain the emperor in power vanished. Republicanism and abolitionism thus coincided during the 1870s and 1880s as the primary forces making the emperor's abdication inevitable. The Republican Party, which gathered regionalist elites from São Paulo especially, campaigned after 1871 on behalf of a federal republic. As republicanism spread among the educated elites of the south, its adherents readily took up the abolitionist cause as well. Slavery was finally abolished after many incremental steps in 1889. Then, São Paulo coffee elites and the military, combined with Dom Pedro's illness (diabetes) and the absence of a male successor, precipitated the end of the empire and the declaration of the republic in 1889.

The Old Republic (1889–1930) differed from the empire in several key respects. Whereas the imperial period represented an uneasy centralization of military and administrative power, the Old Republic was sustained through the influence of the coffee and ranching elites and the governors of just a few states. Landowners and politicians from São Paulo, Minas Gerais, and Rio Grande do Sul especially collaborated in shaping all of the major national institutions of authority. The republic had a liberal constitution that guaranteed individual and property rights and the separation of church and state, and it retained the legislative assemblies of the empire (the

Chamber of Deputies and the Senate). In lieu of the emperor, the directly elected president would play the role of *poder moderador*. As befitted their influence, elites from the three key states traded control over the presidency during the Old Republic. The larger political class, which had long replaced the Portuguese aristocracy with landowners and bureaucrats, remained largely unchanged. They came from the ranks of the dominant economic groups in each state and led parties defined more by their allegiance to the interests of their home states than to any national organization. The political class remained an oligarchy even though the republic invoked universal suffrage, except for illiterates, beggars, enlisted military men, and all women. The effects of the expansion of the franchise were limited by the capacity of local landed elites – *coroneis* (colonels) – to control voters' choices through patron–client networks. In this way, the colonels provided the votes that local political bosses and their beneficiaries required. In return, the landowners received the favors of their elected officials.

The collaborative trading of political power among coffee and ranch elites that typified the Old Republic is regarded as the period of *café com leite* (coffee with milk). The metaphor is especially apt since it represents the close linkage of economic interests and the exercise of government decision-making. The Brazilian governments during this time embraced economic policies that favored the access to foreign loans and external markets of São Paulo coffee plantation owners, the preferences of meat producers for protection against imports, and the desire of the political class of states such as Minas Gerais to gain positions of authority in the growing central state bureaucracy. To be sure, the "coffee and milk" metaphor also obscures the extent to which conflict among elites weakened the system over time. Disagreements over the openness of trade policy and credits for coffee, the composition and command of the military, and the rise in 1929–30 of a unified movement in the southernmost state of Rio Grande do Sul behind an ex-minister of finance, Getúlio Vargas, led to the end of the constitutional republic. These changes coincided with socio-economic transformations that threatened the oligarchy's privileges. Waves of immigrants had already transformed the cities and energized Brazil's first worker movements. Economic modernization empowered both the middle class and wage laborers in the cities and in the countryside. In this context, Vargas's campaign for greater national unity not only seemed the right antidote to the deepening conflicts within the economic and political elite; his movement also affirmed the need to integrate these emerging social classes into a new political order. Widespread revolts in the northeast, in Minas Gerais, and in Rio Grande do Sul quickly became a revolution that swept Vargas to power in 1930.

THE ESTADO NÔVO AND THE POPULIST PERIOD

Getúlio Vargas's revolution replaced the old decentralized system of oligarchic and regional power with institutions that centralized authority in the national state. Economic policy, now freed from the control of the landed elite, promoted industrialization and urbanization. Social welfare policies meant to protect professional and industrial workers brought the urban middle and working classes into the new system. Both the state bureaucracy and the armed forces were modernized and professionalized as never before. Political parties, which up to this point had been representatives of local, economic elites, became the products of Vargas's state and they served the larger mission of developing the national political and economic order.

Vargas's state, as it was conceived between 1930 and 1937 and then fully constructed after 1937 as the *Estado Nôvo* (New State), represented an authoritarian project for reorganizing the polity and Brazilian society. Upon seizing power in 1930, Vargas closed the congress and replaced all of the governors, save in Minas Gerais which remained loyal to the dictator, with appointed administrators (*interventores*). The government invoked widespread censorship of all media. Vargas's Law of National Security (1935) outlawed illegal demonstrations and strikes and virtually all political organizations independent of the state. Labor unions and the armed forces were brought into line. Vargas codified the control of the former under a new Ministry of Labor that oversaw all collective bargaining. A new labor code in 1943 guaranteed workers official protections, including workplace safety regulations, regular paid vacations, equal pay for the same work, a minimum wage, and social security. The establishment of the Superior War College (*Escola Superior de Guerra*, ESG) in Rio de Janeiro years later in 1949 consolidated a decade of Vargas-era professionalization of the armed forces. This infused the officer corps with a clear sense of national mission and administrative and technical skills that would prove essential in expanding the role of the armed forces in Brazilian economic development and politics in succeeding decades.

The *Estado Nôvo* made fundamental changes in the Brazilian economy. First, Vargas nationalized the country's major natural resources, including mining, mineral deposits, and hydroelectric resources. Second, he nationalized and established public firms in key sectors such as steel and mining. The National Steel Company (*Companhia Siderúrgica Nacional*, CSN) (1941) and the Vale do Rio Doce Company (*Companhia do Vale do Rio Doce*, CVRD) (1944) were particularly important for the third major economic impact of the *Estado Nôvo*: the overall direction of economic policy. Vargas's dictatorship coincided with the international collapse of global trade during the Great Depression. Like the other large Latin American economies, Brazil began to substitute manufactured goods imports which it had previously paid for with the receipts of coffee exports, with consumer non-durable and durable goods produced at home. High tariffs on imports of manufactured goods such as textiles and footwear, coupled with import subsidies for the foreign technology needed to produce these products at home, expanded Brazil's light industrial base. The new development model based on import-substitution industrialization (ISI) moved quickly from the promotion of consumer non-durable products, such as apparel, to consumer durables, including appliances and automobiles. Public firms such as CSN and CVRD provided the raw materials and basic commodity inputs (e.g., steel) at subsidized prices to promote heavier forms of industrialization. During the 1950s especially, foreign multinationals such as the auto assemblers General Motors and Ford produced automobiles in Brazil for the domestic market. These companies took advantage of cheap commodities supplied by the public firms and auto parts provided by domestic Brazilian firms, who themselves took advantage of subsidized credit from the national development banks. Import licenses and high tariffs on car parts and finished automobiles protected these manufacturers from foreign competition. As a result of economic policies initiated during the *Estado Nôvo*, Brazil's ISI experience expanded the urban industrial working class and deepened the industrialization of the country.

The state's leadership in the industrialization process coincided with Vargas's reorganization of the state's role in the political system. After 1937, the Brazilian state became the central coordinator of virtually all major aspects of the polity, including political parties, unions, major business associations, and the court system. The principal organizer just below the president himself was the Administrative Department of Public Service (*Departamento Administrativo do Serviço Público*, DASP). Created in 1938, the DASP was responsible for reorganizing the civil service along the lines of a *state corporatist* model. Following the DASP's legislation, the major economic ministries were connected with socio-economic entities normally autonomous from the state in liberal market economies (e.g., unions, business associations, corporations). State ministries, development banks, and public firms decided what would be produced and how production would be linked to a strategy of using foreign capital, including multinational corporate and domestic investment. Unions would be run by civil servant union bosses, known as *pelegos*, who represented the state's interests more than those of workers. In this way, both state and society were organized in a connected and hierarchical fashion.

Although the institutions of the state-led economy and state corporatism would continue to shape Brazil's politics through the 1980s, the *Estado Nôvo* itself as an authoritarian project to modernize the country had a much shorter life-span. It ended in 1945 when, under growing social resentment of authoritarian practices, Vargas acceded to elections and turned over power to a former war minister and military officer, Eurico Dutra, who was elected president. Political competition from this point until 1964 would be shaped by the parties that Vargas created in 1945, the Social Democratic Party (*Partido Social Democrático*, PSD) and the Brazilian Labor Party (*Partido Trabalhista Brasileiro*, PTB), and the opposition to the *Estado Nôvo* that formed the National Democratic Union (*União Democrática Nacional*, UDN). The PSD and PTB united bureaucrats and pro-Vargas unions, respectively, while the UDN gathered assorted liberals who supported the independence of state governments and local elites.

Lacking a history of party identification or mass support, the leaders of these parties, including Vargas, appealed directly to the people through their charisma and promises of material gains. *Populism* – the practice of mobilizing popular support through the distribution of material guarantees – became the basis for modern Brazilian politics at this time. Vargas, who was popular during the 1930s as the *pai do povo* ("father of the people"), employed the model most adeptly. The familiar and avuncular attributes of the once dictatorial Vargas helped him win the presidency in 1950. The reinvented Vargas ruled from January 1951 until August 1954, when overzealous Vargas supporters in the president's inner circle attempted to assassinate their patron's chief political rival, Carlos Lacerda, a Rio de Janeiro newspaperman and politician. The bizarre events surrounding the failed assassination of Lacerda culminated in Vargas's suicide in the presidential mansion in Rio later that month.

After a short military caretaker government, Juscelino Kubitshek, a PSD politician and former governor from Minas Gerais, was elected president in 1955. A PTB politician and former Vargas labor minister, João Goulart, assumed the vice-presidency. Under Kubitshek and Goulart, Brazil experienced its most rapid period of industrialization. "JK," as Kubitshek was known by all, implemented ambitious industrial goals in six key sectors: energy, transportation, food, basic industry, education, and construction. In this last category, the hallmark project was the building of a new capital in the center of the country, Brasília. The *Plano de Metas* (Plan of Goals), as JK's industrial policy was called, accelerated and deepened the process of ISI on a scale that the president himself claimed would produce "fifty years of progress in five."

In contrast to the record of industrialization, the development of democracy during the 1945–64 period proved more shallow. The "populist democracy" of the time is best described as an "experiment in democracy" (Skidmore 1967). The major political parties – PSD, PTB, UDN – and a rising number of minor parties were defined more by the personalistic elites who led them than by distinct ideologies or constituencies in Brazilian society. The UDN's Carlos Lacerda, a perennial opposition leader, Jânio Quadros, a São Paulo-based politician with ties to both the left within the PTB and the anti-Vargas forces in the UDN, and Goulart became the towering personalities of Brazilian politics after JK's presidency ended in 1960. Quadros's presidential victory in that year produced a short-lived government: Quadros resigned only seven months after he was inaugurated in the new capital city of Brasília. João Goulart, his vice-president, assumed the presidency under intense opposition from conservatives and the military, who were displeased with the accidental president's erstwhile ties to labor and the political left. In the white-hot context of the Cold War, the wake of the Cuban Revolution, and a growing mobilization of peasants, urban workers, and students who took to the streets in record numbers on behalf of land reform, pro-union issues, and an expansion of political rights, Brazilian politics became dangerously polarized. Along with a slowdown in the economy, the political context became increasingly precarious for democracy itself. After Goulart attempted to implement a wide-ranging (but not radical) agrarian reform, the president's political enemies on the right made their move. The "experiment with (populist) democracy" ended in March 1964 when the armed forces removed Goulart and launched a twenty-one-year authoritarian regime.

THE BUREAUCRATIC-AUTHORITARIAN REGIME AND THE ABERTURA (1964–85)

The military came to power with the intention of consolidating its political and economic projects over a long period of time. The generals sought to put in place a government that would root out subversive (communist) elements in the polity and stabilize and deepen industrialization. Based on new doctrines developed at the ESG under the directorship of General Golbery do Couto e Silva, Brazil's military government would differ fundamentally from the previous caretaker regimes or "revolutionary" projects that typified the armed forces' earlier involvement in politics. Since it was a "bureaucratic-authoritarian" regime, no single general would rule as dictator. Instead, a series of senior commanders would hold the presidency, with the power behind the throne being held by a small coterie of the heads of the different services (army, navy, and air force). Both military and civilian "technocrats" – engineers, administrators, economists, technicians – some trained at ESG itself, would assume the reins of the state's now broadening role in the economy and in controlling civil society. The generals ruled through "institutional acts" (*atos institucionais*) that expanded the powers of the executive and reduced the authority of the congress, which remained open but under tight control. Legislation, all of it initiated by the president, could be considered in the Chamber of Deputies and the Senate, but the executive could exercise its fiat and implement new laws if congress failed to act or staged opposition. Legislators' own seats could be taken from them arbitrarily, making the congress a powerless debating society. Opposition from other sectors of society could elicit far worse treatment. Summary judgments, imprisonment, and torture were routinely carried out on suspected "subversives." In order to find their enemies, the military launched the National Information Service (*Serviço Nacional de Informações*, SNI) as an intelligence agency designed to maintain a network of surveillance over an increasingly terrorized society.

The war against the subversives, while important, became less so after the most repressive period (1968–72) passed. Managing the economy, and particularly the industrialization of the country, was far more important to the bureaucratic-authoritarian regime. Once in power, the military faced heightening inflation and expanding deficits that required a quick response. Trade deficits also threatened the continuation and deepening of the ISI model, which required heavier forms of public subsidization. At first, the military governments were successful in reducing some of these imbalances through cuts in spending and increases in taxation. A modest currency devaluation in 1964, trade liberalization, and efforts to promote exports prompted higher rates of growth, particularly during a period called the "Brazilian miracle" (1968–73), when average annual rates of growth topped 11 percent. Yet maintaining this growth meant greater fiscal commitments by the state. Since the bureaucratic-authoritarian regime sought to spend on infrastructure at unprecedented levels, billions of dollars had to be poured into massive public projects, including dams, bridges, and Amazonian development. Lacking sufficient domestic sources of capital, the generals turned their efforts to intensifying the inflow of foreign capital in the form of loans from commercial banks in the US and Europe. By the mid-1970s, Brazil was running large trade deficits that it financed with more foreign borrowing. The "miracle" might have been sustained on this formula but, when international oil prices shot up following the first oil price shocks of 1973 (and then again in 1979), the costs of financing this growing foreign debt became too onerous. Central banks in creditor countries increased interest rates to restrain inflation, thus increasing interest costs on the Latin American debtors. This then set the stage for a severe fiscal crisis in Brazil, a debt crisis throughout the region, and a macroeconomic meltdown during the 1980s that ended the developmentalist experience.

The rise and fall of developmentalism/ISI in Brazil was closely tied to the politics of the Brazilian state. More than any other factor, the Achilles' heel of the developmentalist state was the pervasiveness of clientelism throughout the public bureaucracy. "Clientelism" refers to the sustained exchange of favors among private actors, which includes the misappropriation of public resources for political or personal gain. Blatantly illegal examples include corrupt practices, but clientelism also involves nepotism and other forms of favoritism that are not technically illegal but distribute personal and political resources nonetheless. During the developmentalist experience, clientelism produced numerous inefficiencies that protected many industries from foreign competition, rewarded unproductive entrepreneurship, and stifled domestic competition.

Some agencies, such as the National Development Bank (*Banco Nacional de Desenvolvimento Econômico e Social*, BNDES), proved that they could be "pockets of efficiency" in the Brazilian state by employing skilled technocrats and seeing through well-planned projects (Evans 1979). But these agencies were the exceptions. More typically, development banks and federal ministries became the domain of connected politicians who distributed public jobs to their cronies and public resources to local bailiwicks and other supporters. Despite the efforts of the most professional minds in the armed forces, traditional politicians and clientelistic exchange continued to trump the best laid plans of the technocrats (Hagopian 1996). And the larger the military's vision, the greater the costs of clientelism. Some of the grandest developmentalist projects were so riddled with kickbacks and other forms of clientelistic exchange that immense amounts of capital were wasted on sometimes grandiose projects. The political liberalization of the bureaucratic-authoritarian regime beginning in 1973 deepened these costly inefficiencies as the generals sought to bolster their control of the state by inserting political appointees in positions that had previously gone to technocrats (Weyland 2000: 38–9). The expansion of clientelism within the state was also a function of the increasing penetration of the bureaucracy by private lobbies. Business associations and firms, most notably public contractors and health-care companies, extended their influence within the state during a time that the military was gradually allowing private associations more voice in Brazilian politics.

Over time, not even the heroic actions of the state's various pockets of efficiency could cope with the extensive clientelism that pervaded the economic bureaucracy, limiting its efficiency and strangling its fiscal sustainability (Evans 1989). Private businesses used their influence to lock in subsidies and tax breaks permitted by the ISI economy, and they blocked reform-minded technocrats who sought to reduce these benefits. The combination of increasingly costly subsidization of inefficient domestic producers and declining tax revenues as a result of extensive tax breaks and tax evasion set the stage for the fiscal crisis of the Brazilian state (Pereira 1993). Once the center of the developmentalist model, the state was incapable of generating or sustaining growth because of exploding public debt and rising financial costs. The state also suffered from a leadership that failed to take market-oriented reform seriously. Elites sustained the illusion that the "deepening" of ISI was still possible.

Accompanying the worsening economic problems of the country was the growth of popular opposition to the continuation of military rule. Beginning in 1973–4 with the military government's own initiatives to liberalize the regime under President Ernesto Geisel, large segments of Brazilian civil society mobilized against the bureaucratic-authoritarian state. This mixture of regime-initiated gradual political liberalization from above (*distensão* – literally, "depressurization") to reduce opposition tensions combined with the mobilization of civil society produced a gradual "opening," or *abertura*, of the bureaucratic-authoritarian regime. This transition eventually returned Brazil to democracy in 1985.

Middle-class actors, professional associations, church-based groups, opposition politicians, and working-class unions gradually challenged the fundamental institutions of authoritarianism, including press censorship, arbitrary gag orders, torture, and unwarranted detention (Alves 1985; Della Cava 1989; Keck 1992). The Church added its considerable moral authority in denouncing repression. The National Conference of the Bishops of Brazil (*Conferência Nacional dos Bispos do Brasil*, CNBB) played a key role as moral whistleblower in publicizing cases of torture and decrying income inequalities (Serbin 2000). The contradictions of the import-substitution model also helped to mobilize businesses and entrepreneurs against the regime (Payne 1994). Most important, the decision by the military to allow the opposition a political space in congress opened the door to the possibility of opposition electoral victories, which began with the 1974 elections in São Paulo and culminated with the loss by the pro-military party ARENA (*Aliança Nacional Renovadora*; National Renovation Alliance) of its absolute majority in the federal Chamber of Deputies in the 1982 elections. These contests were also the first to allow Brazilians to elect their governors directly, and ten states went to the opposition as a result.

These opposition victories occurred despite the best efforts of the military to create numerous obstacles to the organization of the opposition. In 1979, the government passed an electoral reform that split the Brazilian Democratic Movement (*Movimento Democrático Brasileiro*, MDB) into numerous opposition parties – the Party of the MDB (PMDB), the Democratic Worker Party (*Partido Democrático Trabalhista*, PDT), the PTB, and the PT (see chapter 4). The ARENA reorganized as the Democratic Social Party (*Partido Democrático Social*, PDS), a social democratic party in name only, as it remained conservative and pro-military. Later, dissident factions split off into the Liberal Front Party (*Partido da Frente Liberal*, PFL). Yet opposition parties, and especially the catch-all PMDB, continued to take seats in the legislature and win gubernatorial races, thereby paving the way for the free election of the president in 1985. Mass mobilizations throughout the country during January–March 1984 and widespread calls for direct elections for the presidency (the *Diretas Já* or "Direct Elections Now" movement) produced a crisis of legitimacy in the authoritarian regime that guaranteed that the bureaucratic-authoritarian experiment could not be sustained (Sallum 2003: 181–2).

What is most notable about the Brazilian transition to democracy is how unsuccessful efforts to displace the conservative elites of the bureaucratic-authoritarian period were. First, the military succeeded in keeping the first elections indirect by requiring that the president be selected through an electoral college rather than the popular vote. And although the PDS's candidate, Paulo Maluf, lost to the PMDB's Tancredo Neves, the opposition could not get its candidate elected without the support of the PFL and other conservatives who left the PDS in the weeks preceding the election. Finally, the cruelest joke foisted upon the democratic opposition came when Neves died suddenly before his inauguration. His vice-president, José Sarney of the PFL, a man who had close ties to the bureaucratic-authoritarian governments, became president, and he ushered in a decidedly conservative version of democracy, the New Republic.

THE NEW REPUBLIC

José Sarney was a reflection of the past and a harbinger of things to come for Brazilian democracy. Unlike Fernando Henrique Cardoso, Sarney was a member of a cohort of politicians that fled the PSD to join the PFL once it was clear that a PMDB–PFL alliance would be successful. Like other members of this group, who had extensive backgrounds working on behalf of the authoritarian regime, Sarney found himself at the helm of the new, civilian government. His opportunism seemed to know no bounds as he made generous use of presidential patronage to reward his backers and garner additional support for an extension of his own presidential term by one year to a total of five. In this way, Sarney was a model for other Brazilian politicians to follow. He knew that the development of a personal following, the distribution of patronage, and the cultivation of clientelistic networks were the keys to longevity in Brazilian politics. Sarney would prove it by extending his political career to the present day, outlasting those who attempted to attack the system, such as his immediate successor in the presidency, the disgraced Fernando Collor.

Yet Sarney and his tactics would not play a role in Brazilian politics today if it were not for the way in which the democratic transition itself institutionalized these practices. The first, salient institutional legacy of the transition emerged from the pervasive attempt by civilian leaders to put the authoritarian past behind them. Since the military had so extensively manipulated electoral institutions and the political party system to extend the generals' rule, virtually any restriction against party formation and cross-party alliances during elections was seen by most members of the civilian opposition as resuscitating authoritarian mechanisms that Fernando Henrique Cardoso once called the "authoritarian debris" (*entulho autoritário*). But this widespread attitude also went too far by allowing and even encouraging the proliferation of political parties and the extensive personalization of politics (Power 2000a: 20). Individual politicians emerged during this time as the main agents of change and democratic legitimacy. That in itself was not problematic, but the fact that personalities displaced the importance of building political parties was. The major political parties, especially the PMDB and the PFL, were ideologically indistinct and amorphous, catch-all organizations. Worse still, many of the politicians that adhered to these parties were themselves former members of the ARENA/PDS (Power 2000b; Hagopian 1996). These were the salient indicators of an evolving political system in which partisan insignias would mean less than personal affiliations, access to patronage, and support by private interests. The transition would result in the continuation of a conservative political order.

The drafting of a new democratic constitution between February 1987 and September 1988 institutionalized many of these perverse aspects of the Brazilian political system. The National Constituent Assembly (*Assembléia Nacional Constituente*, ANC) itself reflected these erstwhile elements of the system as it became the focus of relentless lobbying by a host of entrenched economic and social interests. Not surprisingly, the ANC has been described as "parochial," "chaotic" (Rosenn 1990), and a "free-for-all" (Power 2000a: 19). It was in many ways a triumph of democracy in that a number of voices that had not been heard in Brazilian politics took the opportunity to shape the basic law of the land. Grass-roots movements, environmentalists, women, racial minorities, and workers, particularly those organized through the Workers' Party (PT), impressed their interests on the constitution. As a result, the ANC produced a constitution that became all things to all people. It guaranteed a host of civil, political, and social rights that Brazilians had never imagined they would have. But it also created many problems. For example, the ANC granted public employees almost unassailable job security, it decentralized tax collection to the states, and it expanded pension benefits beyond what was fiscally sustainable (Fleischer 2004: 117). As Brazil's macroeconomic and particularly its fiscal crises became more acute after 1988, reform would focus on undoing what many interests had achieved during those nineteen months (Reich 1998). Yet these reforms-cum-constitutional amendments would be all the more difficult to secure against the organized interests that benefited from the "rights" bestowed by the constitution.

The first of these reform attempts produced little in the way of major change. One adjustment to the political system that would have dramatically altered the nature of the New Republic was the choice of presidential or parliamentary system. The ANC had itself been unable to resolve this issue, leaving it to a plebiscite in 1993 to determine the outcome. Sarney's campaign to keep the presidential system and extend the term to five years was hard-fought and succeeded in keeping the system presidential. The campaigns on behalf of a switch to parliamentarism in 1993 produced much spilled ink and debate, but in the end the actual vote favored continuation of the status quo. Later, in 1993, a corruption scandal in the Chamber of Deputies that involved the annual budget bogged down another attempt at constitutional reform. Congressional investigations and the advent of the campaign season paralyzed the special constituent assembly of March 1994 (*Congresso Revisor*). Thirty thousand amendments were proposed in the run-up to the assembly, but only five were passed. The two most noteworthy were the reduction of the presidential term to four years and the creation of an emergency fiscal fund that would be used strategically in subsequent years by the Cardoso government as a bargaining chip in negotiations with state and municipal governments over fiscal reform.

While the elites of the New Republic fiddled with the constitution, the economy burned. Inflation soared as the fiscal crisis of the Brazilian state became more intense. By 1988–9, annual inflation rates approached 1,000 percent. Price instability and declining public investments slowed down the economy and increased urban unemployment. Sarney's government attempted several anti-inflation plans, only to see each fail in the midst of persisting hyperinflationary conditions (more than 50 percent inflation *per month* on average).

Sarney ended his extended presidential term in March 1990 when he passed the presidential sash to a popular outsider in the 1989 presidential race, Fernando Collor de Mello. Collor had beaten Lula da Silva in the run-off by guaranteeing center-right and business interests that only his government could root out the extensive corruption and clientelism of the Brazilian state. Regarding the instability of prices, the new president boasted that he would "kill off inflation with a single shot!" With his declaration, Collor enacted draconian new measures that froze prices, wages, and savings accounts. Yet neither this, his first plan, nor his second corrected Brazil's hyperinflationary spirals. Collor's promises of extensive reform of the state and his bombastic rhetorical attacks against the "*majarajahs*" of clientelism fell on deaf ears as his maverick political style alienated politicians in congress. Although he enacted important structural reforms such as privatization, Collor's inability to garner sustained legislative support limited his reforms. The president's disregard for tradition and the game of clientelistic expectations pushed him to work outside the system. It all caught up with him in 1992, when a growing campaign finance scandal involving his former associate Paulo César Farias brought down his presidency.

Collor's vice-president, Itamar Franco, served out the remainder of his term, but he produced little in the way of consolidating reform. His most notable achievements occurred after he appointed Fernando Henrique Cardoso as finance minister. Cardoso was well known as a world-class sociologist who turned to politics during the *abertura* period. In 1988 he led PMDB politicians discontented with the party's relationship with the government into the new *Partido da Social Democracia Brasileira* (Party of Brazilian Social Democracy, PSDB). He joined Franco's government in May 1993 and within months crafted a stabilization measure that promised to rid Brazil of high inflation for good. The *Plano Real* (Real Plan) was fully enacted in July 1994 after a period of some months during which the Central Bank floated the Brazilian currency within monetary bands linked to the dollar as a flexible exchange-rate anchor. As inflation fell, Cardoso became the favorite to win the presidential elections in October 1994, a position he had been campaigning for since April of that year. Cardoso beat Lula and all other contenders in the first round, and the PSDB led a loose coalition of parties in congress that offered the new president the support of 60 to 70 percent of all seats in the Chamber of Deputies.

Cardoso employed the success of the Real Plan to initiate an ambitious structural reform agenda that focused on extending the national privatization program, tackling fiscal, administrative, and pension reform, and addressing pervasive clientelism in Brazilian politics through political institutional reform. Most of the necessary legislative changes were introduced as amendments to the 1988 constitution and therefore required supermajorities to pass both houses of congress. Given the failure of the *Congresso Revisor* before Cardoso's first term began in January 1995, the prospects of seeing through this reform agenda were not good. In the Brazilian system, constitutional amendments must be approved by *two* three-fifths votes in both the Chamber of Deputies and the Senate, and this must be done without the convening of a conference committee between chambers to work out a common draft. This institutional impediment, one of many in the Brazilian legislative system, greatly tempered the political practicality of Cardoso's reforms. However, the administration made notable advances on the national privatization program, liberalization of the domestic market, and further regulation of the financial practices of subnational governments (see the next chapter).

More than any of his predecessors, Cardoso constructed the basic strategy for enacting reform in Brazil's inefficient and clientelistic political system. Like Sarney, Cardoso was not shy in distributing patronage to garner the support of potential backers. Yet, like Collor, he stuck to an ambitious reform agenda and boldly pursued institutional changes that would increase his own power, as was notably the case with the successful fight in 1997 to amend the constitution to grant the president the right to be re-elected. In 1998, Cardoso employed his right to re-election by running a tight campaign against Lula for the second time, and once again he bested the ex-labor leader in the first round. But the months that followed the presidential contest would be trying ones for Cardoso's reforms: Brazil was forced to abandon the original Real Plan under duress as foreign investors fled the country in the wake of the continuing financial crisis engulfing many developing countries in 1998–9. Administrative and social security reforms would stall for months in congress, only to be significantly watered down after the president's distribution of patronage in return for votes. To be sure, any balanced assessment of the Cardoso administration requires careful analysis of the areas in which Cardoso engineered meaningful change, particularly regarding economic and fiscal reform, as well as areas that were left to his successor, Lula da Silva (see chapter 3).

In October 2002, Lula, the perennial bridesmaid in Brazilian presidential politics, finally won the right to serve his country as president. Beating out Cardoso's hand-picked successor, the ex-health minister José Serra, Lula began where Cardoso had left off, with an agenda of welfare, fiscal, and administrative reforms. The new president crafted alliances between the leftist parties that supported him and the center-right parties he would need to govern the congress. Like his predecessor, Lula invoked a pragmatic approach to Brazilian politics that employed concessions to particular politicians and groups in order to generate substantive but not fundamental reform of the economy and the state.

CONCLUSIONS

This chapter's survey of the political history of Brazil underscores the thematic discussion introduced in the previous chapter and used throughout this text. The first theme is the central role of the Brazilian state in the country's political and economic development. The state's capacity for reshaping society around a corporatist project during the Vargas dictatorship and the state's role at the center of the ISI experience represent the most prominent examples of the state's importance in Brazilian history. Yet the state was also the center of political conflict in the nineteenth century, most notably in the struggle between imperial and local forces over the organization of power. Ironically, the failure of the Old Republic's coffee and ranching barons to resolve these erstwhile tensions led to the centralizing 1930 revolution and the *Estado Nôvo*. In the New Republic, the fiscal crisis of the state ended the developmentalist experience, but state reform and new forms of state intervention and regulation of the economy continued to be at the center of economic development.

Clientelism and the uneven distribution of the benefits of growth are the persisting socio-economic conditions that reinforce a political system that has never shed its strong oligarchical characteristics. Social inequalities, while certainly more stark in the nineteenth century, remained problematic during the ISI period in the twentieth century. Industrial workers, professionals, entrepreneurs, and civil servants were the main beneficiaries of the rapid industrialization of Brazil, but clientelism, state corporatism, and, finally, bureaucratic-authoritarianism limited the extent to which most Brazilians would benefit from the fruits of industrial growth and modernization. Landless peasants and the growing ranks of urban marginals and shantytown dwellers remained largely outside the distributive networks of the ISI experience.

Another cause of the uneven empowerment of Brazil's people and the continuation of oligarchical rule and clientelism is the central role of the state in the creation and operation of the Brazilian party system. The oligarchs of state governments first created political parties during the empire, and they continued to shape national partisan politics during the Old Republic. Although Getúlio Vargas's *Estado Nôvo* banned all of these parties, he created two of the three major parties that dominated the 1946–64 populist period, the PTB and the PSD. Similarly, the military governments used state-created parties, ARENA and MDB, in a semi-open political society to keep a grip on power. In all of these cases, and especially during the most recent democratic period, the close and clientelistic relationship between the political class controlling the state apparatus and the political parties was a core attribute of Brazil's politics. Scott Mainwaring (1999: 56) observes: "The Brazilian case illustrates the general point that states and political elites shape party systems from above." The chief implication of this observation is that elite-run political parties do not develop strong interests in representing the voters, but rather are vehicles for the empowerment (and, in some cases, enrichment) of the political class.

Despite these overarching tendencies in Brazilian politics, civil society also demonstrated a capacity at times for enacting change. The rise of the anti-authoritarian movements of the 1980s and the more routine activity of thousands of non-governmental organizations on environmental, social justice, and ethnic and gender issues during the 1990s are signs that Brazilian politics can change in new ways (see chapter 6). The transition to democracy broke with many of the old orthodoxies of the past, although many of the elites who came to dominate the New Republic were affiliated with the preceding military governments. The transition did not stall with the rise of a new authoritarian movement, and it did not lead to a more oligarchical political structure like the Old Republic or the exclusively populist politics of the 1945–64 period. The politics of the New Republic were a mixture of all of these tendencies – clientelism, populism, developmentalism and liberalism, and oligarchy, but also social mobilization. With the emergence of organizations such as Lula's Workers' Party, the new democracy would amount to more than a renewed "experiment in democracy."

Finally, it is apparent from Brazilian history that what happens in world politics and in the global economy has a direct effect on domestic politics. From the colonial period to the present, Brazil's political order and economic system have been affected by change on the outside. The country's independence, the decline of slavery, the political and economic transformations of the 1930s and 1940s, industrialization, the rise of bureaucratic-authoritarianism, and the transition to democracy represented major transformations of state and society, and each was catalyzed or reinforced by events in other countries and in the global economy. Yet it is only in the most recent period that Brazil has asserted a larger role for itself in the world. This contrasts with the era of the Cold War when Brazil aligned itself with other developing countries as part of an effort not to be subsumed into one or the other of the superpowers' camps. Brazil today is trying to define itself on the global stage as a power in its own right. As this role develops, Brazil might instigate change in other countries and around the globe.

3

STATE-BUILDING AND STATE REFORM AS A CHALLENGE TO DEMOCRATIC POLITICS

The Brazilian state structure is organized to disperse power. Although the *Estado Nôvo* and the military regime of 1964–85 attempted to concentrate authority, these experiments eventually succumbed to the dominant tendency of multiple interests, many of them powerful "veto players," to shape governments and policy. Fernando Henrique Cardoso himself once coined the term "bureaucratic rings" to describe the self-serving exchange of favors and positions linking agencies of the state and segments of Brazilian business, organized labor, multinational firms, and other powerful actors. So even during authoritarian periods, when the central state could act under the direction of dictatorial presidents, it was infused with private (special) interests. The political order was centralized but the state itself was porous and so political power remained diffuse.

Brazil's state structure also reflects societal structures. Despite the heterogeneity of interests, Brazilian society is not fragmented along deep ethnic, linguistic, or religious lines. Such cleavages have been known to make the task of governing much more difficult in other developing countries. Nor are the classic urban–rural and rich region–poor region divides or the persisting racial and class cleavages of Brazilian society so intractable that they call into question the legitimacy of the state. Apart from the politics of the governors and the particular experience of São Paulo and Rio Grande do Sul earlier in the twentieth century, secessionist sentiments have been weak. As a result, Brazilian society is unlikely to create a "crisis of statehood" in which the authority of the national state bureaucracy is likely to be challenged by violent opposition.

The Brazilian state is a complicated object to study because it has played a central role in the politics of modern Brazil. Nevertheless, several key lessons may be gleaned from its study in a variety of areas. These lessons are summarized in **box 3.1**, which follows the order of the rest of the chapter. First, we will examine the most general and enduring characteristics of the Brazilian state, then look at the area of economic reform. Understanding the Brazilian state's role in the country's economic development is most important for grasping the politics of state formation and reform. This section encompasses the subjects of macroeconomic reform, privatization, the regulatory apparatus including the judiciary, and federalism. National security and the promotion of governability, key areas for the development of democratic citizenship as well as a democratic state, are the focus of the final section.

Box 3.1   The characteristics of the Brazilian state

- The politics of the Brazilian state is shaped by the logics of patronage, sustained clientele networks, and patrimonialism. Therefore, the Brazilian state does not act in the "public interest" and state elites are not normally accountable to one another or to the public. The state acts, instead, on behalf of elite groups with privileged access to it.
- Political elites in the contemporary democratic period struggled most with the problem of inflation. Their success hinged upon their ability to curtail clientelistic influences on spending decisions while building popular support through demonstrated initial success (e.g., Fernando Henrique Cardoso's Real Plan).
- President Cardoso had some success with structural reforms following the Real Plan, specifically privatization, but he struggled to control the growth of public debt.
- Cardoso's failure to get legislative approval for extensive tax and social security reform, which presents numerous ongoing problems for the fiscal health of Brazil, catalyzed a financial crisis in 1999 that brought down the Real Plan but did not bring back hyperinflation.
- Judicial reform has progressed very slowly. The problems of an overly political court system and the intervention of the courts in political decisions have deepened the inefficiencies of public policy-making and threatened the regulatory powers the state must have in a more market-oriented society.
- The evolution of federalism in the New Republic presented fundamental challenges to the economic reform agenda of the national government. Since the Cardoso presidency, however, some elements of centralized control have reversed the most perverse aspects of the Brazilian state's highly decentralized fiscal and policy-making apparatus.
- The armed forces have become less of a threat to democracy as they search for a new professional identity within Brazil's national security and defense policy.
- Police violence is a major cause of domestic insecurity and human rights violations. Without reform, official violence will continue to undermine democratic citizenship and reinforce a culture of impunity among elites.

THE CORE ASPECTS OF THE POLITICS OF THE BRAZILIAN STATE

The politics of the Brazilian state follows several enduring logics that are also reflected in the system of democratic representation (see chapter 4) and in the economic and class structure (see chapter 5). The first and most persistent aspect of the Brazilian state is that it is both an arena for political actors to fight over authority and resources and a provider of resources to a broader arena of social and economic life. What links these two dimensions more than anything else is the logic of patronage politics – the dispensing of favors and public resources to cultivate political allies and gain greater authority and wealth for those in power or for those who seek power. Jobs, public contracts, access to public services, and the distribution of fiscal and regulatory protections have historically been the mechanisms of patronage politics. All of these mechanisms have involved the state apparatus in one form or another.

A second enduring logic of the Brazilian state is the tendency for patronage politics to create ongoing political networks among individuals. The most common have evolved around powerful "patrons" who have cultivated bonds with less powerful "clients." As in the traditional patron–client relationship described in Brazil by Victor Nunes Leal (1976), the patrons are dependent on the continuing support of their network of clients to gain and retain political power. In Leal's description of patron–client ties in the countryside, landed elites – "colonels" (*coroneis*) – manage the political activity of their peasant clients who work their land and are dependent upon their favors. The *coroneis* provide essential public services such as justice and protection, thereby equating private interests with public functions. Scholars following Leal argued that these mutually reinforcing clienteles were not limited to rural counties. They expanded to urban areas and they continued even as the Brazilian state modernized and became more sophisticated in regulating, distributing, and protecting society and the economy (Weyland 1996; Hagopian 1996; Samuels 2003). Clientele networks adapted to modernization by moving from parochial local politics in which allies shared kinship and extended family ties to more elaborate cross-class, national networks based in both state and society. For example, the enduring and pervasive private business–state networks, which Cardoso described as "bureaucratic rings," represented the interests of capitalists and the state in a modern system of political-economic domination.

The third enduring logic of the Brazilian state is an extension of the second: patrimonialism. Political elites who believe that the resources of the state are theirs to command as they would their own personal property are engaged in patrimonial politics. Corruption is a natural outgrowth of patrimonialism for it opens the door to politicians gaining undue access to state resources for their own personal gain. Patrimonialism also feeds clientelism in that it provides some of the resources that reinforce clientele networks. But corruption is not the only manifestation of clientelism, nor is it necessarily the most common. Politicians in modern-day Brazil dispense patronage in a more or less apparent fashion (especially for the trained observer). One common method, known as *empreguismo*, involves the doling out of public jobs to political cronies and supporters. The scope and depth of *empreguismo* is difficult to gauge, but scholars of Brazil agree that the number of jobs assigned to political allies exceeds the hundreds of thousands and may well be in the millions (e.g., Mainwaring 1999: 184–5). Another example of patrimonialism is the use of "pork-barrel politics," a term used in the US context to describe the tendency of members of congress to alter legislation to provide their voters back home with federal money. The implications of this practice are more severe for Brazilian democracy than for a venerable and wealthy democracy such as the US. The dispensing of patronage, the cultivation of clientele networks, and patrimonialism combine to reinforce the oligarchical tendencies in

Brazilian politics that are at the heart of the country's enduring political and social inequalities.

In a nutshell, the Brazilian state cannot be said to act in the "public interest." It is, instead, an arena and an apparatus for protecting and strengthening the interests of the few over the many. A couple of examples will serve to illustrate the general principles discussed above. During the Sarney presidency, the minister of communications, Antônio Carlos Magalhães, the most powerful political broker from the northeastern state of Bahia, distributed licenses for television and radio stations to friends and backers of the president. "ACM," as he is called in Brazil, treated these licenses as his own personal property, dispensing them to whomever he decided deserved consideration. Many of these individuals were politicians themselves who would be able to use their own media to favor their own campaigns and those of their allies. The patronage transactions, however, would not be finalized until the recipients signed pledges endorsing Sarney's bid to extend his presidential term to five years. This clientelistic exchange of favors solidified an unstable political pact between Sarney's presidency and the many interests of the center-right parties that nominally supported his policies in the congress, but only at a price. In this story, clientelistic networks, built by the dispensing of patronage and justified by the patrimonial privileges of ACM's cabinet position, helped sustain the first democratic government Brazil had seen in twenty-one years.

One necessary condition for explaining the continuation of patronage politics, clientele networks, and patrimonialism in Brazil is the absence of any real state apparatus with the resources and the interests to cause elites to be accountable. Regulatory agencies and watchdog groups have, until recently, been hollow institutions. Congressional oversight of the system is rendered toothless by the fact that, since most politicians benefit from the status quo, few have incentives to generate any real change. The universal norm in congress is to preserve the multiple avenues that politicians and their allies have to escape charges of influence peddling and corruption. This guarantee of impunity is the product of weak or non-existent oversight by the bureaucracy, the legislature, and the courts. It manifests itself not only within the political class, but also among officials charged to implement the law. Police officers, judges, and even attorneys regularly skirt legal requirements, often to the detriment of the poorest and weakest members of the citizenry.

The end result of these multiple and enduring logics of patronage politics, clientelism, patrimonialism, and the absence of accountability (the "culture of impunity") is that the Brazilian state is a fragmented and inefficient actor. It is also an arena in which an oligarchy of business, financial, and political elites achieve and protect their particular interests with little regard for the common good. This subverts democracy by placing the interests of the many below the parochial concerns of the few. These themes will emerge in the following sections as we discuss different aspects of how the reform of the state has evolved during the democratic period.

THE POLITICAL ECONOMY OF STATE REFORM

For most of its history, the Brazilian state has functioned as the central actor in the economic development of the country. The state produced the first key commodity industries in the post-World War II economy that allowed Brazil to industrialize and deepen ISI (Baer 1965). That model of "state-led" development depended upon the cultivation of enduring ties between the state and domestic and foreign capital or, as one author has famously called it, the "triple alliance" (*o tri-pé*) (Evans 1979). The inefficiency and division produced by clientelistic exchange plus the advent of the Latin American debt crisis, the erosion of the ISI economy, and the systematic fiscal crisis of the Brazilian state during the 1980s dismantled the old triple alliance (Abranches 1978; Evans 1989; Frieden 1991; Weyland 1998). Domestic producers could no longer rely on a ready and available stream of public investment to finance and sustain their market positions at home or abroad. The increasing openness of the economy to foreign imports, in part a response to escalating inflation rates, removed the protection that had guaranteed the profits of many ISI industries. Privatization and administrative reform threatened the previously unassailable jobs of state bureaucrats and the managers of public firms. Yet these changes did not occur all at one time, nor did they run their full course during the first years of the crisis of ISI. Brazil's post-ISI economy emerged slowly over the course of two decades. It remains a work in progress, its eventual shape far from certain in all its aspects.

The 1980s were for Brazil a "lost decade," as they were for the other large debtor states of Latin America. These countries faced bouts of high inflation, growing unemployment, and eroding public finances as a result of the burdens of servicing the huge external debt and coping with domestic fiscal imbalances (Sallum 2003). Brazil's new civilian leaders responded to these crises in a piecemeal fashion, always with a mind to preserve elements of the old political coalition of developmentalism that was the source of the central state's legitimacy (Barros de Castro 1994). Many of these leaders were themselves veterans of developmentalist civilian and military governments in the previous decades (Hagopian 1996). Because they were limited by this experience, their attempts to stabilize prices, promote growth, and deal with the fiscal crisis of the state were halfway measures at best (Pereira 1993). Yet each of the administrations following the transition to democracy made some progress in particular areas of the reform agenda. The Sarney administration began the opening up of the domestic market to foreign trade; the Collor government inaugurated an extensive privatization program; the Franco administration under the leadership of Fernando Henrique Cardoso's Finance Ministry tamed hyperinflation; and Cardoso's government deepened and expanded structural reforms, which his successor, Lula da Silva, is now charged with finishing. The aggregate effect over the course of the last twenty years has been a "rebuilding of state capacity and improving federal control over government finances" (Kingstone 2000: 186).

No other aspect of the political economy of state reform proved more troublesome than the persistence of macroeconomic instability during the first years of the New Republic. The failure of macroeconomic reform was concentrated in a period stretching from 1986 to 1993, in which no fewer than seven major plans collapsed. The beginning of this period began hopefully in February 1986 with an initially successful stabilization effort by the Sarney government's first Cruzado Plan, which created a new currency (the *cruzado*) and attempted to eliminate memories of inflation by freezing prices and, temporarily, wages. Yet widespread violation of price controls and Sarney's penchant for increasing wages to buy popular support made the effects of Cruzado I ephemeral. Growing budget deficits, the lack of structural reform such as privatization, and the new constitution's protection of insolvent social security and exorbitant civil service payrolls spelled the demise of the plan's successors, Cruzado II, the Summer Plan, and the Bresser Plan (Cardoso 2004: 29–30; Pereira 1993). The Collor administration's own plan was more extreme than anything Sarney had tried. Collor froze private bank accounts, increased taxes, froze prices and wages temporarily, and created a new currency. These measures only produced widespread discontent, massive opposition in congress, and a deepening recession that undercut Collor's subsequent attempts to make deals with the opposition to get structural reforms passed through the legislature. In the end, inflation soared again, up to 2,477 percent by the end of 1993 (see table 3.1).

Sarney's and Collor's record of failure reflected the contradictions of the Brazilian state in the neoliberal era. In order to reduce hyperinflation, these presidents had to pass structural reform such as privatization, civil and administrative reform, and social security and pension reform to reduce high, unsustainable levels of government spending that pushed prices up. But in order to get such reforms passed through congress, presidents had to promise substantial patronage expenditures to get the support of legislators. While Sarney's willingness to dispense patronage and engage in populist distribution ruined his inflation-control measures, Collor's stubborn disregard and outright disdain for patronage undercut his reforms in congress. When in 1992 Collor was finally willing to play by these erstwhile rules of Brazilian politics, his time had

Table 3.1   Macroeconomic indicators, 1986–2003

Year	Annual real % change in GDP	Annual inflation	External debt (US$ billion)	External debt as a % of GDP
1986	7.5	59	111	49.4
1987	3.5	395	121	50.3
1988	−0.1	993	114	46.9
1989	3.2	1,862	115	40.2
1990	−4.3	2,739	123	40.6
1991	1.0	472	123	37.9
1992	−0.5	1,119	136	37.2
1993	4.9	2,477	146	33.0
1994	5.9	916	148	29.2
1995	4.2	22	159	30.5
1996	2.7	9	179	33.3
1997	3.3	5	200	34.5
1998	0.1	2	242	42.6
1999	0.8	9	242	46.8
2000	4.4	6	236	49.4
2001	1.3	8	210	52.6
2002	1.9	13	211	55.5
2003	−0.2	9	216	58.7

Sources: Banco Central do Brasil and *Indicadores DIESP*, May/July 2004.

run out and he was impeached in December of that year under the shadow of a growing electoral campaign finance scandal.

Neither president could reverse the deepening fiscal crisis of the state that made pursuing the old ISI model impossible. Yet old practices died hard. Despite Collor's promises to eliminate the "*majarajahs*" – the fat cat civil servants who collected multiple salaries for little work – extensive *empreguismo* continued during his truncated term. This added substantially to burgeoning budget deficits, especially at the state level, where spending on civil service salaries exceeded on average 70 percent of annual revenues. Assigning lucrative public contracts to politically connected contractors and businesses generated untold millions in additional costs, costs that would otherwise have been limited under a system of transparent and competitive bidding.

These practices became even more codified in Brazilian political institutions during the New Republic as the politics of the Constituent Assembly played a key role in undermining attempts to stabilize the economy. While the Sarney government attempted nominally to cut the domain of state intervention in the economy, including subsidies and state ownership, the assembly established prohibitions against privatization in several strategic industries such as petroleum. Sarney also struggled with the inflationary effects of larger budget outlays for social security and unemployment support that were required by the new constitution (Mainwaring 1997: 93).

Despite the impediments, the Sarney and Collor governments generated some piecemeal progress on structural reform that set the stage for future efforts. Collor's liberalization of trade consolidated many of the attempts at tariff reduction initiated by Sarney. More important, his government's concerns for improving the competitiveness of Brazilian industry shaped the national privatization program (*Programa Nacional de De-estatização*, PND) (see table 3.2, p. 35). Using subsidized pricing and industrial restructuring policies, privatization was implemented as an effective industrial policy to rid the state of some failing firms and reconvert others into market leaders (Montero 1998). These efforts did not reduce the country's mounting debt burdens but they did infuse scarce capital into industries – steel-making, fertilizers, and mining – that proved immensely profitable later in the decade. Then, Collor's efforts to expand exports and end monetary correction of wages (indexation) helped stave off an acceleration of the external debt.

Understanding that inflation control was both economically necessary and politically essential to develop the popular support that would move congress on the reform agenda, Fernando Henrique Cardoso implemented the only macroeconomic stabilization effort that successfully tamed hyperinflation. As Itamar Franco's finance minister in 1993–4, Cardoso laid out a new index of inflation (the unit of real value, URV) that stabilized prices by maintaining the exchange rate within a moving band linked to the US dollar. On July 1, 1994, the URV was converted into a new currency, the *Real*. Instantly, inflation fell to as low as 2 percent by 1998 (see table 3.1). The Real's stabilizing effects on prices were strengthened by the unprecedented openness of the economy to foreign imports that dissuaded domestic firms from raising prices. Moreover, the earlier passage of a Social Emergency Fund that withheld 20 percent of fiscal transfer payments from the states and cities capped the growth of public spending, at least temporarily. That produced an operational fiscal surplus in the first year of the plan. Economic growth returned to reasonable levels (4 percent during the 1994–7 period) (see table 3.1). Most important, wages increased 25 percent in real terms after the Real Plan was implemented, thus laying the foundation for Cardoso's first-round victories in the presidential elections of October 1994 and 1998, both against Lula da Silva of the Workers' Party.

More than his predecessors, Fernando Henrique Cardoso focused on the core institutional impediments to economic reform by tackling constitutional reform. Cardoso's economic team understood that the stability of the Real could not depend indefinitely on an overvalued exchange rate, which the Real Plan provided by anchoring the currency, albeit flexibly, to the dollar. The government also maintained high real interest rates to keep inflationary pressures weak while it also increased government borrowing and assumed greater amounts of state and municipal government debt. Foreign entrepreneurs invested billions in Brazil but, without substantial fiscal and state reform, their confidence in the economy would remain shaky. Brazil's mounting trade deficits (US$6.8 billion in 1998) and high debt service payments already had them doubting that the Real's value could be kept stable. The slightest hint of trouble would cause them to pull their money out and thereby force the Central Bank of Brazil to devalue the Real and risk a return of inflation. To stave off that fate, Cardoso attempted unsuccessfully in 1995–6 to pass meaningful reforms to the welfare system and the civil service to reverse Brazil's gaping deficits. Then, in 1997, Cardoso's reform agenda took a temporary backseat to his efforts to amend the constitution to allow for the re-election of the president, governors, and mayors. The effort proved expensive, as the president had to disburse massive amounts of patronage to collect the necessary congressional support for the amendment's passage. Having run out of time in his first term, Cardoso could still claim that he was the father of the Real Plan, and that was sufficient to win re-election in October 1998. But events in Brazil and elsewhere were already moving against the stability of the Real. Following a crisis in Asian financial markets in 1997 and the collapse of the Russian economy in August 1998, increasingly skittish foreign investors began pulling money out of Brazil to the tune of several billion US dollars every few days. On January 15, 1999, sustained capital flight forced the Central Bank to abandon the band system and devalue the Real. Within a month, the value of the Real fell by 35 percent. While hyperinflation did not return, as many had feared, the government still had to scramble to face up to the underlying fiscal problems that continued to concern anxious investors and threaten the currency.

These problems would remain severe. After the financial crises of 1997–8 and the January 1999 devaluation of the Real, debt service payments exploded.[1] As table 3.1 shows, total public debt (domestic and external combined) increased from 29 percent of GDP in 1994 to 58.7 percent in 2003. By 2004 it was apparent that Brazil's fiscal situation remained grave as the country's interest payments on its debt totaled US$50 billion per year, or 8 percent of GDP (the fourth largest debt service to GDP

---

1   A comparison in *reais* for 1998–2003 illustrates this escalation of debt service payments: R$72.6 billion in 1998, R$87.4 billion in 1999, R$78 billion in 2000, R$86.4 billion in 2001, R$114 billion in 2002, and R$145.2 billion in 2003.

ratio in the world), and its primary surplus remained at half that amount. Foreign investors and capital markets continued to doubt whether the total debt burden exceeded Brazil's capacity to repay. Moreover, capital flight continued as a problem after the January 1999 crisis, reaching a high point in 2003 as US$6 billion exited Brazil. Thus Cardoso's inability to pass fiscal reform set in motion a worsening of public accounts, despite his Real Plan's initial success against inflation and its stabilization following the 1999 crisis.

In other areas, Cardoso's reforms proved more successful. More than his old boss, Itamar Franco, Cardoso was dedicated to deepening the national privatization program first launched by Collor. The president secured the support of a growing majority of legislators for deregulation of sectors off limits to foreign investment (Almeida and Moya 1997). In 1995–6, the congress passed constitutional changes that allowed petroleum refining, telecommunications, electricity, and natural gas to be privatized. The once sensitive area of telecommunications was sold in large chunks between 1998 and 2001 and even the state development and savings banks, once the sacred cows of the governors, were sold at auction, while the least viable ones were simply closed down. Based on aggregate numbers, privatization provided a tremendous infusion of resources. Between 1991 and 2004, sales of public firms (federal and subnational combined) produced US$105.3 billion for the public coffers, US$70.5 billion of which was the result of the sale of national firms (Almeida 2004). As **table 3.2** shows, privatization under Cardoso expanded remarkably, encompassing telecommunications and subnational public firms not previously included in the national privatization program (PND).

Nevertheless, these numbers do not tell the whole story regarding the fiscal effect of these sales. The practice of using public resources to subsidize sales and restructure

Table 3.2   Privatization, 1991–2004 (US$ billion)

Year	PND	Telecoms	State government assets	Total
1991	1.9			1.9
1992	3.3			3.3
1993	4.2			4.2
1994	2.3			2.3
1995	1.6			1.6
1996	4.8		1.7	6.5
1997	7.8	4.7	15.1	27.6
1998	2.7	23.9	10.9	37.5
1999	0.1	0.4	3.9	4.4
2000	7.7		2.9	10.6
2001	1.1	1.8	0.03	2.9
2002	1.9	0.3	0.24	2.4
2003				
2004	0.03			0.03
Total	39.4	31.1	34.8	105.3

Sources: BNDES and *Indicadores DIESP*, May/June 2004.

some industries also represented a fiscal drain. Between 1992 and 2003, the National Development Bank (BNDES) pumped over $10 billion in monies to finance productive restructuring, including investments in new technologies and reduction of the debt of firms in the most export-competitive industries. The ten largest newly privatized firms in aircraft engineering, telecommunications, steel, and utilities received over 68 percent of these monies. Although many of these firms are now competitive, with the state still holding minority shares in some, the overall fiscal effect of privatization proved modestly positive, but no windfall (Pinheiro and Schneider 1995; Almeida 2004; Giambiagi and Ronci 2004: 29). Privatization reduced some of the unproductive going concerns, but it also contributed to the long-term debt burden of the state even as it paid out some one-off fiscal rewards.

The relative success of the national privatization program underscores several lessons about the political economy of state reform in Brazil. First, privatization reform enjoyed a growing degree of support within the Brazilian political class, and particularly on the right and center-right. Market-friendly ideas gradually emerged among members of the catch-all parties – PFL, PMDB, and PSDB – during the early to mid-1990s (Power 1998a). Second, the Brazilian business class made a similar ideological and strategic transition. Although large industries associated with the powerful Federation of São Paulo Industries still preferred state ownership in some sectors, dissident business groups gradually chipped away at these ideas in favor of more competitive practices (Kingstone 1999; see also chapter 5). Finally, key segments of the Brazilian economic bureaucracy advocated privatization. It was none other than the BNDES, the National Development Bank once at the center of the state-led growth model, that administered the national privatization program. The thinking of its leadership throughout the 1990s reflected a sea-change from developmentalism to market-oriented ideals based on competition, technological and productive innovation, and fine-tuning the role of the state in a supportive but secondary position (Montero 1998; Almeida 2004).

The factors that proved salutary for privatization reforms were weak or non-existent for tax reform. Over the course of the 1990s, it became increasingly certain that macroeconomic stabilization and privatization would be overshadowed by the need to engage in tax reform as the core of any lasting and effective fiscal reform. In this area the degree of taxation is not the problem. The tax/GDP ratio in Brazil is high (40 percent) for a developing country, and it achieved this level as the governments of the New Republic cracked down on tax evasion and strengthened the national tax collection agency, the *Receita Federal*. But more than the degree of taxation, the complicated structure of the tax system presents more troublesome concerns. The Brazilian tax structure is formed by six federal taxes, nine major mandatory contributions to federal programs such as social security, four major state-administered taxes, and four major municipal (county) taxes. The constitution grants states the power to collect the largest single tax, the value-added tax on goods and services (*Imposto sobre Circulação de Mercadorias e Serviços*, ICMS), while the federal government handles income, trade, financial, and industrial taxes. The chief problem presented by this complex tax structure is that it burdens businesses, especially those that pay multiple taxes on different stages of production and distribution. This "cascading taxation effect" reduces profits and investment values (Cardoso 2004: 47). Firms that pay the industrial products tax (a value-added tax on industry) also pay the ICMS tax administered by states. Moreover, since the states set their own ICMS rates, firms that organize their production and distribution activities across state boundaries suffer from differences in interstate tax rates. This complicates efforts to plan production schedules and initiate new investments over the medium and long term.

Another problem of the tax system is its regressive nature (see chapter 5). The federal income tax, which was simplified during the Sarney administration in 1988, affords the highest tax brackets extensive loopholes and exemptions. Profits on capital gains are untaxed and even property taxes can be reduced through creative accounting. Tax evasion, which has skyrocketed in the last few years, also allows the wealthy to hide their income and avoid taxation. By contrast, members of the middle and working classes must dedicate a larger share of their household incomes to the tax bill, which has grown only in recent years. The growth of indirect taxes (e.g., ICMS, social security taxes, etc.), which fall on all income levels at the same rate, increases the relative tax burden on the middle class and the poor. During the New Republic every effort reformers made to remedy the regressive nature of the tax structure was overturned by concerted business and landowner lobbying as well as the opposition of governors and mayors, who feared a reduction in their share of tax revenues (Weyland 1996: 112–23). Current attention focuses on reversing some of the most regressive aspects of the indirect taxation system, which makes up two-thirds of the total tax burden. However, since the growth of these taxes forms most of the increase in federal shares of taxation vis-à-vis states and cities after 1996, federal authorities are unlikely to reduce these revenues soon.

This last point highlights another problem in the structure of taxation: the organization of fiscal transfers. The constitution obligates the federal government to transfer almost half of its tax receipts to the states and municipalities. During the Sarney, Collor, and Franco administrations, these transfers were often misappropriated by the governors, who utilized these funds to shore up failing state pension plans and state-owned banks. Untold billions were also lost to pork-barrel politics. So when the Cardoso administration began, the focus was on ways to keep a larger share of tax revenues in federal coffers. The congress had already authorized the creation of a Fiscal Stabilization Fund (*Fundo de Establização Fiscal*, FEF) to allow the federal government to retain 20 percent of constitutionally mandated transfers to the states and cities in an "emergency fund." Cardoso would use the FEF and new taxes free of transfer requirements as a means of reconfiguring the state's fiscal structure. Tax increases, especially on indirect taxes such as the Contribution for the Financing of Social Security (*Contribução para o Financiamento da Seguridade Social*, COFINS), and improvements in tax collection coincided with the creation of the new tax on checks in 1997, the Provisional Contribution on Financial Transactions (*Contribução Provisória sobre Movimentação Financeira*, CPMF). In this way, Cardoso improved the federal share of tax revenues, but this was only a partial solution to the problems of fiscal federalism (see below), and, as previously noted, these taxes exacerbated the regressive qualities of the system.

On the spending side, the social security system presents the most severe fiscal problems and it contributes to Brazil's inequality. The social security system guarantees pensions and disability and life insurance for three categories of workers: private workers who contribute to a pay-as-you-go government-managed plan known as the National Institute of Social Security (*Instituto Nacional da Seguridade Social*, INSS), the accounts dedicated to the civil service, and a supplemental plan available to workers on a voluntary basis. Before recent changes, the average retirement age for public employees was fifty-five for men and fifty-three for women. Early retirement (before sixty for women and sixty-five for men) was possible if a worker put in at least thirty years (for men) or twenty-five years (for women) of service regardless of age. Retiring civil servants were also guaranteed a pension indexed to the salaries of regular civil servants, which was adjustable whenever the salaries of these workers were raised. As a result, the benefits retired civil servants received were six times greater than the contributions they paid into the system. Yet it was the fact that workers could receive some pension benefits for as little as five years of service that contributed the most to the exponential growth of deficits in the public pension system after 1995 (Madrid 2003: 141). Consequently, the total fiscal burden of the public social security system is heavy. For example, in 2002, the government paid out R$39 billion (US$14 billion) in benefits to retired civil servants, a sum R$9 billion (US$3.2 billion) larger than it spent on the entire national health-care system. Comparatively this represents a huge imbalance in spending commitments. While developed economies spend just 1.7 percent of GDP on public pensions, Brazil spends almost three times that amount, and its retirement age population is only 40 percent that of the developed economies. The system is also very unequal. Currently more than 70 percent of all income transfers are retirement benefits that go to middle-class and upper-class individuals. The indigent, the bottom decile of the population, receive only 1.5 percent of these monies. Civil servants, including politicians, judges, and military officers, receive more than 50 percent of all social security payments, but they constitute only 5 percent of all retirees. The disparity is clearest when one notes that R$39 billion (US$14 billion) in pensions goes to a total population of retired civil servants that is just 3.5 million strong, while R$17 billion (US$ 6.1 billion) in the INSS system is distributed to 19 million retirees. Needless to say, the vast majority of elderly and retired people in Brazil receive no social security whatsoever.

In 1998 and 2000, the government was able to secure modest changes to social security that imposed minimum retirement ages of sixty for women and sixty-five for men; it also increased contribution periods and amounts while reducing benefits. These changes helped reduce some of the projected problems in the private system (INSS), but they were less effective on public pensions. The pension system's guarantees of replacing 100 percent of retirees' final salary were changed to allow the government to allot public pensions based on a longer period of employment and therefore a reduced average salary base. But the public pension systems still require much more aggressive reforms to bring them into fiscal health. Currently the social security system consumes 35 percent of public expenditures, but only 58 percent of this is covered by current contributions. This has caused the federal government to increase the main social security taxes in recent years, yet a significant shortfall remains that must be financed with public debt. Privatization, either partial or complete, has been floated by policy-makers since at least the Collor presidency, but relatively high domestic savings rates (22 percent in Brazil, 16 percent in Latin America as a whole) made this option unnecessary. Moreover, the exploding debt of the system would have made privatization too costly in the short term to pull off (Madrid 2003: 146).

The overall state reform efforts of the Cardoso years have been described as "muddling through gridlock" (Kingstone 2000). Yet the amount of reform actually enacted in the eight years of Cardoso's two terms suggests that this period remained one of considerably more gridlock than muddling. Part of the problem was that all the major reform initiatives had to take the form of constitutional amendments, since the constitution of 1988 remained the chief institutional roadblock against the political economic reform Cardoso's government saw as necessary. After privatization, all of the major structural reforms – civil service, fiscal, and social security reform – required multiple constitutional amendments (Couto 1998; Reich 1998). Appropriately, Timothy Power (2000a) has evoked the image of a "permanent constitutional convention" to describe Cardoso's (and now Lula's) dilemma. This made an already difficult task, given the numerous institutional impediments of Brazil's political system (see chapter 4), more difficult. It should be recalled that each constitutional amendment must clear both houses of the legislature *twice* with three-fifths majorities and without the benefit of a conference committee between the chambers to iron out differences beforehand. Such obstacles are not insurmountable, as recent governments have shown, but they make dealing efficiently with Brazil's worsening economic and social problems a painstaking process.

THE REGULATORY STATE

The Brazilian state's developmentalist role in the economy favored the mechanisms of industrial planning, public ownership, and state corporatism. As a result of the transition to a more market-oriented economy, the state's regulatory, adjudicating, and watchdog roles have become more important. But these functions have had to be constructed, some of them from scratch, since they mattered little during the decades of import-substitution industrialization.

The most difficult questions concern the judiciary, a cumbersome, multi-tiered and inefficient structure that is ill-suited to solving the country's problems. Brazil has a federal court system with an eleven-justice Supreme Federal Court (*Supremo Tribunal Federal*, STF), a second-order national appeals court, the Superior Court of Justice (*Superior Tribunal de Justiça*, STJ), which has thirty-three justices, an Electoral Supreme Tribunal with authority over the electoral system, superior labor courts, superior military courts, state courts of appeal, state supreme courts, and district courts. The labor and electoral courts have regional courts that operate alongside the regional federal courts. This diffuse structure produces a system of conflicting and ambiguous judicial review. The highest courts, the STF and the STJ, share the authority to hear challenges to the constitutionality of state and federal laws, although increasingly the STF's interpretations of the constitution have become more influential. Lower courts, however, are not obliged to follow the precedents of the STF or STJ, a fact that undermines judicial review.

Observers of the Brazilian judiciary claim that it suffers from the twin evils of the "judicialization of politics" and the "politicization of the judiciary" (Lamounier 2003: 276). Regarding the former, the 1988 constitution produced a highly detailed set of areas, ranging from civil rights to social and political questions, in which the courts have primary jurisdiction. This integrated the Brazilian courts into the political system not as arbiters and mechanisms of oversight but as actors in their own right with the authority and the responsibility to intervene in political decisions (Macaulay 2003: 87). Even lower court decisions routinely overturn or stall legislative decisions made at the federal level. Lower court judges are free to set new precedents not only on civil and criminal matters but also on constitutional questions. For example, federal privatization initiatives during the Cardoso administration and social security reforms that limited benefits to judges were delayed by the need for federal attorneys to fight constitutional injunctions in dozens of state courts simultaneously. The resulting inefficiency of this system makes any major reform slow and arduous.

The "politicization of the judiciary" is even more problematic, for it refers to the impression of political interests on the decisions made by judges. Relatively speaking, the Brazilian courts were never as politicized as courts in other Latin American countries were and still are. For example, during the military regime, the courts were not always compliant with the will of the generals. In 1968, the STF declared the government's National Security Law unconstitutional, which was a key sign that the courts would maintain a degree of independence during even the bureaucratic-authoritarian project (Pereira 1998). This independence was underscored even more in the 1988 constitution, which reflected the powerful influence of judges and lawyers who wished to keep politicians from meddling in their business (Macaulay 2003: 86). The key result of this heightened political and operational autonomy for the judiciary was that it undercut democratic oversight and accountability by creating opportunities for judges and other court officials to engage in nepotism and cronyism, if not outright corruption.

In recent years, however, it can be said that the higher courts have functioned more professionally and in keeping with their position as increasingly more influential interpreters of the constitution. The STF's eleven judges may only now be forming a coherent set of ideological perspectives, with a minority (usually four justices) tending to vote against reforms and a majority of seven justices in favor of the reform agenda. This was apparent in mid-2004, when Lula's social security reforms were ruled constitutional by the STF. Given that the members of the STF are appointed by the president and approved by the Senate, the justices have tended to be compliant. The vast majority of the constitutional challenges to presidential or congressional legislative initiatives are unsuccessful, but each must nonetheless be dealt with by the high courts, thereby clogging the latter's dockets. Moreover, since the STF's precedents are not binding on lower courts, many of the 70,000 cases on the high court's docket each year are duplicative injunctions. The STJ receives 5,000 such cases on appeal per week. Many on the Brazilian left argue that each of these cases represents a legitimate exercise in judicial review, but the aggregate effect on the court system has been to paralyze it.

The court system's weakest links are at the local level. Brazil has too few judges to attend to the growing docket of civil and criminal cases and constitutional injunctions that must be heard. There are a mere 6,000 judges for the entire population, a fact that undermines the rule of law. Their distribution is another problem. In the poor north and northeast, the ratio of judges to citizens is smaller than what it is in the richer states. These "rural judges" are often the most poorly trained and the most beholden to their political benefactors, local landowners, and the governors. Consequently, few cases of crime, including those involving rural violence, are prosecuted by the authorities.

Efforts in recent years to reform the judiciary have been meager. The most substantial reforms were undertaken in 2002 with the elimination of injunction requests that tend to clog court calendars and the decision to end the practice of having unions place judges (*juizes classistas*) on the labor courts, which presented numerous conflict of interest problems (Fleischer 2004: 121). But the most crucial reform – the establishment of a binding precedent for the STF's decisions – has yet to be passed. This change would go a long way toward unclogging the courts and making both lower and higher courts more efficient. Finally, regarding corruption, recent crackdowns, as discussed in chapter 8, have started to counteract nepotism and malfeasance in the ranks of judges and state and local prosecutorial authorities. Each investigation, however, reveals the existence of wider networks of corruption that have yet to be fully disassembled. So much more must be done to really take a bite out of corruption in the justice system.

One area that will increasingly require a more robust role to be taken by the courts and the larger state bureaucracy is market regulation. The most notable advances to date in this domain have involved the Ministry of Justice's anti-trust unit, Cade, which regulates competition in the domestic market. Cade has become much more active in recent years as it has approved several mega-mergers, such as the union in 2000 of the three largest Brazilian brewers, Brahma, Antartica, and Skol, into AmBev. It has also blocked proposed mergers such as Nestlé's aborted attempt to buy the Brazilian confectionery firm Garoto in 2004. The regulatory powers of Cade were built up under the directorship of Gesner Oliveira, Fernando Henrique Cardoso's point-man for anti-trust activity. Under Oliveira, Cade's decisions had tremendous impact on the structure of sectors such as steel, agriculture, and consumer non-durables. The courts and the congress cannot overrule Cade, although the justice minister can block any decision and Cade can revise an earlier decision, as it considered doing in the Nestlé case. The agency's power has become more relevant as market forces play a bigger role in Brazil's economic development.

Yet Cade cannot do it alone without the support of the court system. The role of the judiciary in regulating business practices is the subject of great concern. Over 90 percent of business leaders consider the efficiency of the courts to be bad or terrible and an impediment to productive investments (Fleischer 2004: 122). Corruption and nepotism play a role here as well, since many in the business world believe they must bribe or benefit the family members of sitting judges in order to get favorable rulings on commercial matters.

Given the weaknesses of the judiciary, it is not surprising that other institutions have taken a more direct role in rooting out corruption. Congress has played a leading role, especially following the impeachment of President Collor in 1992. Parliamentary inquiry commissions have investigated and sparked reforms to practices or punishment of wrongdoing in several cases since then, including the "budget mafia" scandal of 1993–4 that involved corrupt legislators on the Chamber of Deputies budget committee, corruption in public bidding, bank scandals, fraud in the accumulation of state and municipal debt bonds tied to judicial credits in 1997–8, and numerous sting operations and investigations of corrupt judges and police officers. Congressional sanctions on their own members are generally weak, so politicians are still more able to engage in corrupt practices under the cover of impunity than is the case for judges, whom state and federal prosecutors have targeted increasingly in the last few years. There are encouraging signs that the prosecutorial and investigative actions of the Brazilian state have been effective in catching some of the most egregious cases of corruption, but the weaknesses of the judiciary and widespread wrongdoing in that branch continue as key concerns. Moreover, the limited investigative capacity of congress and the federal police (*Polícia Federal*, PF), who as the Brazilian federal bureau of criminal investigations number only about 3,000, constrains the ability of these actors to investigate corrupt practices by the largely autonomous governors and mayors. As a result, the corruption discovered to this point may be only the tip of a very large iceberg.

FEDERALISM

The Brazilian state is federal, with twenty-six states and a federal district and approximately 5,500 municipalities. Yet the degree of decentralization has varied over the entire history of the country. During periods such as the empire, the *Estado Nôvo*, and the bureaucratic-authoritarian regime of 1964–85, the Brazilian state was generally centralized in its administration of fiscal resources.[2] The state was more decentralized during the Old Republic, the 1945–64 populist regime, and the New Republic. Democratization and decentralization coincided in the last of these periods, but in a manner that I have argued was paradoxical (see Montero 2000). During and after the regime transition, decentralization provided an impetus to democracy but it also complicated state reform and further democratization. The direct elections of the governors in 1982 gave Brazilian voters the first opportunity since 1965 to select chief executives. And while some of these governors produced notable improvements in social welfare provision, industrial policy, and fiscal accounts, most of them did not. The governors became, as David Samuels (2003) has argued, the most important power brokers in the clientelistic game of Brazilian politics. By distributing patronage and mobilizing subnational political machines, the governors not only proved adept at garnering federal resources through congressional pork-barreling, they secured extraordinary fiscal resources of their own by shaping the 1988 constitution. The extensive powers of the governors to tax and spend added to the macroeconomic difficulties of the 1980s and 1990s and impeded more extensive state reforms during the Cardoso and Lula da Silva administrations.

The evolution of decentralization and its effects on the state and democratization developed over three partially overlapping time periods.[3] The first phase spanned most

2   The military government of 1964–85, it should be noted, also engaged in notable fiscal decentralization when it created state-administered taxes through a constitutional amendment in 1967. See Montero (2004: 146–7).
3   To be sure, the military enacted important decentralizing fiscal reforms before the transition to democracy. I focus here on the fiscal reforms that had the most effect on the decentralization period during and after democratization. For other decentralizing policies from the bureaucratic-authoritarian period, see Montero (2002).

of the 1980s. It involved the empowerment of the governors and was associated with the significant strengthening of subnational clientelism and macroeconomic instability. This phase also included the extensive decentralization of taxation to the state governments that was codified in the constitution. The military's 1967 fiscal reform set the stage by creating a new value-added tax on goods (and later services), the Tax on the Circulation of Goods and Services (ICMS), and other taxes to be administered by the state governments. Inevitably, state governors, who were appointed by the military government, created confusion by adjusting ICMS rates without coordination. Spending outpaced tax revenues in many states whose tax bases were either too low or too prone to rampant tax evasion to provide necessary resources. With the advent of the fiscal crisis of the 1980s and democratization, these imbalances became more pernicious. The direct election of the governors in 1982 brought to power many of the old names that had already been involved in state politics during the authoritarian period (Hagopian 1996). Now imbued with the legitimacy that they were the vanguard of the democratization process, and sensing Sarney's particular need to cultivate their support, the governors mobilized powerful subnational lobbies (Sola 1995: 40; Abrúcio 1998). The *bancadas regionais*, as these regional lobbies were called, staunchly defended the states' control over ICMS and they expanded the size of fiscal transfers during the drafting of the 1988 constitution (Martínez-Lara 1996; Souza 1997). The codification of the states' fiscal "rights" under the constitution deepened fiscal decentralization to an unprecedented degree, causing the federal share of tax revenues to drop as state shares increased. Federal shares of taxes and contributions peaked at 72.8 percent in 1980 and then declined to 65 percent in 1990 just after the 1988 constitution was enacted. State shares increased from 24 percent to 29 percent in the same period and municipal shares went from 3.2 percent to 5 percent (Montero 2000: 65). If revenue sharing, which requires that the federal government transfer a portion of its tax revenues to the states and cities, is included, then the adjustment in federal versus subnational fiscal authority is more striking. The federal government controlled 66.2 percent of all revenues after revenue shares were deducted, but that percentage fell to 53.8 in 1990, while that of the states went from 24.3 to 30.4 percent and municipalities did even better, with almost a doubling of final disposition shares of 9.5 to 15.9 percent during the same period. The fiscal power of the states also coincided with their authority to manipulate their state banks. State constitutions made the state banks autonomous from federal regulation, a move that would produce perverse effects for the economy in the short term.

The second phase of decentralization spanned the early 1990s to the advent of the Cardoso administration. This period was marked first by the realization that the states' extensive control over fiscal resources and the open-ended nature with which they could spend, accumulate debt, and even print money through their own state banks could not be sustained in the face of hyperinflation. Without re-equilibration of the fiscal powers of the central and subnational governments, Brazil's hyperinflation could not be attacked. The precipitous worsening of the state budgets created an opening for a partial recentralization of fiscal power when the Central Bank under the Collor administration began to offer bailouts in return for the imposition of adjustment programs on the state banks. State banks were prohibited from rolling over their debts to the Banco do Brasil, the second of the three national monetary authorities. The National Monetary Council (*Conselho Monetário Nacional*, CMN), the major regulatory commission of the financial system, stepped in to impose other restrictions on the growth of state debt. Although these were partial steps, they were sufficient to halt a total collapse of the financial order. But the fiscal crisis remained grave. By 1992, the debt of the state banks alone was twice their total liquidity, and state debt as a whole represented half of Brazil's operational deficit (Afonso 1996: 37).

The third phase of decentralization included most of the Cardoso administration and the beginning of the Lula government. During this time, restrictions on destabilizing state and municipal fiscal practices became more concrete. The worsening fiscal accounts of the state governments, coupled with the inability of the governors to present a united front against Brasília, afforded Cardoso some leverage to coerce and cajole the states to implement financial and fiscal reforms, restructure or sell their banks and utility companies, and enact cuts in their wasteful civil service payrolls (Montero 2004; see table 3.2). Cardoso's macroeconomic and structural reforms also enjoyed a measure of popular support since the failure of previous stabilization plans by 1994 had created an acute sense of crisis that brought together business interests, a majority of politicians in congress, and most of the population in a pragmatic consensus in favor of the Real Plan (Mainwaring 1999: 314–15; Kingstone 1999; Melo 1997). The Real Plan itself ended the erstwhile state government practice of using inflation to keep down the real costs of civil service payrolls. In 1993, the Senate passed constitutional restrictions on the emission of new bonds to finance the spending of the states. This would be the first of several federal restrictions during the 1990s on the growth of state indebtedness. In the meantime the Central Bank's high interest rate policy to keep the Real stable made rolling over state debt more costly (Dain 1995: 359). The governors could also not turn to their cash-strapped state banks, which were cut off from inter-bank credit by federal authorities and were each forced to negotiate the terms of bailouts offered by the Central Bank. Bailout terms often required substantial scaling back of financial operations and, increasingly, outright privatization. Finally, the passage of the Fiscal Stabilization Fund (*Fondo de Estabilização Fiscal*, FEF) in February 1994 allowed the federal government to hold back 20 percent of constitutionally mandated transfers to the states and municipalities.

Perhaps the most pernicious problem involving state tax policy was the tendency to utilize differences in ICMS rates across states to attract foreign investors. Since the 1980s, state governments, especially those neighboring industry-rich São Paulo, used tax abatements, rebates, property and utility concessions, and subsidized finance through state banks to cajole companies to relocate. The escalation of these trends became a veritable "fiscal war" among the states, as competing investment plans hurt some state revenues and produced investments of dubious value over the long haul (Cavalcanti and Prado 1998; Arbix 2000). Yet the fiscal war also had another, more positive, dimension. Some investment plans were organized well, integrating subnational industrial policies with fiscal reform to make the mixture more sustainable (Montero 2000: 69–70). Fiscal war also kept the governors divided, thus facilitating the efforts of the Cardoso administration to impose additional restrictions on subnational spending.

The Cardoso administration's fiscal federal reforms came together around two projects: the Program to Support Restructuring and Fiscal Adjustment in the States and the Law of Fiscal Responsibility (*Lei de Responsabilidade Fiscal*, LRF). Under the first program, the federal government negotiated debt workouts with each state individually, thus preventing the governors from forming a common front against the national government. Each workout involved exchanges of state bonds for treasury and Central Bank bonds. The states contracted federal loans to pay off payroll and contractors' obligations while they worked to limit the growth of new debt. As a result, the federal government assumed 87 percent of all subnational debt, which included bailouts of states involved in a US$22 billion public bond scandal that erupted in 1999. Then, with the passage of the LRF in June 2000, many of the measures the president used to constrain state spending were codified and made permanent. The LRF set stringent spending ceilings on the states and cities, it prevented governors and mayors from passing unpaid public bills to their successors, and it empowered the federal government to punish flouters by freezing federal transfers and applying criminal penalties to subnational administrators. Under the law, states cannot accumulate debts more than double their annual tax revenues. The LRF also stopped the federal practice of bailing out heavily indebted states, thus imposing much harder budget constraints on the governors.

The advent of the LRF during the final phase of decentralization created additional incentives for states and cities to develop elements of good government, and not just good fiscal management. Some subnational governments responded by innovating partial solutions to enduring social and economic problems. Even before the LRF, states such as Ceará had already implemented effective programs in preventive health care, public procurement, and agriculture, despite their relative poverty (Tendler 1997). Richer states located closer to the economic center of São Paulo took advantage of the deconcentration of industries there to attract new investors and provide other incentives to move whole supply chains and industries to areas such as the southern region of Minas Gerais, Paraná, and the metropolitan center of Rio de Janeiro (Montero 2002). These policies not only created new employment opportunities, they expanded tax bases, thereby redressing some of the enduring regional inequalities among many states.

Despite the promise of good government reflected in these cases and the overall efforts of national regulators, the fiscal health and quality of public services of Brazil's states and cities remain parlous. In 2002, the balance of state debt stood at over R$158 billion (US$56 billion), or 1.79 times their annual revenues. The poorer states and cities cannot meet the LRF's stringent standards, so many are in flagrant violation of the spending and debt limits. This is the case even with the most advanced states of São Paulo, Rio de Janeiro, Minas Gerais, and Rio Grande do Sul, all of which have debt/revenue ratios well over 2. Management of government resources is another problem. Most subnational governments in Brazil are ill-equipped to take on the policy responsibilities that higher levels of government are devolving to them. Staff are poorly trained or they have outmoded skills. Many governments suffer from outright corruption and mismanagement. In 2004, the Federal Controller General's Office investigated the 281 largest cities and found cases of misdirection of funds in 70 percent of them (198 cities). National education program monies are one target of fraud investigators, since many believe that as much as 20 percent of the US$10 billion annual fund is being misallocated (Hall 2003: 280). This must remain one of the chief areas for reform in the near future if the LRF and other regulations hope to reverse the enduring harm caused by earlier periods of irresponsible public management in states and cities.

NATIONAL SECURITY AND GOVERNABILITY

The armed forces have played a key role in contemporary Brazilian politics. Like all modern militaries, the Brazilian armed forces developed a significant capacity for fighting and winning wars, internal and external, but that was only one aspect of their mission. The military regime of the 1964–85 period was based on a comprehensive project to advance the country's industrialization while restraining the autonomy of a developing civil society. That project was based on a military convinced that it had both the administrative and the technical capacity to run Brazil (Stepan 1971). So one of the crucial dimensions of the transition to democracy during the mid-1980s was reorganizing civil–military relations in a way that would allow civilians to assume responsibilities for areas of policy-making that were for twenty-one years managed by the generals. Military and civilian leaders negotiated the transfer of authority over economic and social policy, the prerogatives of the generals over the military budget, and the downsizing of arms industries owned by the state (Stepan 1988). Initially, the Sarney government, which was led by many elites with close ties to the outgoing authoritarian regime, ceded prerogatives such as control of the Defense Ministry to the military. Over the course of the administrations of Collor and Cardoso's first term, the armed forces gradually lost many of these prerogatives, as tighter military budgets and uncompetitive military industries weakened the autonomy of the generals and increased civilian control over defense matters (Hunter 1997; Conca 1997). The culmination of this change was the replacement of the three ministries controlled by each service branch – the ministries of the army, the navy, and the air force – and the creation of a unified, civilian-led ministry in June 1999 by the Cardoso administration.

Yet it would be mistaken to believe that these accomplishments mean that the military has no current relevance to politics. The armed forces still retain some prerogatives that place limits on civilian "ministerial control." Under the constitution's article 142, the armed forces retain ultimate authority to intervene in the democratic process in the face of threats to "law and order," a problematically ambiguous justification. This curtails the authority of the president as "commander-in-chief" of the armed forces, since the generals can interpret threats to "internal security" and move against a president perceived to be acting above the law. Most troubling, the Brazilian legislature has developed little capacity for overseeing or even understanding military projects to build new weapons systems, the Amazonian satellite surveillance system (*Sistema de Vigilância da Amazônia*, SIVAM), and, of greatest concern, the national nuclear industry (Hunter 2000: 119–22). Therefore, civilians remain obstructed by legal, regulatory, and technical constraints from exerting complete control over the armed forces.

Civilian leaders themselves have also prompted the armed forces to expand their role in Brazilian internal security in new ways. Amazonian defense continues to be a focus of the military, which is also linked to civilian efforts to interdict transfer shipments of drugs from Colombia and Peru. Once called by Fernando Henrique Cardoso "our eye on the Amazon," SIVAM has greatly expanded the capacity of the armed forces to survey the large, mostly unguarded expanse of the Amazon against incursions by Colombian guerrillas, Venezuelan National Guardsmen, and drug traffickers (Wittkoff 2003: 545). Brazilian presidents have also employed the armed forces against urban crime. In 1994–5, President Cardoso authorized the army to invade some of Rio's *favelas* in an effort to end gang violence, gun running, and drug trafficking. Operation Rio (*Operação Rio*), as this mission was called, was tremendously popular with Rio's long-suffering law-abiding middle class, but the generals remained reluctant to take on such missions for any sustained period of time.

The external security mission of the armed forces has also expanded in recent years. The armed forces have participated in numerous foreign peacekeeping missions, most notably the United Nations-sponsored interventions in Portuguese-speaking East Timor and in Haiti. Brazil's commitments in these cases are part of the country's aspirations to play a greater role at the UN itself, perhaps with a permanent seat on the Security Council (see chapter 7). Since Brazil does not face any serious external threats on its borders with other South American countries, the armed forces will most likely focus their external mission in the years to come on multilateral peacekeeping efforts of this type.

By contrast, Brazil's internal security problems are far worse than its external concerns. Urban crime is among the worst in Latin America. The mortality rate by firearms between 1991 and 2000 for men between the ages of fifteen and twenty-four increased by 95 percent, from 36.8 deaths per 100,000 to 71.7 (IBGE 2004). The homicide rate nationwide increased between 1980 and 2000 by 130 percent, one of the highest in the region. Gangland-style shootings like those depicted in Paulo Lins's novel *Cidade de Deus* (*City of God*) and in the eponymous Oscar-nominated movie are all too common in the *favelas* in urban centers such as Rio de Janeiro and São Paulo. Drug dealers in the *favelas* wield both legitimacy and military violence effectively against their rivals and against official law enforcement. The most successful *favela* kingpins provide protection to people in the community as a popular cover for their illegal activity (Leeds 1996; Arias 2004). They also gather extensive armaments to secure their positions. Organized bands of gangsters regularly invade army and air force facilities to steal caches of assault weapons and even explosives, or they purchase these armaments from unscrupulous brokers with ties to the police and the armed forces. Although the vast majority of the urban poor do not participate in these gangs, they are the chief victims of gang and official violence. The average *favelado* (resident of a *favela*) is more likely to die from violence than from *any type* of cancer and cardiovascular disease (Pinheiro 1997: 270–1). Even though Cardoso and Lula periodically employed federal troops to quell trouble in the most violent *favelas*, the salutary effects on urban violence as a result of these operations were for relatively short periods and could not be sustained without generating high costs, both human and economic. Once troops were pulled out, the gangs returned to their internecine warfare.

Not all violence in Brazil is perpetrated by criminal elements in society. Official forms of violence committed by the police are almost as common. The most notorious acts occur against street children, who are routinely attacked by off-duty security and police personnel known as *justiceiros*. Urban merchants, who regard these urchins as a public menace, often hire *justiceiros* to "clean up" areas surrounding their stores. Violence against children in rural areas is more poorly documented, but good estimates have for the past decade held that no fewer than four children are murdered in this way every day in Brazil. Another example of official violence is that committed against criminals, some of whom are brutally tortured after arrest or even summarily executed at the crime scene. Human Rights Watch has documented that the incidence of homicides committed by on-duty military police is appreciable. In 1992 alone these constituted one-third of all murders in São Paulo (1997: 13). Other statistics for Rio de Janeiro and São Paulo estimate that the police contribute to over 10 percent of the homicide rates in those cities, a figure that is more than double the rate of the most violent US cities (Cano 1997). The lethality rate is also much higher than in the US, indicating that when the Brazilian police shoot they do so to kill (Carneiro 2003: 244). Extra-judicial killings also occur in the major prisons and jails. One of the most notorious occurred in the Carandiru prison in São Paulo in 1992, when 111 prisoners who participated in a riot were slaughtered by invading military police. Torture and other forms of mistreatment occur daily in the prison system, with some of the most egregious examples existing in detention centers reserved for minors.

Some scholars regard such acts as the products of a political culture that makes a distinction in the application of the law between those who "deserve citizenship" and those who are "unworthy, non-citizens" on account of their social marginality (Pereira 2000: 220–1). This quality is one of several that some observers see as Brazil's problem of "democracy without citizenship" (e.g., Pinheiro 1997). Brazilians enjoy the right to elect their leaders, but not all Brazilians share in the fruits of a democratic order, including freedom from arbitrary state-sponsored violence. The resulting culture of impunity imbues the police and other security forces with a sense that they can protect some while engaging in extra-judicial actions against others they deem non-citizens. Other analysts blame the weakness of rules regulating official violence. Since most cases of police violence go undetected, and even those that are discovered are not consistently punished by the courts, the police enjoy an institutionally sanctioned impunity in dispensing street-level justice (Human Rights Watch 1997; Carneiro 2003). Another institutional factor is the way the urban police force is organized into two branches, the plainclothes civil police and the uniformed military police (*polícia militar*, PM). PMs, who are most responsible for official violence, are only nominally under the control of civilian governors. The armed forces train, equip and manage these forces directly, thus limiting the extent to which democratically elected leaders can change the behavior of the PM (Pereira and Ungar 2004). The constitution of 1988 also preserved the authoritarian regime's separate system of justice for crimes committed by PMs. These crimes are not even subject to the armed forces' judicial oversight but are tried in courts maintained by the *polícia militar* itself.

The Cardoso administration took several modest steps to address the problems of police violence, but a great deal more must be done to avoid continued abuses. The president launched a National Program for Human Rights in 1996 that used incidences of human rights abuses to restrict funds from cities and states guilty of looking the other way. Police academies were also required by federal law to integrate a human rights curriculum. In 1998, the Ministry of Justice inaugurated a national training program implemented through the International Committee of the Red Cross to educate PMs on human rights law. But attempts to legislate lasting solutions have heretofore been derailed. Nevertheless, São Paulo state adapted some of the national provisions, notably the retraining of police cadets in human rights principles and the suspension of officers involved in abuses. The state also created an ombudsman's office headed by a human rights activist to improve relations between the police and civilians. Although these changes generated some improvement in police–civilian relations, levels of police killings and human rights abuses increased over time nonetheless (Pereira and Ungar 2004: 11). Community policing projects, which sprang up throughout Brazil beginning in the 1990s, have shown some promise in improving police–civilian relations, although the results have varied based on local political support and community involvement (Mesquita Neto and Loche 2003). Finally, the federal police have focused their scarce resources on anti-narcotics and anti-corruption activities. If this force expands its current investigation capacities then more cases of abuse and malfeasance by state and local law enforcement might be detected and prosecuted.

Given the extensive impunity with which officers of the law seem to employ violence and political corruption, one might ask to what extent this is a sign of a deeper, cultural problem. The profound weakness of the law in everyday life in Brazil is a subject of much cultural as well as political and sociological analysis of the country. Brazilianists recognize the *jeitinho* – literally, the "little Brazilian way" – that allows all Brazilians to ask all other Brazilians for a momentary suspension of a formal rule in order to accomplish some task. The *jeitinho* can be helpful in a highly bureaucratized society weighed down by inefficient institutions, but it has a dark side in that it helps to cultivate a common perception that the application of the law is always informally negotiable (Barbosa 1995). Its extreme understanding takes the form of impunity that allows political, economic and security elites to engage in systematic corruption.

Conclusions

Much of the work on the Brazilian state has focused on whether the state is "strong" or "weak." The state seems strong on many of the dimensions of state capacity examined in this chapter. During the developmentalist period, the Brazilian state played a singularly important role in coordinating and planning the industrialization of the country. While the fiscal and bureaucratic capacity for such state-led strategies is now greatly eroded, the state has implemented extensive reform. Privatization, macroeconomic stabilization after 1994, improved tax collection, increasing market regulation, and the reversal of many of the perverse effects of fiscal federalism are all indications that the Brazilian state remains capable of reshaping political and economic institutions. Yet the weak side of the Brazilian state is still present and it is growing. The fiscal crisis of the state, which debilitated the ISI model during the 1980s, has continued in the form of an exploding public debt, precarious entitlement budgets, and an inefficient tax structure that erodes the competitiveness of business. The culture of impunity that sanctions arbitrary and extra-judicial police killings is another dimension of the weakness of the state. A weak system of judicial review and official corruption among the ranks of law enforcement debilitate any attempt to counteract the culture of impunity or restore the citizenship rights of much of the population that falls victim to it.

Patronage, clientelism, patrimonialism, and a general lack of elite accountability to the people and the law weaken the state fundamentally. More democracy and a stronger rule of law are apt to change these aspects of the Brazilian state more than anything else (Weyland 2000). Democracy itself sheds more light on the everyday practices that protect the interests of the elite few. That in itself helps the cause of greater transparency and accountability that will make the Brazilian state more professional and efficient. Yet the reform of the state so that it no longer disperses power to particularistic interests will only be possible if the representative structure that determines who the reformers are is also changed.

Brazil's network of political parties, electoral institutions, legislative procedures, and presidential authority tends to disperse power. These institutions have weakened the efficiency of decision-making and failed to mitigate the historical dominance of clientelism and patrimonialism in policy-making. Without political institutional reform, state reform is likely to continue as it has during the New Republic, as a process of punctuated periods of muddling through otherwise permanent gridlock.

GOVERNMENT BY AND FOR THE FEW: THE PERSISTENCE OF OLIGARCHICAL POLITICS IN THE REPRESENTATIVE SYSTEM

Oligarchical rule in all of its forms continues in modern-day Brazil because of the pervasive use of clientelism, patronage, and patrimonialism. The role of these central aspects of the country's politics is most apparent in the representative institutions of contemporary Brazilian democracy. The political use of public resources is the lifeblood of legislative practice, interest-based lobbying, political party organization, and the process of building political careers. Politicians and parties that are most capable of dispensing patronage and cultivating clientele networks are the most successful in the Brazilian system. While this benefits some voters who are the periodic recipients of these favors and resources, more often than not the main beneficiaries are a small number of elite economic and political interests who develop ongoing relationships with legislators, governors, and presidents. In this way, the "representation of the few," even in an era of supposedly mass electorates and representative democracy, continues to provide the basis for policy-making and implementation.

The most enduring aspect of contemporary Brazilian political institutions is the capacity of minority interests to block institutional change. This tendency is consistent with the logic of oligarchical rule ("representation of the few") and the conservative preference to undercut any attempt to alter the structure of political and social inequality. The persistence of this "unholy alliance" between the rules of political representation and the economic interests of conservative oligarchs was reflected in the transition to democracy itself. Despite the upsurge of civil societal organization manifested in the "new unionism" and the *Diretas Já* campaign, the rules and institutions of the new democracy were shaped by many of the same clientelistic civilian and military elites that benefited from previous experiences with limited democracy.

This chapter will explore these themes by examining institutions (formal rules) and the kinds of political behavior that they foster in the elite and the voting public. The first section focuses on the Brazilian party system and the legislature. Brazil is often said to have the weakest parties in the developing world, if not the globe. Multiple legacies of state-created parties, the persistence of personalism and populism, and the erstwhile predominance of clientelistic exchange undermine partisan identities and loyalties. The governing styles of presidents in the democratic period have also contributed to these tendencies. Subsequently, we will explore the seemingly exceptional example of the Workers' Party (PT) and ask if it might not be an "exception" that proves these general rules of Brazilian politics true. Finally, the chapter examines the changing nature of the electorate. The key lessons of the chapter are summarized in **box 4.1** for reference.

Box 4.1   The dynamics of oligarchical politics in the representative system

- The creation and manipulation of political parties by the state undermined the development of mass parties based on societal groups. Personalism, clientelism, and populism rather than ideological or socio-economic identities shape the current configuration of most of the parties.
- The party system suffers from "extreme multipartism" – fragmentation, which is shown in a high effective number of parties, and weak partisan identity, which is reflected in extensive party switching and the failure of the partisan rank and file to follow the orders of party leaders.
- Private and societal interests exert extensive influence on legislative representatives through lobbying, campaign finance, and directly placing politicians in the congress who represent their interests (e.g., landowners, evangelicals, etc.).
- Institutional factors that make representation uneven and cause representatives to pursue their own interests or those of a minority of elites include the malapportionment of seats in the legislature, open-list proportional representation, the structure of electoral districts, and decentralized nomination procedures.
- Presidential decree authorities and *fisiologismo* have reinforced clientelistic tendencies and weakened accountability norms in Brazilian policy-making. These factors are reflected to differing degrees in the distinct presidential styles of Sarney, Collor, Franco, and Cardoso.
- While the PT is far more disciplined than the average Brazilian party, Lula as president has also made extensive use of *fisiologista* politics under the banner of "pragmatism." The vote-buying corruption scandal involving PT leaders in 2005 demonstrates that some in Lula's party are even willing to commit illegal acts to achieve their interests. Finally Lula has been less capable of employing decree authorities to the same extent as his predecessors on account of legal reforms.
- Two-thirds of the Brazilian electorate do not have consistent partisan loyalties or clear socio-economic bases for their choices. Voters from the same social categories may opt for candidates of the catch-all parties, the PSDB, or the PT. The most salient discernible tendency among the electorate is an antipolitical one.

POLITICAL PARTIES AND THE LEGISLATURE

The historical dominance of the state in Brazilian political history is the primary factor explaining the relative weakness of parties and party systems. In Brazil, parties did not emerge as representatives of class interests or organizations capable of shaping the state apparatus as they did in many of the countries of Western Europe. Instead, the state created parties. Most notably, the *vargista* state corporatist tradition was most responsible for the creation of parties in the 1945–64 period (Souza 1976). The military employed it in the shaping of the modern political party system, and the current spectrum of parties is the direct product, for the most part, of the political class and the organizations that participated in the party system orchestrated by the armed forces between 1965 and 1985. It will be recalled that the military first created two parties, an official government party, ARENA, and an official opposition party, the MDB. In order to fragment the opposition, in 1979, the generals split up the opposition into separate parties, the centrist party of the MDB (PMDB) and several other parties to the left of it. Meanwhile, the ARENA reformed itself under the banner of the Social Democratic Party (PDS). The weakness of virtually all of these parties was that they bore the political imprint of the Brazilian state; they were focused on the distribution of patronage and the building up of clientelistic alliances.

The military's attempts to control the proliferation of parties notwithstanding, the number in the lower house increased following the 1982 congressional elections, in which the military required straight party voting. After 1985, civilian leaders removed these restrictions and the number of parties and the volatility of the vote soared. With low electoral thresholds, an open-list proportional representation system, and frequent switching of parties by politicians, Brazil has a system that is one of the most volatile in the world (Mainwaring 1999: 108–9). Yet parties still remain relevant arenas and agents in Brazilian politics, if only because individual politicians cannot run for office legally in the country without a formal partisan affiliation.

The Brazilian party system can be subdivided into traditional ideological categories, although the coherence of any of the parties can vary substantially and in general is not very high. With the exception of some of those on the left, the main parties have a strong catch-all nature. That is, they encompass a variety of ideological strands. If, however, we use surveys of Brazilian politicians and party manifestos and positions, we can place each party on a three-tier ideological scale (see **table 4.1**).

The four major leftist parties – the PT, PDT, PCdoB, and PPS – are also the most internally disciplined and ideologically coherent. Yet these are the exceptions in the Brazilian party system. The other parties either subscribe to a moderately disciplined program of action or are more personalistic and clientelistic. The Workers' Party (PT) is the largest leftist party in Latin America and, as of the 2002 elections, is the single largest party in the congress. The Communist Party of Brazil (*Partido Comunista do Brasil,* PCdoB) and the Popular Socialist Party (*Partido Popular Socialista*, PPS) represent the traditional Marxist left, although the PPS's leadership recently has gone to social democrats such as the ex-finance minister and governor of Ceará, Ciro Gomes. The Democratic Worker Party (*Partido Democrático Trabalhista*, PDT) has been a vehicle for populist leaders such as the late Leonel Brizola. But the PT towers over

Table 4.1   The main political parties in Brazil, 2004

Left	Center-left	Center/center-right	Right
PT (Workers' Party)	PSDB (social democrats)	PMDB (catch-all)	PFL (catch-all)
PDT (populist)	PSB (independent left)		PL (evangelical, pro-business)
PCdoB (communist)			PPB (old PDS, ARENA)
PPS (communist)			

these other leftist parties and its rank and file is growing, while the base of these other parties has not changed. And even if these other parties are on the ideological left, they have not always been consistent in their support of Lula's reform agenda. Since the PPS and PDT in particular are led by individuals with presidential aspirations themselves, these organizations are notably untrustworthy allies for Lula.

Two center-left parties and one conservative party satisfy the "moderate discipline" category (Mainwaring 1995: 376). These are the PSDB, PSB, and PL, respectively. The Party of Brazilian Social Democracy (*Partido da Social Democracia Brasileira*, PSDB) is Fernando Henrique Cardoso's party. Cardoso led the dissident movement within the PMDB that split off in 1988 to create the PSDB. The party groups social democrats and progressives, pro-business politicians, and some liberal economic thinkers, a rank and file that reflects Cardoso's pragmatism. The PSDB has many of the dynamics of the catch-all parties on the right and center-right in that it does not have the internal discipline of parties such as the PT. It also lacks the PT's unifying, progressive ideology. Even so, its members tend to vote together on roll-call votes in congress more often than is the case for the catch-all parties, so it is more internally disciplined than the PMDB. The Brazilian Socialist Party (*Partido Socialista Brasileiro*, PSB) and the Liberal Party (*Partido Liberal*, PL) are reformist organizations like the PSDB and highly dependent on personal leadership. The PL, which is in coalition with the PT, is a party that speaks for a mixed constituency of business and evangelical sectors of Brazilian society. Its leader, the textile entrepreneur José Alencar, runs an organization in which more than a quarter of those who vote for it do so because their pastors asked them to (Monclaire 2004: 82). The PL provides the PT with this evangelical support and with business sector support, which has been useful in calming the fears of capitalists apprehensive about Lula's presidency.

The two largest catch-all parties, PMDB and Party of the Liberal Front (*Partido da Frente Liberal*, PFL), are the least disciplined, but they nonetheless have an identifiable ideological profile (Figueiredo and Limongi 1995). The members of the PMDB and PFL tend to support business interests and liberal trade policy (although a substantial minority champion protection for some industries and subsidies for agriculture), and these rightist parties back a reduction in entitlements. These positions are generally consistent with the Cardoso and Lula reform agendas, but then actually acquiring the consistent backing of these parties in congress is a difficult task. As catch-all parties with low levels of discipline and coherence, the PMDB and the PFL have many seats and they are mostly for sale. In roll-call votes, PFL looks more disciplined than PMDB, but that is limited to important votes and only when presidents offer access to patronage in return for the vote of party members. The PMDB and PFL, along with Cardoso's PSDB, had the greatest say on the evolution of the reform agenda between 1985 and 2000 (Power 2000b). That fact alone helps to explain several enduring characteristics of the Brazilian party system.

The dominance of the PMDB and PFL on the eve of the democratic transition in 1985 might have produced a much more manageable number of parties in the democratic period, but several forces led to the further fragmentation of partisan structures and loyalties. First, sensing the failure of pro-military affiliations, dozens of politicians from the ARENA and PDS found their way into the PMDB and PFL. This served to undermine the avowed democratic credentials of the PMDB especially. The heterogeneous PMDB could not retain its coherence with both rightist and center-left politicians as members. In June 1988, a center-left "social democratic" faction, led by Fernando Henrique Cardoso, split off to form the PSDB. Second, the PMDB further discredited itself by forming alliances of convenience with the increasingly unpopular Sarney government. It repeatedly cut deals with the government in return for patronage during the Constituent Assembly. Despite that, it was not able to stop 130 of its 261 deputies and twenty-three of its forty-five senators from switching to rival parties. Neither the PMDB nor the PFL could hold together in an ideologically coherent manner. Even after the splitting off of the PSDB from the PMDB, and the increasingly more "right-wing" profile of the PFL, both parties continued to fracture around distinct internal interests. For example, the PMDB and the PFL contained pro-protectionist *and* statist industrial and landowning interests and anti-protectionist export-oriented industries and commercial agriculture. In all of these ways, the PMDB and PFL reflected the essence of incoherent, undisciplined, and clientelistic party behavior.

More than the internal incoherence of the catch-all parties (a subject explored in greater detail below), the Brazilian party and legislative systems suffer from what Scott Mainwaring has called "extreme multipartism." The more political representation is divided between a large number of small parties and some internally fragmented catch-all parties such as the PMDB and PFL, the more unstable, polarized, and unpredictable the entire legislative and electoral process will be (Cox 1990). The most studied Brazilian legislature, the Constituent Assembly (1987–8), was fragmented by parties as well as by factions. Although two large parties, the PMDB and PFL, occupied the majority of seats (64 percent), eleven other parties held seats, with four of these retaining less than 1 percent of all seats. Mainwaring and Pérez-Liñán (1997) found that the decentralized nature of decision-making, coupled with the weak internal discipline of the catch-all parties and the large number of factions that acted through the small parties, produced a sprawling, 200-page constitution with an incredible 315 articles. Defections from the PMDB in the 1986–8 period left the Brazilian system even more fragmented. **Figure 4.1** shows that seat shares for the PMDB, the largest party in the Chamber of Deputies, exceeded 50 percent in 1987 but then fell to 20 percent by 1995. No single party held more than 21 percent of the Chamber's seats in each subsequent legislature. **Figure 4.2** shows that the PT's current share of 19 percent puts it in the same position as the PMDB (1991, 1995) and the PFL (1999) found themselves, during the 1990s, as the party with the most seats but an insufficient number to sustain reform legislation without making alliances. In the Senate, which is equal in power to the Chamber of Deputies, the PT's position is even worse, since the center-right and rightist parties control a larger share of total seats.

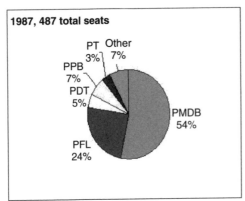

1987, 487 total seats

PT 3%
Other 7%
PPB 7%
PDT 5%
PMDB 54%
PFL 24%

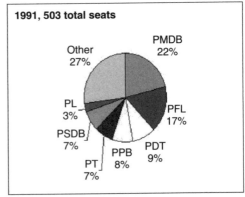

1991, 503 total seats

Other 27%
PMDB 22%
PL 3%
PFL 17%
PSDB 7%
PT 7%
PPB 8%
PDT 9%

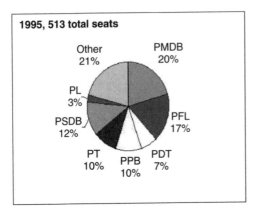

1995, 513 total seats

Other 21%
PMDB 20%
PL 3%
PSDB 12%
PFL 17%
PT 10%
PPB 10%
PDT 7%

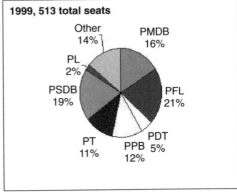

1999, 513 total seats

Other 14%
PMDB 16%
PL 2%
PSDB 19%
PFL 21%
PT 11%
PPB 12%
PDT 5%

Figure 4.1 Seat shares per party in the Chamber of Deputies, 1987–99

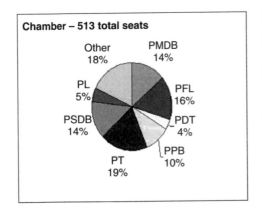

Chamber – 513 total seats

Other 18%
PMDB 14%
PL 5%
PFL 16%
PSDB 14%
PDT 4%
PT 19%
PPB 10%

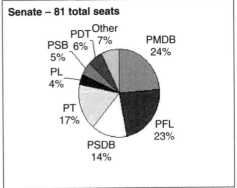

Senate – 81 total seats

PDT 6%
Other 7%
PSB 5%
PMDB 24%
PL 4%
PT 17%
PFL 23%
PSDB 14%

Figure 4.2 Seat shares in the 2003 legislature, Chamber and Senate
Source: Calculated from final Superior Electoral Court (*Tribunal Superior Electoral*; TSE) numbers.

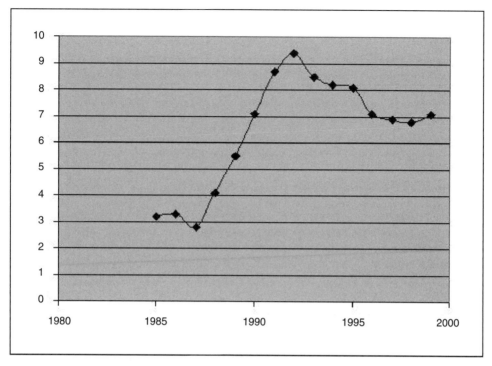

Figure 4.3   Effective number of legislative parties, Chamber of Deputies, 1985–99
Source: Amorim Neto (2002: table 3.3).

Another factor evident in the snapshots of seat division in the assembly over time is the appreciable number of seats captured by the "other parties" category. The figures report the share of seats of the major parties, but not all parties that had seats. These numbers fluctuated during the New Republic, reaching a high count of twenty-one separate parties with seats in the 1991 legislature. Yet the absolute number of parties in the lower house overstates the degree of fragmentation by discounting the weight of large parties. Only by taking the square of parties' seat shares and formulating a measure called the "effective number of parties" in a system is it possible to gauge the true fragmentation of legislative representation.[1] By this measure, as shown in **figure 4.3**, Brazil's lower house suffered from a marked proliferation of parties following the drafting of the 1988 constitution. Also striking is the fact that the effective number of parties remained high even as Cardoso attempted to forge coalitions among the center-left, center-right, and right-wing parties. Comparatively speaking, Brazil's effective number of parties makes the Chamber one of the most fragmented assemblies in the world (Lamounier 2003: 275). This is somewhat surprising given that party creation

1   This formula was developed by Laakso and Taagepera (1979) and is represented as $N = 1/\Sigma\, x^2_i$, where x_i is the percentage of seats held by the i-th party. Following this formula, if the distribution of seats favors two parties in similar proportions, with a third minor party taking the remainder of seats, N will be some number between 2.0 and 3.0.

is not easy. It requires 500,000 signatures spread over at least nine states in order for a new party to be included in the permanent registry of parties maintained by the electoral courts. The most recent example is the PESD, the Party of the Socialist and Democratic Left, which was created by several politicians who were formally expelled from the PT in late 2003 as a result of their voting against Lula's reforms in congress.

Another dimension of partisan fragmentation is that politicians can easily switch their party affiliation. As part of their attack on the authoritarian rules governing the party system, civilian elites in 1985 removed laws requiring politicians to remain loyal to their party. The result was a growing tourism of politicians among parties. From 1987 to 1995, there were 459 separate instances of party defections (Mainwaring 1997: 81); that is, one in three federal legislators changed parties (Power 2000a: 29). Ticket-switching is so common now that party leaders, let alone constituents, have a difficult time identifying who is in their party at any one time. The fact also that many of these changes do not conform with the ideological tendency of the first party (e.g., PMDB representatives shifting to the pro-military party PDS/PPB) is evidence that politicians are relatively free to follow their particular interests and ignore their party label. Candidates have incentives to move to parties with ample television time, name recognition, and clientelistic connections that can provide the means for re-election. Parties have incentives to woo politicians over to their organizations, especially if these individuals have demonstrated electoral followings. To be *bom de voto* in Brazilian politics, "good at attracting votes," is one and perhaps the only real factor determining the marriage of certain politicians with certain parties. Political divorces also demonstrate that individual politicians have the upper hand. Under the "birthright candidate" (*candidate nato*) rule, incumbents are guaranteed a place on the ballot regardless of their loyalty or relative *lack* of loyalty to their party. So incumbents might vote consistently against the recommendations of their party leaders and still end up on the ballot for the next election under their party's affiliation.

The rate of change of deputies' partisan affiliations as well as other factors that cause each party's share of seats to change make the composition of the congress highly mercurial. Reshuffling of cabinet ministries also causes partisan seat shares to change. Since presidents need to cultivate the support of multiple parties in congress, cabinet appointments usually reward party leaders who are supportive of the president's reform agenda. The movement of these individuals into the cabinet involves having their replacements (*suplentes*) take possession of their seats, and, in the case that replacement positions belong to another party in compensation for alliance support, the partisan composition of seats in congress changes.

Brazilian deputies have a high rate of turnover in the chamber. Most leave after serving only one term. David Samuels (2002, 2003) has shown that, instead of seeking re-election and a long legislative career, Brazilian deputies are *progressively ambitious*, that is, they seek to move on after a stint in the congress to an executive office, usually a subnational one (see also Mainwaring 1999: 246). In this way, federalism and the relatively low rewards of a career in the legislature undermine experienced leadership in the congress and add to the perils of fragmentation.

Given the fragmentation of legislative politics and the indeterminacy of who is in the "government" at any one time, Brazilian voters are easily confused about their choices and unaware of how to make representatives accountable to their needs. The exception is the presidency, which is an office that all Brazilians fill directly with their votes. But how presidents govern is entirely left to the machinations and horse-trading of support for resources of individual political leaders.

This situation violates several core aspects of democratic representation. First, it disables the ability of the electorate to *identify* their representatives and therefore their capacity to hold these politicians accountable (Morgenstern 2004). Second, it causes voters to disengage from the political system by not voting (not going to the polls or submitting a blank ballot) or by spoiling their ballots (null voting). The incidence of blank and null voting increased from 1986 to 1998, and turnout rates have fallen steadily since the completion of the democratic transition (Lamounier 2003: 275; Power and Roberts 1995).

Another factor weakening the legislature and partisan identities among both the political class and the electorate is parties' lack of internal discipline. The prevalence of ticket-switching is only one indicator of the devalued status of party labels. In undisciplined party systems, rank-and-file congressional representatives do not vote together on the same pieces of legislation, and they often defy their partisan leaders or whips. Once again, in the Brazilian experience, the Constituent Assembly serves to illustrate the overall tendency. The catch-all parties, the PMDB and PFL especially, held the majority of seats, but their delegations split repeatedly on important votes (Mainwaring and Pérez Liñán 1997). Another indicator of indiscipline is that deputies do not strictly follow their party leaders' recommendations on votes. Barry Ames (2002) has shown that the formal recommendations on most votes (yea or nay) that party leaders are asked by the president of the Chamber of Deputies to declare before votes are taken (known as the *encaminhamento*) do not correlate with actual voting behavior. That is, leaders' *encaminhamentos* do not explain cooperation, especially when compared to the greater effect of the distribution of pork, ideology, and other factors.

Recent work by mostly Brazilian scholars has contested the extent to which party leaders have weak control of their party organizations. Argelina Cheibub Figueiredo and Fernando Limongi have spearheaded this line of argument with substantial empirical work on roll-call votes in the 1988–94 period that show a high level of unity among co-partisans in the Chamber of Deputies. They argue that party leaders organized a "college of leaders" in the congress that doled out committee appointments and other perquisites that gave these leaders some leverage over their rank and file. Scott Morgenstern (2004), in his study of Brazil and three other Latin American countries and the United States, demonstrates that Brazilian parties appear relatively coherent on roll-call votes in the Chamber of Deputies, and more coherent than the two parties in the US.

Such studies are important, but their findings are subject to diverse interpretations. Does the relative cohesion of Brazilian parties in the congress indicate that their leaders have any real power over the outcome of votes? That is, are these parties *disciplined* by their leaders or is the apparent cohesion reflected in roll-call votes an optical illusion, the result of extensive distribution of pork behind closed doors prior to the voting? Barry Ames (2002: 188) argues that the data reflect indiscipline and costly pork-barreling, since other Latin American countries such as Argentina and Venezuela have much higher legislative unity scores and party leaders in these systems do not need to dole out favors in order to produce these results.

In the Brazilian legislature, many other actors compete with party leaders over control of the average politician's vote. The progressive ambition of deputies and the structure of Brazilian federalism enhance the power of governors and even mayors as power brokers in the system. These actors along with the rural caucus compose the two most powerful socio-economic groups within the congress. Given their control over subnational resources useful for gaining municipal or state office for progressively ambitious deputies, the governors shape the behavior of many deputies. Consequently, groups of deputies organized in *state delegations* have exerted increasing influence over legislation, and particularly annual budgets (Samuels 2002). The mayors of the major cities have comparable influence, as demonstrated by the fact that José Serra, the PSDB's candidate to succeed Cardoso as president in 2002, focused on running for mayor of São Paulo after he was beaten in the presidential race by Lula. Deputies in the rural caucus represent not only their states' interests but those of the agrarian industries, and, of course, many of these individuals are landowners themselves. Landowners held about 30 percent of the seats in the Chamber of Deputies during the Cardoso administration (Hunter 2003: 156). If the rural caucus votes as a bloc, its members have more seats than any single party in the Chamber. Not surprisingly, the president and his ministers must directly negotiate the details of economic stabilization, administrative reform, and tax reform routinely with these deputies. Other cohesive interest groups include the growing evangelical/"born again" bloc of mostly Pentecostal deputies. These individuals held fifty-three seats in the Chamber in 2004.

The interests of these factions, which cross party lines, must be weighed in any assessment of how votes will be taken in congress (Morgenstern 2004). For example, efforts by Cardoso and Lula to push through fiscal reform legislation met with heavy resistance by governors and "their" deputies in congress, who opposed giving up control of the states' value-added taxes. Cardoso's efforts to get landowners to pay their debts to the Banco do Brasil were stymied by unified landowner interests in congress. Inter-bloc disputes are also important. For example, the born again bloc clashed repeatedly with the rural caucus on federal funding and regulation of genetic research, which has positive implications for the agrarian sector but raises moral and religious concerns involving work on stem cells from human embryos.

One prominent way that these interests shape the behavior of elected officials in Brasília is through campaign finance. Public financing of campaigns was meager before 1995 and then increased following the Law of Political Parties in that year to US$36 million (Mainwaring 1999: 163). Yet these monies, which are channeled to the parties, remain a small amount of the total spent by individual politicians. Since most electoral campaigns tend to emphasize the individual characteristics of the politician and not the party's program, politicians most often must raise their own money. Donations coming from firms, organized interests, and family members of politicians go directly to the candidates and not to their parties. This not only weakens the party leadership's influence, it expands the leverage that special interests have over politicians. Candidates endeavor to represent their benefactors' interests when attempting to form ties with governors and mayors, who are major sources of patronage. In this way, Brazilian politicians broker private and public resources through personal networks designed to advance their own particular political careers while they satisfy the concerns of executive politicians and special interests.

Although the tendencies outlined above are true throughout Brazil, they are especially apparent in the poorest and more rural regions of the northeast and north. In these regions, tax bases are shallow and states, cities, and towns depend more on programmed fiscal transfers from Brasília and discretionary outlays. Federal representatives must broker these much-needed resources for their *municípios* and defend the interests of their governors if they wish to be included in the clientelistic patronage networks that guarantee their future in politics. In this way these politicians are both producers and consumers of patronage in a self-serving circle that reinforces the interests of the political elite.

The malapportionment of seats in the congress amplifies these region-specific tendencies in Brazilian politics at the national level. The Senate is one of the most malapportioned upper houses among federal democracies, with the most populous state, São Paulo, having 144 times more inhabitants per senator than the least populous state (Mainwaring 1999: 267). Even the lower house, which allocates seats based on population, caps the maximum number at seventy but provides a minimum of eight to the least populous states. As a result, sparsely populated states are overrepresented as much as thirty-three times more per voter than is, for example, an urban area such as São Paulo (Nicolau 1992). If seats were allocated on a strictly proportional basis, then São Paulo should have 114 seats and Roraima would have one. Instead, São Paulo has seventy and Roraima has eight (Stepan 1999: 24). **Table 4.2** illustrates the gap between population and seat shares per region. The most glaring differences occur between the developed southeastern region and the underdeveloped and poor northern and center-western regions.

Finally, several salient aspects of the electoral system add to the fragmentation of the legislature, undermine the discipline of parties, and enhance the influence of subnational power brokers such as the governors. The eighty-one senators in the congress are elected in first-past-the-post contests, as are governors, mayors of the largest cities, and presidents, with second-round run-offs for the top two finishers. However, elections for the 513-member Chamber of Deputies and the state legislatures use a proportional representation (PR) system that differs from the "closed-list" variety used in most legislatures around the world. In the closed-list system, party leaders determine the placement of candidates on lists in each electoral district. Voters select a list of candidates but cannot change the order or, in most cases, provide a preference for any one candidate.[2] In Brazil's open-list system, voters may write in their favored candidates or choose a party instead, but few voters do the latter. Parties gain seats based on votes for their candidates, but it is the voters' preferred candidates that get the seats. Campaigns are focused on the personal qualities of the candidate and so politicians seek out resources that might make them distinctive even in comparison to members of their own party (Ames 1995, 2001; Samuels 2003; Power 2000a;

---

2 Brazil figures prominently in many studies of comparative electoral systems as an exemplar of open-list PR. See Carey and Shugart (1995).

Table 4.2   Malapportionment in the Brazilian congress, 1998

Region	Chamber seats %	Senate seats %	Population %
Center-west	8.0	14.8	6.4
Northeast	29.4	33.3	29.2
North	12.7	25.9	6.8
Southeast	34.9	14.8	42.5
South	15.0	11.1	15.1

Source: Samuels (2002: table 11.1).

Mainwaring 1999). Gaining access to the clientelistic networks of governors and mayors is one of the salient ways in which politicians can garner the support needed to cultivate a personal following within the electorate. These incentives undermine the control that party leaders would otherwise enjoy over their rank and file and they enhance the role of governors and mayors as brokers within the parties. Such tendencies also undermine party identity among members of the political class and the electorate.

The structure of electoral districts contributes to the weakness of party identity. Electoral districts are whole states (twenty-six plus the federal district). On average, each district has upwards of nineteen or twenty seats, so the "district magnitude" (the number of seats per district) is high. There is no national threshold (a minimum percentage of the vote a party must acquire to gain one seat). To obtain a seat a party must garner a percentage of the vote just above the electoral quotient in a state (the number of votes divided by the number of seats). Parties may form alliances with other parties, and these alliances, if they make the quotient, give each member party a right to a seat. So, in practice, Brazil's electoral system is one of low thresholds and high district magnitude. Individual candidates with strong personal followings need only affiliate themselves with a party likely to gain a seat in order to get elected. This undercuts accountability and identifiability since voters cannot know who they are electing and to which party or constituency that person is responsible (Power 2000a: 26).

The process of acquiring an affiliation and then a party's nomination enhances both the personalist nature of candidacies and the highly decentralized character of the political system. Parties hold nominating conventions for all state-wide and federal positions (e.g., governor, vice-governor, senators, and federal deputies). Therefore politicians with ambitions for national office must negotiate with subnational party leaders (governors, gubernatorial candidates, mayors, etc.) who control the delegates that compose the party's electoral lists. Candidates who are *bom de voto* and are supported by party notables are the most likely to do well in this negotiation process. That leaves party leaders in congress as secondary players in the shaping of an ambitious politician's career. If the voters back home and the governor like the candidate, the deputy or senator can afford to ignore party leaders in congress unless these elites have something to offer the local bailiwicks.

THE PRESIDENCY

According to the constitution of 1988, the president is elected by majority vote. If no candidate obtains an absolute majority, the top two in the ballot go to a decisive second round of voting. Between 1985 and 1994, presidential terms were five years in length and then they were shortened to four years by constitutional amendment. Presidential elections in 1985 and 1989 were non-concurrent with legislative contests but were made concurrent thereafter. Incumbent presidents (and governors) are allowed to run for a second and final term as of the elections of 1998, a contest that went then to the incumbent Cardoso in the first-round vote.

Presidential elections have become referenda on the policies of incumbent presidents and their chosen successors. That principle was tested in 1998 when Cardoso sought re-election after changing the constitution in 1997 to allow him to run again. Voters, although not completely happy with the progress of Cardoso's reform agenda, returned him to office based on his previous success in controlling inflation. The currency crisis of 1999 and the eroding status of the economy in the wake of the Argentine financial crisis in 2001 and 2002 caused these same voters to turn against Cardoso's hand-picked successor, José Serra, the former minister of health, and his party, the PSDB. Votes went to Lula based more on a rejection of Cardoso's second-term performance than on the electorate's devotion to the PT leader (Hunter 2003: 154).

The powers of the Brazilian presidency are considerable. The president may initiate legislation (and the office retains a monopoly of initiation over many areas of policy-making). Over the last decade, more than 75 percent of all legislation has originated in the presidency. The president has both a line-item and total veto that may be exercised against any legislation. Although the jointly assembled congress (Chamber and Senate) may override a presidential veto with an absolute majority vote of all members, high absenteeism usually means that more than an absolute majority of *members present at the time of the vote* is necessary to effectively override a presidential veto (Mainwaring 1997: 60). Cabinet ministers and their top subordinates are hand-selected by the chief executive, who maintains one of the most expansive powers of appointment among all democracies. Most important, the president may *legislate* through the submission of the annual budget that congress can only amend within the guidelines defined by the presidency. The president may also legislate in other areas through "provisional measures" (*medidas provisórias* – MPs), also known as decree powers, that have the force of law but must be approved by congress in thirty days or they become null and void. Presidents since Sarney gained the power to issue and, most important, reissue MPs in 1988 (Power 1998b: 204–5). They used these decree powers to implement economic and administrative reform, including Collor's stabilization plans and Cardoso's Real Plan. During the Cardoso presidency especially, the right to reissue MPs was used to its maximum effect. Re-editing and reissuing MPs kept pressure on the congress to move the reform agenda forward. Although the right to reissue was curtailed by constitutional amendment in 2001, Lula has kept pace with his predecessor's rate of MP use. While Cardoso issued an average of 3.2 MPs per month, Lula's average during the first two years of his presidency was 4.5.

Beyond the use of decree authorities, Brazilian presidents shape the legislative agenda. They may label bills before the congress as urgent, thereby moving them automatically to the top of the legislative docket. MPs that congress fails to address in thirty days are also taken to the top of the agenda.

The relationship between the executive and the legislature in democratic Brazil has become in recent years a focus of much debate. While some scholars claim that presidents have depended upon executive decree authorities and agenda-setting powers to initiate and shape reform legislation, others have argued that presidents have pieced together workable "coalition governments" with congressional parties to work collaboratively on reform. This debate revolves around the extent to which presidentialism in Brazil has become more parliamentary.

Both perspectives share the same analytical point of departure: the problems of multipartism greatly complicate the executive's relations with the legislature. Given the fragmentation of the congress, the president's party is unlikely to enjoy a majority of seats and must therefore cultivate the support of parties with similar policy positions. This leads to two costly activities for presidents trying to organize legislative support: (a) forging cross-party coalitions and (b) reinforcing intra-party discipline. The higher the level of multipartism, the greater the expense to the president of cultivating consistent partisan support in the legislature, and Brazil's Chamber of Deputies is one of the most fragmented in the world.

The costs of garnering legislative support and partisan discipline are paid in the form of "pork" – patronage appointments, distribution of budgetary allotments and discretionary monies, and changes in the timing and execution of policies so as to favor interests that will generate votes for the president's reform items. In contemporary Brazilian politics, these tactics have been described as *fisiologismo*, a term with no direct English translation, but meaning a mixture of old-fashioned clientelism and pork-barrel politics. *Fisiologismo* is a necessary by-product of a fragmented legislature and weak party system in which support can only be cultivated through the costly and unstable mechanism of offering legislators pork in return for their votes. In a system of disciplined parties, heads of government can ask for and reasonably expect to receive the loyalty of their party's or alliance's rank-and-file legislators by referring to ideological messages or their own control over nomination procedures for future elections. The compliance of co-partisans in such systems comes "cheaply" in contrast to the doling out of pork required in a weak party system such as Brazil's. This is especially important in parliamentary systems in which the government relies on the continued confidence of its legislative majority.

It is significant then that some scholars have recently argued that the increasing and more tactical use of *fisiologismo* in Brazil is associated with an evolution in presidential–legislative relations in a more "parliamentary" direction (e.g., Amorim Neto 2002; Amorim Neto et al. 2003). A brief survey of differences in presidential governing styles during the democratic period suggests some support for this proposition but also some essential caveats.

Sarney's initial and all too brief success with his Cruzado Plan gave him the strong support of a substantial center-right alliance in congress represented by the PMDB and the PFL. His powers during the first three and a half years of his mandate were defined by the 1967 constitution, which gave him extensive decree powers. Sarney used these powers with little opposition or even debate in congress, which retained the right to veto decree laws. Yet the erosion of the president's macroeconomic reforms, his declining popularity, and the overshadowing of partisan affiliations by supraparty sectoral, regional, and interest-based blocs in the Constituent Assembly (February 1987–October 1988) weakened executive–legislative collaboration. When, in 1987, the center-left within the PMDB split off to form the PSDB and factions of Sarney's PFL became critical of the government, the president could not hope to piece together a stable partisan coalition. Not surprisingly, Sarney began the practice of reissuing MPs as a means of circumventing the fragmentation and opposition of congress. The president also distributed patronage to traditional elite networks. In his campaign to lengthen his own mandate to five years, Sarney doled out discretionary monies and rolled over the exploding debt of state governments in order to cultivate the support of the governors and their allies in congress. This contributed to the fiscal crisis of the Brazilian state and the accelerating hyperinflationary spiral that marked the final year of Sarney's term.

Collor had even less support in congress than Sarney and he had much less respect for the need to cultivate traditional support. His Party of National Reconstruction (PRN), which was largely a vehicle for him, had only 5 percent of all seats in the Chamber of Deputies when Collor was inaugurated. More than his predecessor, Collor took to issuing and reissuing presidential decrees to implement his economic reforms. He spun out 163 decrees in the first year of his presidency, which according to the constitution meant that in 1990 Brazil suffered a substantial emergency requiring an MP approximately every two days! Collor also initially appointed non-politicians to his cabinet, thereby eschewing the tendency to use cabinet appointment to reward rival party leaders and thereby cobble together congressional majorities. Collor's tendency to rely on decrees and abandon the use of political appointments no doubt contributed to congress's antipathy toward his presidency and the fervor of the effort to impeach him in 1992 (Weyland 1993).

Collor's vice-president and successor in 1992, Itamar Franco, governed in the traditional *fisiologista* style. His initial cabinet reflected a broad range of ministers from parties on the left (PT) to the right (PFL) and center (PMDB and PSDB). Yet Franco also overcommitted himself to hundreds of pork-barrel projects that limited the extent to which he could engage in crucial fiscal and structural reforms. Had it not been for the success of finance minister Fernando Henrique Cardoso's Real Plan, Franco's government would have been a dismal failure. Even so, Franco's two years in office provided much proof that *fisiologismo* could easily become an end in itself, thereby compromising a president's reform agenda.

Cardoso's governing style, while even more dependent upon decree powers than Collor's presidency, was more "parliamentary" than that of his predecessors. An emerging pro-market reform majority in congress, coupled with an appreciation of Cardoso's success in taming inflation and the president's own strategy of doling out cabinet and subcabinet appointments to the notables of the largest center-right parties in rough proportion to their share of seats in the congress, enabled the president to pass reform legislation. More than his predecessors, Cardoso employed his power of appointments to cultivate congressional support, a tactic that shaped the behavior of "government parties" that tended to support reform legislation on repeated roll-call votes (Amorim Neto 2002).

While Cardoso's relations with congress suggested a transition to a more "parliamentary" style, this point must be qualified with reference to the substantial costs of this approach and its limited effectiveness. Cardoso was forced to distribute significant patronage to his political allies to reinforce these legislative alliances. Given weak party discipline and the undue influence of interests outside of congress on deputies' behavior, the president often had to cultivate the support of individual deputies by satisfying a broad array of interests – governors, mayors, business elites – with substantial disbursements of pork. The dangers of relying on such loose congressional affiliations were demonstrated periodically throughout Cardoso's two terms in office. No fewer than three attempts by the administration to reform the inefficient and expensive social security system fell by the wayside in the months leading up to the exchange-rate crisis of January 1999. Each failure of legislative support sent signals to investors that Brazil's overvalued currency could not be maintained, thus precipitating the crisis of the Real Plan.

The debate between those scholars who see parliamentary tendencies in executive–legislative relations and those who see the lack of party discipline and legislative fragmentation as disabling any kind of true presidential leadership in congress will not likely be resolved soon. One of the most recalcitrant problems is the kind of data scholars use to support their arguments. Some have relied on roll-call votes in congress, but others have pointed out that these votes reflect only legislation that is actually considered. It does not represent legislation that the president fails to submit to a vote owing to his perception that he does not have the necessary support in congress (Ames 2002: 189–90). In true parliamentary systems with disciplined governing parties and coalitions, prime ministers always know that the legislation they pursue will get the necessary support. Roll-call votes are largely uninteresting, relatively dull events. In Brazil, high degrees of support on roll-call votes may be an optical illusion, as these outcomes are produced by the president's substantial distribution of pork (Mainwaring and Pérez-Liñán 1997: 473). Even if we accept certain differences in presidential style, Brazilian legislators as a whole, and particularly those on the right, during the democratic period have tended to support the government to retain access to the sources of pork.

It may be most useful to think of presidential power as playing in several arenas at once. Timothy Power (2000a) has evoked this idea by arguing that each policy question in the Brazilian political system involves several actors with different powers. Presidents play in a "decree game" in which iterated decrees give the office a legislative power. The "appointment game" allows presidents to cultivate some support in the legislature from ambitious politicians (Amorim Neto 2002). Finally, the wider "patronage game" gives presidents the ability to distribute pork and jobs in an effort to muster support for reform from business actors (Kingstone 1999), subnational governments (Montero 2004), and the many private interests that lobby or sit directly inside the congress (Ames 2001). Brazilian presidents, therefore, are neither kings nor king-makers, but they have considerable resources at their disposal to cobble together, albeit in an inefficient and costly manner, political support for reform. Perhaps this more than anything else explains the slow, sometimes contradictory, but generally progressive pattern of reform during the Cardoso and Lula administrations.

THE PT EXCEPTION

Scholars of the Brazilian party system always set aside the Workers' Party as the exception to the undisciplined, incoherent, and poorly led organizations that typify the political parties of Brazil (e.g., Mainwaring 1995: 382; Weyland 1996: 73). Although these same scholars point to the internal factionalism of the PT, a somewhat fanciful devotion to socialism among some of these groups, and internal procedures that are sometimes not very democratic (e.g., Azevedo 1995), the consensus is that the PT is the very model of the disciplined and participatory party (Lacerda 2002). It is, perhaps, the most disciplined and well-organized party in Latin America. Moreover, it is a party that by its examples of "good government" at the municipal and state levels has done much to strengthen Brazilian democracy overall (Nylen 1997, 2000). This makes the revelation in 2005 by a former member of the PT's governing coalition of parties of a vote-buying scheme led by Workers' Party leaders so shocking. No event in the twenty-five year history of the party has cast more doubt on the PT's unique role in building Brazil's democracy.

Before 2005, the organization of the PT and its leadership of good governments provided ample support for the idea that it was an exception in the Brazilian party system. First, the origins of the PT defy the model of state-created parties. The PT was formed in 1980 by the leaders of the union movement in the industrial areas of São Paulo (Keck 1992; Meneguello 1989). This mass base infused the party with a combination of organizational discipline and strong grass roots that gradually expanded during the 1980s to include environmental, agrarian rights, progressive ecclesiastical movements, and urban social organizations. Excepting the traditional communist parties, all other Brazilian parties lack a similar mass base. Second, as **table 4.3** shows, the PT's electoral successes have grown steadily since its founding. PT mayors now number 411, whereas the party had only about thirty during the 1980s. PT shares of seats in the Chamber of Deputies now make it the largest single party in that body. Moreover, its members do not switch parties frequently as other politicians do, nor does the party leadership have to distribute patronage to keep their rank and file aligned to the party platform. Finally, the range of substantive issues that have consistently been the focus of the party has not wavered from a concern for social equity, environmental sustainability, and the accountability of elected officials. These matters consistently shaped the voters' perceptions of the PT as the least corrupt party and the one most likely to be concerned for the issues that are central in the lives of most Brazilians (Nylen 2000: 139).

Nevertheless, the "PT exception" must be qualified, especially now that its leader is president. Lula and the dominant faction within the PT, *Articulação*, sought to expand their electoral base during the 1990s in a way that would make a PT government acceptable to elements of business, the middle class, and the landowning elite, the social groups most likely to turn to center-right or right-wing parties for fear of the "radical left" (Lacerda 2002). Lula moderated his image in 1998 and again in 2002

Table 4.3 The PT in government, 1982–2004

	Deputies			Municipal offices	
Election	Federal	State	Election	Mayors	Councilors
1982	8 (1.6%)	13 (1.4%)	1985	3 (0.5%)	118
1986	16 (3.2%)	40 (4.1%)	1988	38 (0.9%)	900
1990	35 (7.0%)	81 (7.9%)	1992	54 (1.1%)	1,100
1994	50 (9.7%)	92 (8.8%)	1996	110 (2.0%)	1,895
1998	59 (11.5%)	90 (8.6%)	2000	187 (3.4%)	2,485
2002	91 (17.7%)	142 (13.4%)	2004	411 (7.5%)	3,679

Sources: Samuels (2004: table 2) and Partido dos Trabalhadores (2004).

by proclaiming his dedication to IMF-style economic policies, the free market, and modest social reform without challenging the property rights of landowners and industry. Most telling was the fact that all references to "socialism" were struck from the PT's electoral propaganda in the run-up to the 2002 elections (Hunter 2003: 153). To a great extent, this moderation at the top was made possible after 1995 on account of the growing moderation at the base of the party. Industrial unions, long opposed to privatization and pension reform, became participants in these efforts by the middle of the decade. As the PT gained more and more municipal responsibilities, its elected leaders forged a pragmatic governing consensus with academics and social activists in non-governmental organizations who were concerned with the practicalities of managing local budgets. In this way, the growth of practical concerns within the base took the party away from the classist, opposition rhetoric that characterized its early years (Samuels 2004). The PT did not abandon its priorities, just its fiery ideology. So practical approaches coincided with initiatives by PT governments to expand popular participation in municipal budgeting, improve access to public services, and guarantee transparent and trustworthy leadership This moderation trend was a product of a larger effort by social movements, unions, and non-governmental organizations, the once and current base of the PT, to replace sustained protest with activity in formal institutions (see chapter 5).

Nevertheless, Lula's appeal to the middle class and to business introduced some significant contradictions into the party's image and, more important, its policy choices. For example, Lula's current emphasis on maintaining IMF fiscal deficit/surplus targets undermines his government's promises of redistributing land to hundreds of thousands of families and compensating landowners at the same time. Lula's commitment to defending industrial employment is also being tested by his government's pursuit of free trade accords that bring cheaper foreign imports into the Brazilian market. On these and other points, the tension between pragmatism and core beliefs has created problems between the PT's leadership and parts of its base such as landless peasants and workers.

Several institutions and structures in the Brazilian political-economic system will likely constrain the extent to which even the progressive-minded PT can expand democratic representation and, as a result, produce policy outcomes that improve the lives of most Brazilians. First, in the Brazilian system of representation, the temptation to play off various groups against one another and to buy support that cannot be garnered more cheaply through partisan discipline and ideological appeals is overwhelming. Since the PT stands alone as a disciplined party, the PT president must elicit support outside his party to pass reform legislation. *Fisiologismo*, which was a tactic Lula and the PT once condemned during Sarney's, Collor's, and Cardoso's administrations, is now central to the Lula government's ability to organize a heterogeneous coalition of parties in support of the reform agenda (Palermo 2004). Given the supermajorities that are needed to pass the constitutional amendments that are the core of the government's reforms, building support for each vote on each piece of legislation is an involved game of horse-trading of votes, pork, and promises of pork. These were the forces that allegedly compelled a dozen party leaders, including Lula's chief of staff, José Dirceu, to resign in mid-2005 following accusations that they distributed or condoned cash payments to the legislators of allied parties in return for their votes on key pieces of legislation. The main accuser, Roberto Jefferson, a leader of the Brazilian Labor Party (PTB), an organization nominally in the government coalition, held Brazilians spellbound as he provided televised testimony in June to a congressional board of inquiry. Jefferson's very public outing of top PT officials and subsequent congressional investigations have erased the line between Lula's and the PT's "pragmatism" via *fisiologismo* and outright corruption. Yet even without blatant corruption, *fisiologismo* is a most undemocratic and unaccountable mechanism of government. Since these transactions occur in the legislative arena where only the most organized social groups are represented – business, agro-industry, landowners, finance – most Brazilians, and especially the poor, who are those most in need of greater representation of their interests in the policy-making process, are excluded from the game of *fisiologismo* and therefore shut out from the real arenas of power.

Perhaps the most threatening impediment to the PT's chances of changing Brazilian politics for good is the pervasive view in the electorate that the very things the PT is fighting against – clientelism, corruption, inequality – are so entrenched as to make Lula no better than a Don Quixote jousting at windmills. The PT's own concern with "ethical politics" reinforces the view of many Brazilians that all politics is corrupt and that no single party can change the system (Nylen 2000: 140). And now that the PT itself has been tarnished by accusations of corruption, it is likely that these perceptions will become even more entrenched. Yet it should be recalled that such public cynicism is a product of weak partisan identities in the electorate, which view parties and voting as mere formalities that provide no real hope of changing the country.

THE ELECTORATE

The inauguration of the New Republic constituted the single largest expansion of the franchise in Brazilian history. All illiterates were given the franchise in 1985, while in 1988 the voting age was reduced from eighteen to sixteen and voting was made compulsory for those eighteen and older, except illiterates and those citizens over seventy. This makes the Brazilian electorate about 120 million strong, larger than Germany's, France's, or Britain's.

Why Brazilians vote the way they do is a subject that has only recently received scholarly attention, in part because new survey data has made rigorous analysis of political culture more possible. The conventional reasons why individuals vote usually refer to how they identify with particular parties or follow an ideology. Using early surveys of the Brazilian electorate in 1987–8, Mainwaring (1995: 385) shows that well over 60 percent of the voters expressed no party identification, and of those expressing some affiliation the main answer was the amorphous PMDB. Analyses by Meneguello (1994) and more recently by Samuels (n.d.) demonstrate that partisan identity for the 1989–2002 period is strongest for those affiliated to the PT (23 percent of all respondents in the latest surveys). Overall partisanship stands at 40 percent, which some scholars interpret as low (e.g., Mainwaring 1999) while others claim it is as high as that of some institutionalized party systems such as Chile's (Samuels n.d.). Given the mixed data it is difficult to say whether partisan identities are relatively "weak." Nevertheless, all these studies confirm that how voters see their situation at the time of the survey is the strongest predictor of their avowed preferences. In other words, voter choice in Brazil is not shaped by partisan identity. Instead, it is shaped by voters' objective socio-economic situation. This may be the most relevant indicator for a somewhat unstable base of partisan identity.

Assessing the reasons why two-thirds of the electorate has no party affiliation is important. The main causes are likely related to the aforementioned lack of coherence and internal discipline of parties, the tendency of politicians to switch their party allegiances, and the incentives the electoral system creates for politicians to cultivate personal support among voters. One might add to this list certain historical factors. First, the parties in the current system in Brazil emerged primarily after 1979 (the PMDB is the one exception): Brazilian voters do not have generational affiliations to particular parties as do the voters of the Chilean Socialist Party or the Mexican Institutional Revolutionary Party (PRI). Second, the salience of the personal vote in Brazil has a long history. Figures such as Getúlio Vargas and Juscelino Kubitschek persist in voters' memories for who they were as opposed to the parties to which they were affiliated. By contrast, Juan Perón cultivated a vast personal following in Argentina but he also launched a political movement spearheaded by his own *Partido Justicialista* (PJ). The fact that Peronism and the PJ have persisted and adapted to the times so many years after Perón's death in the mid-1970s contrasts with the absence of a similar level of partisan identity associated with the Brazilian political giants of the twentieth century. Finally, the ineptitude and corruption associated with the Sarney and Collor governments, which were mostly supported by the large center-right and rightist parties PMDB and PFL, badly eroded Brazilians' faith in these parties (Mainwaring 1995: 383). This may be one of the reasons why reported partisan affiliations involving the catch-all parties have waned as consistent support for the PT, the party of opposition until recently, has increased.

The voting behavior of the Brazilian electorate, like that of many "third wave" democracies that emerged in the post-1974 period and in Latin America in particular, is not based on salient social cleavages, including class (Dix 1989, 1992; Roberts 2002). Despite running very different campaigns in 1994 and again in 1998, Cardoso and Lula had very similar social bases (Mainwaring 1999: 42–4). Although conservative parties tended to support Cardoso and leftist parties sided with Lula, both candidates drew support from the same groups and in more or less even proportions across education, religious affiliation, and social levels. In general, the personal background of the candidate is a poor predictor of how Brazilians will vote. Collor, who was a scion of a major northeastern oligarchical family, received most of his electoral support in 1989 from the poor.

Ideology may form a more relevant basis for partisan identities than social categories. The ideological component in voters' choices has typically been discounted since the coherence of the parties is low and the average voter is too poorly educated to place them meaningfully on a left–right ideological spectrum (e.g., Mainwaring 1995: 376; Mainwaring 1999: 131). Yet surveys do consistently detect a marked ideology in the Brazilian voters: a decidedly anti-political one! Over 90 percent of Brazilians tend to believe that all politicians "always or usually lie" (Mainwaring 1995: 386). Parties and congress consistently rank last or next to last on the list of political institutions Brazilians trust. While that is true for Latin America as a whole (Lagos 2001), Brazilian parties and legislators are either at the bottom or in the penultimate place on the *regional list* (Mainwaring 1999: 127; *The Economist* 2004). More global assessments that compare Brazil to countries in other regions also consistently place Brazil *last* on indicators of trust (e.g., Knack and Keefer 1997; Inglehart 1999). Of course, these anti-political sentiments are precisely *not* the kind of ideological principles that make voters partial to parties. Widespread cynicism is toxic in a political system already enfeebled by undisciplined parties and personalistic politicians.

CONCLUSIONS

The political class in Brazil is largely autonomous in its ability to frame issues and shape the nature of party and legislative politics. The preferences of voters are only vaguely reflected in the behavior of their representatives, who are more likely to act on behalf of powerful and organized groups such as the rural lobby or the state governors than on behalf of the broad and heterogeneous electorate who selected them. So the fundamental problem examined in this chapter can be summed up as one of "democracy without representation."

The implications of Brazil's oligarchical system of representation for deepening democracy are mixed. On the one hand, the presence of conservative interests in congress gives these powerful interests a stake in maintaining the system. So long as policy reflects their preferences, these actors need not embrace anti-democratic values as many did in 1964 when the military initiated the bureaucratic-authoritarian regime. On the other hand, the dominance of these actors in the system of representation excludes the voice of other members of civil society who represent a larger percentage of the population. This contradiction, perhaps more than any other, helps to explain the maintenance of what Kurt Weyland has called Brazil's "low-quality democracy" and Scott Mainwaring has termed "feckless democracy." It is a regime that survives largely on the interests of the rich, but it does not deepen democratic representation by including the mass of the poor.

Another fundamental characteristic of the political system is its highly inefficient and unstable character. The combination of a high effective number of undisciplined parties and presidentialism is a singularly unstable one in comparative perspective. Inter-branch conflict, legislative gridlock, and constitutional crises are more difficult to address in an effective manner in these systems (Mainwaring 1993). Meaningful social and economic reforms are either watered down or not implemented in a timely fashion on account of the way formal political institutions work in Brazil.

Given these aspects of Brazilian politics, it is remarkable that reform occurs at all. Without clientelistic exchange, progress in this system would be even more difficult. The dynamics of the party system, the legislature, and the presidency's relationship with the congress come together around the strategic use of state resources. Presidents, governors, mayors, party leaders, and entrenched social and economic interests engage one another in a complex game of distribution and exchange to make political compromise possible. This essential quality of Brazilian politics is unsurprising given the central role played by the Brazilian state in shaping political and economic institutions (Souza 1976; Lamounier and Meneguello 1986). And so it is that "democracy without representation" functions through the parceling out of state resources and authority.

Strengthening Brazil's political institutions is perhaps the most challenging item on the reform agenda because it requires that a highly self-interested set of political groups and individuals alter the very rules that provide them with potentially huge rewards. This is why political reform has been regarded as the "missing link" in Brazil's reform agenda (Fleischer 2004). Yet recent history suggests that some reform is possible. In 1995, the congress passed a set of rule changes meant to strengthen the parties. Under the new law, only parties that gain 0.5 percent of the national vote can take seats in the Chamber of Deputies and only those that garner 5 percent of the national vote (two-fifths of this share must be distributed among one-third of the states) make their leaders eligible for important leadership and committee assignments. Politicians who switch parties can now be penalized by losing their parliamentary privileges, but the law does not make this mandatory and such politicians do not lose their seats. In 2001, the congress approved substantial limits on the president's *medida provisória* power. Under the new law, MPs cannot be reissued after ninety days and must be deliberated by the congress to the exclusion of all other matters on the legislative docket.

Short of a switch to a parliamentary system, certain other reforms can significantly strengthen parties and the legislature, and make the current separation of powers system work more efficiently. If the open-list PR system could be replaced with one favoring closed lists, and were there to be a national threshold at about 5 percent as in Germany, then partisan discipline would improve and the legislature would see a reduction in the effective number of parties. Such changes would help to elevate the influence of the congress and thereby strengthen the accountability of the presidency to the assembly.

The possible institutional reform scenarios for Brazil are virtually endless, with many alternatives satisfying the basic condition that they improve on an already unstable and inefficient system. Political reform, however, remains the most difficult item on the reform agenda precisely because the political class has only weak interests in producing a system that would reduce their individual prerogatives over patronage (see chapter 8). Politicians and their bailiwicks enjoy the benefits of not changing, while the costs are borne by the people, who await meaningful social and economic reform.

THE DILEMMA OF DEMOCRATIZATION IN AN ECONOMICALLY UNEQUAL SOCIETY

The most fundamental contradiction in Brazil's development is the fact that it has periodically enjoyed high rates of growth and is among the most industrialized and modern countries in the developing world, yet it has the distinction of being one of the most unequal societies on earth. This mixed record recalls Oliveira's (2003) metaphor from chapter 1 of Brazil as a duckbilled platypus – a country that grows but does not develop, a Darwinian dead-end.

In comparison to the rest of the developing world, Brazil is not a poor country. With a per capita GDP of US$5,000 at 1998 rates and the ninth largest economy in the world, it stands as one of the larger middle-income societies. It is, however, a mixture of rich and poor, an amalgam exemplified by the economist Edmar Bacha's oft-quoted moniker "Bel-India" – a "first world" Belgium in the industrial south and southeast, with rich urban cores, surrounded by a "third world" India of poor regions in the north and northeast, and rural poverty and urban shantytowns encompassing the modern cities. Part of this contradiction is explained by the pattern of industrial growth during most of the twentieth century. Import-substitution industrialization transferred resources from rural areas to the urban, industrializing centers of the southern regions. At the same time the rate of population growth outpaced the rate of industrialization, so the proportion of urban unemployed and underemployed increased even as the economy became more modern. These problems were exacerbated by rural–urban migration. In 1940, 31 percent of all Brazilians lived in cities and 69 percent lived in rural areas. But those numbers were reversed by 1991, with 76 percent inhabiting cities and 25 percent the countryside (Ribeiro and Scanlon 2003: 206). After the 1960s, millions of poor rural migrants could not find formal sector jobs or adequate housing. Consequently they contributed to the development of the *favelas*, the growing shantytowns that overwhelmed the social services and police forces of the major cities.

These aspects of "Bel-India" only scratch the surface causes and manifestations of poverty and inequality, the twin evils that beset Brazil. In this chapter we will first examine the main indicators and causes of social disparities in Brazil. We will then analyze how the main economic actors in the country's development history have coped with these challenges. Organized labor, the middle class, and business represent large social categories that include a diverse array of different organizations. The relative abilities of these groups to organize collectively and focus their influence on changing Brazil's unequal social legacies provide rich insight into why the country remains a "democracy without equity." **Box 5.1** summarizes the main lessons of the chapter.

POVERTY AND SOCIAL INEQUALITY

Poverty and inequality are the greatest problems the country faces. Any look at the numbers will underscore the persistence of immense social misery. The poorest people

---

Box 5.1   Chapter lessons – key findings regarding inequality and poverty in Brazil

- Poverty and inequality have worsened even as Brazil has democratized. Rural dwellers, inhabitants of the north and northeast regions, Afro-Brazilians, and women are disproportionately the victims of socio-economic inequities.
- The economic causes of inequality and poverty include low growth rates, the increase in informal employment, declining wages and wages failing to keep up with inflation, unemployment and underemployment. Inequality is also a prominent predictor of poverty levels.
- Government policies or the lack of reform increase socio-economic disparities through an unequal distribution of the tax burden, disparate and weak social security support, and poor opportunities of access to education for the working class and the poor.
- Mortality is linked to inequality and poverty through higher incidences of violent crime against the poor and unequal access to health care.
- The Cardoso administration passed important reforms to improve access to education, health care, and rural land ownership, but more must be done in these areas and in the key areas of taxation and social security.
- While organized labor played a key role during the democratic transition and on several industrial relations issues during the New Republic, it has lost much of its mobilizational power after years of industrial restructuring, privatization, and the growth of the informal market. The landless peasant movement, on the other hand, remains a powerful mobilizer in the countryside.
- Middle-class and business associations remain fragmented, although certain organizations have been important supporters of democratization and market reforms.
- Social inequality is an important issue for many businesses. However, the focus of entrepreneurs has been on expanding the semi-public vocational training system to address the wage-skills gap, which is a strong predictor of income.

in Brazil who somehow survive on less than US$1 per day make up 33 percent of the population. Brazil is also one of the most unequal societies on earth. According to the United Nations, the top 10 percent of the population earns eighty-five times more than the poorest 10 percent. By contrast, in other Latin American countries the top decile of the population earns forty to forty-five times more than the bottom decile. In the United States, the most unequal of the advanced capitalist countries, the top 10 percent earns sixteen times that of the bottom ten percent. Brazil's Gini coefficient, an aggregate index of income inequality ranging from 0.0 for perfect equality to over 0.6 (among the most unequal), is 0.59, one of the highest in the developing world (World Bank 2003: 10–11; Deininger and Squire 1996). This Gini score is higher than that of other middle-income large countries such as China, Mexico, and India. Even within Brazil, the income gap picture is reflected in gross regional disparities. For example, per capita incomes in the poor northeast are 45 percent those of the national average (Baer 2001: 325). Whereas less than 10 percent of the residents of São Paulo state live below the poverty line of R$65 per month, more than 60 percent do in the poor northern state of Maranhão. Life expectancy in the poorest states of the northeast is 63.2 while that of the richest states in the south is over 72.

Poverty and inequality are worse in rural areas than in the cities. Average household incomes in the countryside are one-sixth those of urban areas. Well over a third of the rural population lives below the poverty line and these poor, landless peasants are the victims of the greatest inequalities in land ownership in Brazil. In 1985, the beginning of the New Republic, only 1 percent of landowners possessed 44 percent of all the land. That is an area the equivalent of modern-day Venezuela and Colombia *combined*. Worse still, the concentration of land ownership *increased* during most of the twentieth century. The Gini coefficient for land tenure was 0.825 in 1940 and 0.853 in 1985 (Deere 2004: 179). And what land some small landowners do have supports a parlous existence. Those who resettle on plots must farm it themselves with minimal technical or financial assistance from the government. Rural illiteracy and disease is common, as health, educational, and infrastructural services are poorly developed and unequally distributed.

Socio-economic disparities are also reflected in racial and gender terms. At least 12 percent of Brazil's inequality is attributable to income differences by skin color, whereas the same number in the US is 2.4 percent (World Bank 2003). Wage differentials are the notable proximate causes of these social asymmetries. Blacks earn 48 percent of what whites make on average for the same job. This is due to occupational discrimination in which the wages of non-whites are reduced in comparison to those of whites, or non-whites are simply not hired (Silva 1999: 77; Lovell 1994). Brazilian women make only 70 percent of what men make, and black women do even worse at 40 percent. In rural areas, women are substantially disadvantaged in the granting of land titles. Female heads of families are routinely passed over by official agencies distributing land titles to favor oldest sons, even when these are minors (Deere 2004: 186). While still somewhat controversial, studies of the racial and gender dimensions of inequality show that, as income increases, these factors account less for determining access to education and other aspects of social mobility (e.g., Silva and Hasenbalg 1999: 58). So wage differentials remain the key causes of inequality, with racial and gender characteristics explaining some but not most of the effect on social disparities.

The causes of wage differentials and the larger explanations for poverty and inequality in Brazil are legion and together form a complex picture. For clarity, they might be grouped into three categories: (1) economic factors, (2) government policies, and (3) access to quality education.

Among the economic factors, the most fundamental basis for rising levels of poverty is the slow growth of the economy in the democratic period (Barros et al. 2000). The average annual growth rate between 1985 and 2000 was 2.5 percent. That contrasts with an average of 9 percent between 1965 and 1980, when the military ran the country. This periodization reflects the crisis of the import-substitution model and the accompanying decline in industrial labor as a percentage of the workforce. Between 1985 and 2001, the industrial labor force fell by 33 percent even as the total workforce doubled. The difference was made up by private sector service jobs and the growth of the informal market. **Table 5.1** illustrates these shifts for the economically active population in the period 1940 to 1996.

Jobs in the formal service sector and in informal work pay on average less than industrial jobs and provide fewer protections against unemployment or underemployment. Informal sector jobs are particularly precarious since they involve activities with little or no labor market protection and regulation. These semi-legal or illegal services involve a diverse range of professions, such as unlicensed taxi drivers (*perueiros*), street vendors (*camelôs*), large-scale artisanal production often in sweatshops, and the distribution of products involving child labor. Moreover, many businesses utilize informal sector workers as part of their efforts to avoid hiring formal sector workers, who are expensive to fire because of severance payment rules and more costly to retain given that employers are obliged to pay into unemployment compensation funds. Such incentives combined with the desperation of the working poor have expanded the informal labor market in Brazil to encompass 48 percent of all workers, up from approximately 30 percent at the beginning of the 1990s (Portes and Hoffman 2003).

Sluggish growth and inflation, even after the Real Plan's success against hyperinflation, are a cruel mix for workers. Wages have struggled to keep pace with inflation. Most estimates show that over half of all wage-earners in the formal market receive wage increases that are well below the rate of inflation, and recent evidence shows that wage rates continue to decline even as inflation remains substantial. More than half of the population lives on US$166 per month (about twice the minimum wage). Governments since the transition have periodically struggled with the minimum wage, which also acts as a benchmark for all incomes, including social security benefits. Cardoso adjusted the minimum wage upward only modestly during his eight years in power. Excluding an initial increase of 22 percent in real terms in an inflationary context during 1995, subsequent increases averaged about 5 percent. Lula, under greater budgetary pressures, supported similarly limited increases. However, the PT's preferences for larger increases will be offset by countervailing efforts to cap social security benefits that are indexed to the minimum wage (Amann and Baer 2004: 14).

Urban unemployment escalated during the 1990s as industrial employment plummeted 48 percent during the decade (Ribeiro and Scanlon 2003: 207). Formal sector unemployment stands at 20 percent in major centers such as São Paulo and Rio de Janeiro. Between 2.5 and 3.5 million people are unemployed in these two metropolitan

Table 5.1   The economically active population (EAP), by sector, 1940–96 (percent of total EAP)

Year	Agriculture/mining	Industry	Services
1940	67	13	20
1950	61	17	22
1960	55	17	27
1970	46	22	32
1980	31	29	40
1996	26	21	56

Source: Ribeiro and Scanlon (2003: table 9.1).

areas, with most of the economic dislocation being felt by women (52.5 percent), those aged eighteen to twenty-four (34.1 percent), and those without a university education (34 percent). If the unemployment rate is calculated to include informal market employment, then the national rate falls to 7.5 percent. The differential between the formal market unemployment rate and the aggregated rate (formal plus informal) has expanded, indicating that an increasing percentage of workers permanently leave the formal job market and depend for their livelihood on precarious employment. Taken together, the rising dependence of a larger share of the workforce on the informal market, inflation, declining wages, and sluggish growth since the mid-1980s have coincided with a rising and stubbornly high Gini index (World Bank 2003: 12–13).

The discussion to this point has assumed that poverty (which relies on absolute levels of income) and inequality (which is based on relative measures of income shares) are not the same, but they are closely related. Income inequality deepens absolute poverty levels over time. Since income is shared unequally across Brazil, the growth of the economy reduces poverty levels more slowly than would otherwise be the case in a more equal society (Skidmore 2004). This fact is most evident in studies of women and Afro-Brazilians, whose incomes have increased in absolute terms over time but who continue to suffer from enduring economic disadvantages such as occupational discrimination. Women and non-whites, consequently, are the poorest of all social categories in Brazil (Lovell 1994). The lives of these people would be improved by economic growth to a greater degree if income were not so unequally distributed. The World Bank (2003: 62) estimates that inequality accounts for a poverty level in Brazil that is 17 percent greater than the average for a country at its level of per capita GDP. The Brazilian example is thus a cautionary tale to those who would claim that economic growth alone can alleviate poverty.

Government policies, either through action or through inaction, have more often than not aggravated poverty and social inequality. The distribution of the tax burden is one prominent example. The federal income tax offers numerous loopholes, exemptions, and tax incentives that favor the upper tax brackets. Most of the working and middle classes must dedicate a relatively large percentage of their income to tax payments, including indirect taxes that fall on all income levels at the same rate. Indirect taxes such as ICMS, for example, represent 25 percent of the income of the poorest 10 percent of the population, or five times the proportion of tax to income of the richest 10 percent of Brazilians. In general, Brazil has the highest tax burden on salaries of any country in Latin America, approximately 42 percent, a figure that places it among some of the Scandinavian countries.

However, in contrast to the systems in countries such as Sweden and Norway, Brazil's social spending does not justify the high taxes paid by workers. Social security expenditures, for example, do little to ameliorate the plight of the poor. The World Bank (2001: 3) estimates that only 1 percent of all social security spending makes its way to the 10 percent who are the poorest Brazilians, while more than half of all social security allotments go to the wealthiest 10 percent. In comparison to the United States, Brazil's pensions pay more to the wealthy, although the total population of wealthy retired persons is less than half that of the US. Moreover, half of the population of Brazilians receiving public pensions is aged under sixty-five, suggesting that the system unnecessarily favors a segment that usually retires with a public pension and then moves into the private sector to claim additional benefits from further employment. In this way, Brazil's unequal pension system and the extensive economic informality of most of the country's poor combine to keep only privileged workers protected, while most do without even the most modest welfare supports.

Efforts to expand the social safety net during the New Republic fell far short of improving the lot of the vast majority of Brazil's impoverished. One has to look back into the military period, particularly the governments of generals Médici and Geisel during the early 1970s, to find evidence of the last coordinated attempt to expand social protection (e.g., welfare, unemployment support, pensions and health-care insurance). But even these endeavors fell short, as the military directed these supports at organized interest groups already linked to the corporatist state, such as the official unions (Weyland 1996). The Sarney, Collor, and Franco governments did not try to universalize the social security system as the 1988 constitution had called for, since that was not viable given the internal distortions produced by the public pension system. When Cardoso came to power, reforming the parlous finances of social security was a priority. As mentioned in chapter 3, Cardoso's reforms were sensible but partial. Specifically, the effort to limit pensioners' benefits and to move them in line with contributions, a goal that was not completely reached, still helped the fiscal health of the system in the short run (Draibe 2004a: 88; Madrid 2003).

Social security reform looms as the "mother of all social reform" in Brazil, since pensions take up half of all entitlement spending and yet fail to improve social welfare. Most important, if left unreformed, the public pension system with its mounting debt will take up a growing share of monies allotted for social expenditures. This would hurt targeted social spending in education, health care, and other public services that have a progressive effect on poverty and inequality. The contrast between the fiscal commitment to social security versus education is particularly hurtful. Although the population under the age of twenty is *five times* the population over sixty, the latter receive a disproportionate share of the fiscal pie.

What is spent on the young is also unequally distributed. The most important example is the education system, which figures prominently when scholars of Brazil list the main causes of persisting levels of inequality and poverty (Castro 2000). Brazil's education system is three-tiered: primary education for students seven to fourteen years of age is free and compulsory; secondary education for students fifteen to seventeen years of age is also free but not mandatory; and higher education, which includes undergraduate and graduate levels, is low cost, but the dynamics of admission favor the well off. Like the social security system, the education system is based on institutions that both sustain and deepen inequalities of access to primary and secondary educational services. Only 35 percent of Brazil's workforce has a high school education, compared with 52 percent in Mexico and 94 percent in the United States (World Bank 2003: 20). During the early 1990s, combined repetition and dropout rates in the primary schools were 50 percent (Draibe 2004b: 383). The average period of formal education still hovers around five years, which is one of the lowest figures among the large Latin American countries (Hall 2003: 273). This poor access to education explains disparities in wages, since differences in skill sets are the single most powerful causes of income inequalities. In Brazil, workers with a high school education earn 50 percent more than those without a diploma. Not surprisingly, when both unequal access to education and wage differentials are measured together, they demonstrate an increase during the 1990s, one that coincides with the movement of other indices such as the Gini coefficient. These changes alone represent 60 percent of the worsening of income inequality during the period (World Bank 2003).

Overall performance of the education system is a serious area of concern. Only 66 percent of students entering the first grade will complete the eighth, and one of every three students who begin the ninth grade will not graduate (Larach 2001: 4). The quality of education is another problem, as the system suffers from a large number of uncertified and underqualified teachers and obsolete learning materials. In 1997, for example, more than half of all primary school teachers had not completed any post-secondary education (Hall 2003: 273). A related factor is that teachers are underpaid, thus reducing incentives for qualified instructors to enter the public school system (Draibe 2004a: 76). As a result of the vicious circle of poor pay and weak qualifications, falling repetition rates and rising completion rates have not accompanied improved academic results. Evaluations by the Ministry of Education between 1997 and 1999 demonstrated that student performance on language and mathematics skills tests have not improved and in some areas of the poorer regions of Brazil these skills are in marked decline.

Recent reforms hold out some hope for addressing the problems that afflict primary and secondary education. Repetition rates have fallen and completion rates in primary schools have increased for all grades; in the higher grades they have doubled since 1995, thus raising the average period of schooling from 4.9 to 5.8 years (Larach 2001; Hall 2003). This reflects a growth of spending by state governments, who control 70 percent of all primary and secondary schools, and the expansion of direct subsidy programs to families with school-age children under the School Grant (*Bolsa Escola*) program inaugurated in 1995 (Castro 2000; Draibe 2004b). Efforts to reduce grade repetition and expand night-school programs have had the greatest effect.

Beginning in January 1998, the Cardoso administration addressed these problems by launching the Fund for the Development and Maintenance of Basic Education and Teacher Development (*Fundo de Manutenção e Desenvolvimento do Ensino Fundamental e de Valorização do Magistério*, FUNDEF), a program that earmarked

15 percent of total state and local tax revenues for education. The program provided the equivalent of US$300 per child enrolled in school, up to the eighth grade. By establishing a per child spending floor, the FUNDEF program helped to reverse some of the problems listed above by elevating teacher salaries on average 30 percent nationally, hiring new instructors, stimulating student enrollments, enhancing infrastructure, and redistributing state and federal resources to the poorest schools (Castro 2000: 297). FUNDEF reduced the population of unqualified lay teachers by 46 percent, and the number of teachers with secondary and post-secondary training increased by 10.6 and 12 percent respectively (Draibe 2004b: 402). The Cardoso administration also allotted other monies to train municipal education officials in modern administrative techniques. More funding along these lines is clearly needed, and new programs should focus on the higher grade levels. Existing programs have already proven effective at the primary level. In 2001, primary enrollment rates reached 97 percent, or virtual universal enrollment (Draibe 2004a: 79). Reliable estimates of improvements in quality are not yet available, but case reports are encouraging (Hall 2003: 282–3).

Given the problems of primary and secondary education, national literacy remains a concern. Just over 80 percent of the population is literate in the sense that they can sign their own name. During the 1990s, illiteracy rates fell strongly for those aged fifteen years or more, from 21.3 percent at the beginning of the decade to 13.3 percent in 1999 (Draibe 2004a: 79). Yet, despite these overall improvements, some regions and rural areas lag behind the best performing states in the south, and, more alarming still, an estimated 30 percent of Brazilians are unable to read newspapers or write a letter, which are common measures of "functional literacy." These figures are below the median for Latin America. Moreover, poverty and illiteracy reinforce one another, as members of the poorest decile of the population are ten times more likely to be illiterate than members of the top three deciles. Blacks are two to three times more likely to be illiterate than whites (Silva and Hasenbalg 1999). By contrast, female literacy has improved as more girls have attended school over the decades. In fact, the gender gap in education now runs to the disadvantage of males, who on average have one year less schooling than females before they enter the job market.

The greatest inequities in the education system are reserved for the disparities of access to the university system and the distribution of funding among higher, secondary and primary education. Access to the university system is closed to all but the members of the middle and upper classes, with few exceptions. Admission to one of the universally free-tuition federal universities is based on performance in a national exam, the *vestibular*. Competition for one of the slots for the most coveted institutions – the Universade de São Paulo (USP), the Universidade de Campinas (UNICAMP), or the Universidade Federal de Rio de Janeiro (UFRJ) – is especially fierce, and those students with access to preparatory training for the *vestibular* or private secondary training stand the best chances. The top schools in the public system also receive the majority of federal resources for research and scholarships, to the detriment of universities in poorer areas. The university system as a whole receives 43 percent of total education spending (78 percent of all federal education spending), while primary and secondary schools receive 55 percent (Vélez and Foster 2000; Larach 2001). Expenditures on staffing per student are second only to the US and double that of countries such as the United Kingdom and France. But 95 percent of expenditures on university education benefit the top 40 percent of income earners (World Bank 2003: 52–3). This disparity in access opportunities and resources in higher education deepens the skill gaps that are linked to income differentials.

Attempts to redress inequalities of access to the higher education system must recognize that race matters. While whites on average complete 6.5 years of schooling, blacks complete only two-thirds of that, with 4.4 years (World Bank 2003: 15; Silva and Hasenbalg 1999). That is the same gap that existed forty years ago (Draibe 2004b: 383). Wage differentials across racial categories help to explain these disparities, but discrimination is another factor. The Brazilian government addressed this concern in 2002 when it called on the public universities to institute explicit quotas of 20 percent of their annual slots for Afro-Brazilians. This will help those blacks who complete more than the average number of years in high school, but such measures will only work if other programs increase the numbers and improve the performance of Afro-Brazilians at the primary and secondary levels.

Whatever the causes of poverty and inequality, these twin evils rip at the very social fabric of Brazil. Human life itself is imperiled by them. The aforementioned differentials across regions in life expectancy are one indicator. Another is the high incidence of disease, particularly curable viral infections that spread as a result of the lack of access to adequate health care. Between 1960 and 1995, despite the fact that Brazil achieved the highest rates of growth in Latin America, the country made slower progress than most other countries in the region in reducing infant mortality and raising life expectancy (McGuire 2001): forty-one in every 1,000 infants died in 1995, as compared to a regional average of thirty-three per 1,000. Undernourishment and unsafe drinking water are less the cause of infant deaths than is substandard primary health care for the poor, especially in rural areas. Nutritional scores, as measured by daily caloric intake and access to potable water, are above the regional average, but basic health care is problematic. The key issue is the distribution of essential services such as prenatal care and vaccinations to most of the poor. This was a concern that the Cardoso administration addressed after 1995 better than any of its predecessors.

A brief history of public health care is enough to demonstrate the differences between the pre-1995 and the post-1995 periods. Between 1964 and 1985, the military governments created two highly centralized health-care agencies. The first was the National Institute of Medical Care and Social Security (*Instituto Nacional de Assistência Médica da Previdência Social*, INAMPS), which focused on providing health care to civil servants and formal sector workers through INAMPS facilities or private hospitals with INAMPS contracts. INAMPS focused on curative medicine, and it received 78 percent of all federal spending on health care. The second system, which accounted for the rest of the health-care budget, focused on expanding access to primary care. It was governed by the Foundation for Public Health Services (*Fundação Serviços de Saúde Pública*, FSESP). FSESP, which came under the control of the Ministry of Health, was effective in hiring and training health-care workers and sending them into homes and communities during the 1960s and 1970s. However, these initiatives were insufficient and unsustainable for the task. FSESP's thousands of doctors and nurses were unable to attend to the tens of millions of poor Brazilians who required medical assistance. The agency also became a victim of bureaucratic in-fighting and patronage politics, which limited its effectiveness (Weyland 1996). The same fate befell the Ministry of

Health's National Program of Basic Health Services (*Prevsaúde*), instituted in 1980, which was the object of bitter conflicts with the Ministry of Social Welfare before the program collapsed in 1983. Most important, neither the INAMPS nor the FSESP system provided sufficient coverage for most of the population. The INAMPS system suffered from the rising cost of curative care and depended upon private hospitals, while the FSESP system could not provide sufficient preventive and primary care to the poor.

In 1988, the constitution called for the universalization of public health care through the creation of the United and Decentralized Health System (*Sistema Unificado e Descentralizado de Saúde*, SUDS) and the guarantee that all citizens have the right to public health care. SUDS replaced the old social insurance funds that were disbursed and managed by the Ministry of Social Welfare and decentralized the provision of public health care to municipalities. By phasing out the INAMPS bureaucracy and making the Ministry of Health ultimately responsible for both curative and preventive care, the new unified system promised to solve the inequities of the old system. Yet the transition to a newly empowered Health Ministry soon succumbed to the classic problems of clientelist resistance. Former INAMPS officials, now in the Ministry of Health, used auditing and other bureaucratic hurdles to impede decentralization (Arretche 2004: 174). Hopes of universalizing health-care access also fell victim to concerted opposition by the particular interests of professional health-care associations, politicians wishing to keep their access to patronage, private care providers and hospitals, drug makers, and insurers (Weyland 1996: 164–6). SUDS was also terribly underfunded.

Reforming the failing health-care system became a priority of the Cardoso administration soon after it came to power in 1995. Total health-care spending grew during the 1995–2001 period by 30 percent in real terms, and that portion dedicated to primary health care rose from 17 to 25 percent of the total health-care budget. Like the FSESP's programs, Cardoso's comprehensive Family Health Program sent community health agents to visit households and provide basic health-care services to the poor, including cancer screenings, vaccinations, and prenatal care. The new program expanded the number of public health-care workers by four times and increased their coverage from 17 million people in 1994 to 68 million in 2000 (McGuire 2001: 19). By 2000, all of Brazil's municipalities were included in the united health-care system. Cities and towns delivered 80 percent of all primary health services and managed more than 70 percent of Brazil's primary health-care centers (Arretche 2004: 181). At the national level, specialized efforts, such as health minister José Serra's campaign between 1998 and 2001 to reduce the incidence of HIV/AIDS in Brazil by distributing retroviral drugs widely, also played a role in improving health-care services. Public expenditures for all of these programs grew as in 1996 the congress passed a new tax on financial transactions (CPMF). A new system for transferring federal funds to states and cities was also inaugurated in 1997 to finance the continued decentralization of health-care services.

Poverty and inequality threaten human health in other ways. Urban crime, which is linked to rising inequality in developing countries, takes a tremendous toll on the quality of life of most citizens (Portes and Hoffman 2003). Homicide rates alone have increased several times in cities such as São Paulo and Rio de Janeiro during the past

decade on account of growing social desperation (Lisboa and Viegas 2000). This escalating level of violence is closely related to the growing population of street children;
their routine imprisonment and torture in overcrowded urban jails only succeeds in
making these street urchins even more violent (Human Rights Watch 2004). José
Padilha's film *Bus 174*, a documentary of a televised hijacking of a Rio de Janeiro bus
by a former street child, reveals many of the cruel ways in which the degradation of
human beings by poverty and social exclusion leave them with few options. The police
violence that ended the hijacking, with one hostage dead and the summary execution
of the hijacker while unarmed and already in police custody, illustrates how official
institutions interact with social misery to produce a tragic outcome that is all too
common throughout Brazil.

Having analyzed the distinct yet interrelated dimensions of poverty and inequality
in Brazil, it is now important to ask how the country's main social and economic actors
have addressed these problems. Urban and rural labor, the middle classes, and business
associations are the main non-state actors in the Brazilian economy. Their politics have
often coincided with changes in state structures and policy that have affected social
development as well as economic growth and democratization. To be sure, these are
not the only relevant non-state actors. The next chapter discusses the role that other
non-governmental organizations and social movements have played in a range of
issues, including social inequality.

ORGANIZED LABOR

Since at least Getúlio Vargas's *Estado Nôvo*, Brazilian labor organizations have lived
under the shadow of extensive state control. From 1937 until the liberalization of the
bureaucratic-authoritarian regime, labor unions were under the direct command of
state officials and worker militancy was limited tightly by these authorities. The burst
of (illegal) labor militancy in the industrial area of São Paulo during the late 1970s
produced the first major rupture in this system of labor corporatism as official union
stewards, known as *pelegos*, were challenged by the growth of an autonomous union
leadership led by Lula da Silva in the metallurgical and auto assembly sectors. The
"new unionism" was first a movement against state corporatism and then became one
in favor of political liberalization. New union leaders were critical of management's
shop-floor rules but also of the military's wage policies that struggled to keep salaries
on a par with changes in inflation rates. Workers staged strikes in 1977–9 that quickly
became manifestations of popular disapproval of continued military rule. During the
democratic transition, the leading autonomist labor confederation, the Workers' Singular Peak Association (*Central Única dos Trabalhadores*, CUT), established in 1983,
mobilized the most important segments of the "new union" movement and allied itself
to the newly formed Workers' Party (*Partido dos Trabalhadores*, PT) (Keck 1992). The
CUT soon became a modern, anti-corporatist movement that opposed the obligatory
elements of the old labor codes, including the required union tax collected from industrial workers to support the *pelego* system, which no longer had their support.

Despite these auspicious beginnings for the autonomous union movement, the structure of labor activism produced numerous and highly fragmented organizations. First,

because of the long rule of state corporatism, independent labor voices emerged only in the later stages of industrialization. This explains why the first autonomous unions came from the most advanced sectors. The diversity of shop-floor issues across distinct sectors also made the creation of a national and encompassing labor confederation difficult. Second, ideological differences within the labor movement, even in the same industrial sectors, encouraged the rise of multiple organizations. Moderate and conservative voices in the workers' movement formed organizations to rival the CUT. The General Workers' Confederation (*Central Geral dos Trabalhadores*, CGT) emerged as a more moderate alternative during the 1980s and, later in the 1990s, the Union Force (*Força Sindical*, FS) agreed with firms that attempts to satisfy the wage demands of workers must coincide with efforts to enhance the competitiveness of the companies for which they work. Finally, the organizational bases of the major labor confederations were different. While the CUT's unions came from the autonomous "new union movement," the CGT and FS represented many of the old corporatist unions. Therefore these confederations were more reticent about reforming the corporatist labor codes than was the CUT. These and other organizational cleavages played out in the formulation and implementation of structural reforms such as privatization. While the CUT (and the PT) opposed privatization, segments of the CGT and FS embraced the involvement of workers and their pension funds in the sale of state firms.

Labor unions' record of political mobilization through strikes during the 1990s reflected changes in the economy and the shifting organizational capacities of the CUT and the other confederations. As **figure 5.1** demonstrates, the years preceding the Real Plan's stabilization of prices were ones of heightened labor militancy. Fueled by extensive resentment of Sarney's and Collor's failure to tame inflation, the CUT found that its ability to mobilize workers grew markedly. Although the number of strikes fell during this period, the average number of workers who participated exploded, with an average of 7,095 participating in each strike in 1993 (Sandoval 2004: 196). Between 1994 and 1996, the Real Plan had the expected effect of cooling labor militancy, since the reform succeeded in ending hyperinflation. But the growing recession of the Brazilian economy after 1997 and the rising specter of urban unemployment transformed patterns of labor militancy once again. Fewer workers went on strike and those that did shifted the nature of their demands from increasing wages and securing employment to demands for compliance with legal standards. This more defensive focus to workers' demands reflected the real limits to calls for wage increases in a recessionary economy. Moreover, structural changes to production systems caused by automation and information technology as well as the flight of investors from the old industrial core of metropolitan São Paulo led unions to embrace a concern for the competitiveness of existing industries. With the shift in priorities came a strategic shift in organization. The CUT lost rank-and-file adherents who increasingly were dissatisfied with the confederation's opposition to privatization and market liberalization without presenting alternatives (Sandoval 2004: 202).

As the CUT's membership has declined, the FS and CGT have become more important interlocutors, but the overall effect has been that all of Brazil's labor organizations have lost influence. This is ironic considering that the PT is the largest single party in the Chamber of Deputies and its leader is president. Notwithstanding Lula's rise to power, Brazilian labor's loss of organizational power is the product of several long-term

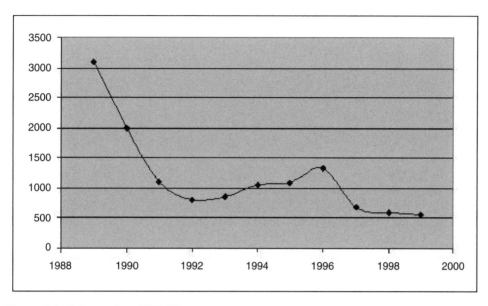

Figure 5.1   Labor strikes, 1989–99
Source: Sandoval (2004: figure 10.1) and DIEESE (2002: 135).

trends. First, the growing emphasis on capital- and technology-intensive production in both industry and agriculture has radically changed the number of workers employed in these sectors. This is reflected in the declining size of the industrial and agricultural sectors, as noted above, and in the growth of the service or "tertiary" sector. Some unions in the service sector retain some influence, a fact that is especially true for government workers. However, since employment in the service sector tends to be more mobile, temporary, and precarious than that in industry, unionization of the service sector has been slow and difficult. Second, the workers that remain in the modernized industrial and agrobusiness sectors retain a high level of skills and are expected to take on multiple tasks that include even management functions. Such "flexible" workers in general tend to side with their firms on many workplace issues and against their union. Many have also opted not to join unions and have settled for negotiating pay and work conditions more directly with their firms. These transformations of production, worker skills, and interests have evolved for at least the last two decades in Brazil as they have elsewhere, making the traditional union a less central actor in negotiating workplace issues (Martin 2001). Presently, only 16 percent of the entire working population is unionized, a proportion that is higher in the southern states (20 percent) and lower elsewhere in Brazil (12 percent) (DIEESE 2002).

Nevertheless, industrial unions scored some important and innovative successes during the 1990s. The most noteworthy occurred in the ABC region of São Paulo, the heart of the metallurgical and auto assembly sectors. During the early 1990s, tripartite "sectoral chambers" formed to enable businesses, unions, and local and federal politicians to plan out long-term responses to workplace and production issues. Ultimately none of these tripartite forums became permanent, but they generated numerous seminars, ideas, and studies that remain the focus of industrial relations reform in the automotive industry today. Moreover, the chambers proved that the tripartite framework could reintegrate the unions in a regular way into industrial reform and provide a viable means for coordinating private and public resources such as worker pension plans in the service of other employment-creating and skill-enhancement programs (Guimarães et al. 2001).

Conditions in the countryside are very different from those in the cities, and so a labor movement has evolved that is quite distinct from its urban counterpart. Inequality of land ownership is the focus for the rural labor movement and it is also at the heart of efforts to improve the efficiency and sustainability of farming. Small, family-owned farms use land and labor most efficiently, employing 77 percent of all rural workers, but they possess only one-third of the total arable landmass. Large landowners dominate the rest, but most of this land, excepting the modernized agro-industrial sector, is inefficiently cultivated. Under the bureaucratic-authoritarian governments, the state channeled subsidized credit, tax breaks, price supports, and other rents to promote capital-intensive and mechanized farming, concentrating these resources in the largest holdings (Deere 2004: 178). Anthony Pereira (1997), referring to this process as the "conservative modernization" of agriculture, notes that the military's agrarian policy stripped thousands of rural peasants of their land, removing sharecroppers and tenants from the commercial agricultural sector and relegating them to a landless status. Millions of these landless peasants migrated to urban areas. But for those who remained in the countryside, the only option was to mobilize for the distribution of land through agrarian reform.

The first major contemporary rural worker organization was the National Confederation of Workers in Agriculture (*Confederação Nacional dos Trabalhadores na Agricultura*, CONTAG), which emerged in 1963 following João Goulart's extension of urban labor rights to rural workers. The specter of a more radical agrarian reform was one of the key catalysts for the coup against Goulart in March 1964 and the consolidation of the bureaucratic-authoritarian project. After the collapse of democracy, CONTAG became useful to the military as a corporatist mechanism for controlling rural workers. CONTAG drew in rural workers with extensions of health programs and pension protection so as to minimize the possibilities of social unrest in the countryside. In this way, the provision of welfare for workers coincided with the conservative modernization of agriculture. CONTAG's peasant base became more sophisticated over time as they garnered access to land themselves and became either small farmers or rural wage workers. The union's success as a form of inclusionary corporatism then laid the foundation for its growing autonomy during the transition to democracy as its broadening membership gave the organization leverage in negotiations with state agencies and private landowners (Weyland 1996: 56; Maybury-Lewis 1996). Yet, even at the height of its organizational success, CONTAG represented only a small fraction of the rural labor force. The vast pool of poor, uneducated, and landless peasants remained without an encompassing labor organization willing and able to speak on their behalf. Like the urban labor confederations, CONTAG suffered from internal heterogeneity. For instance, the union's rank and file of small farmers and rural wage workers embraced legal and legislative pressure, while more radical landless elements favored the more direct actions (e.g., land invasions) of the rival landless peasant movements (Pereira 1997: 148). As CONTAG's leaders became focused more on wage issues than on land redistribution, more of the radical factions left the union.

The Movement of Landless Rural Workers (*Movimento dos Trabalhadores Rurais Sem Terra*, MST) is CONTAG's main rival in the organization of rural laborers and historically the main critic of the government's agrarian reform. The MST got its start in the fall of 1979 when an economist working at the State Secretariat of Agriculture in Rio Grande do Sul assisted a group of 102 families in their invasion of the Macali farm in Ronda Alta. After several such invasions, the MST was formally founded on 20 January 1984 and since that time has used land invasions and judicial appropriations to create 2,350 rural settlements, almost half of all such settlements throughout Brazil. In embracing these direct actions, the MST responded to a long history of violence and oppression in the countryside. The Catholic Church's Pastoral Land Commission (*Comissão Pastoral da Terra*, CPT), which like the MST mobilized peasants and helped settle them, publicized cases of widespread violations of human rights by landowners and public officials who routinely turned their backs to such wrongdoing. From 1985 to 2003, 1,349 rural killings were recorded by the CPT, but only seventy-five of these cases were tried. Hence the MST's agenda of radical land reform through direct actions (land invasions) responded to a no less direct and institutionalized system of political repression in the countryside.

Other forces driving the MST and even CONTAG to employ more radical techniques emerged from the drafting of the 1988 constitution. The constitution represented a turning point in the national discussion concerning land reform, but one that was a mixed blessing. Most important to the agrarian reform movement, the constitution established the principle that land that is not being farmed productively can be designated "of social interest" and expropriated. Yet enforcement of this provision was watered down by the lobbying influence of agrobusiness and the increasing power of landowners in the assembly and in the congress thereafter. These forces reinforced the legal hurdles to expropriation and strengthened the rights of landowners and agrobusiness interests. The fiscal crisis of the state helped their cause since it made the old compensation formulas used in CONTAG's earlier expropriations unsustainable. CONTAG and other unions would have to rethink their strategies. Not surprisingly, the turn to more militant tactics such as land invasions by both CONTAG and the MST in the years following the constitutional assembly was an outgrowth of these institutional changes (Pereira 1997: 164–5). By the middle of the 1990s, the countryside became the focus of the most militant labor actions in Brazil. Even the CUT, which began to suffer declining mobilization in industrial cities, formed an alliance with CONTAG and periodically participated alongside the MST in land invasions.

Not until Fernando Henrique Cardoso became president did agrarian reform become as important an issue as other kinds of structural reform during the New Republic. Somewhat surprisingly, Cardoso made the resettlement of rural families one of his priorities and subsequently referred to what was accomplished as "a veritable peaceful revolution in the countryside" (Pereira 2004: 101). Initially, the government proclaimed that it would settle 280,000 landless families. But Cardoso soon backed off from that promise as he realized that the fiscal costs of compensating landowners and the potential destabilizing effects on concentrated, mechanized agricultural producers could harm the Real Plan. Meanwhile, the congress passed legislation raising the Rural Territorial Tax (*Imposto Territorial Rural*, ITR) on unproductive land while easing the process for land expropriation. According to the law, the compensatory price to the former owners of expropriated land can be determined *after* the property is distributed to landless peasants. The change made the process of expropriation more efficient, but other problems concerning the maintenance of distributed land remained unaddressed. The precarious system of land titling by registration agencies, which can be politically manipulated by local elites, still threatens settled peasants even after they achieve legal ownership (Pereira 2004: 110). Add to this the absence of rural credit and technical assistance for small farmers, and the life of resettled families remains parlous. Rural women are in a particularly difficult position, since land titles that are distributed most often go to the male heads of families rather than to couples (Deere 2004).

Furthermore, Cardoso and the congress were not prepared for the growing resistance of the landless peasant movement, which pressured the administration with its strategy of "occupy, resist, and produce." **Table 5.2** shows that the number of land occupations and the number of families participating exploded during this period. One of the causes of this sustained increase was the deepening recession following 1997 and the frustration of workers suffering declining living standards (Sandoval 2004: 207–8; Martins 2000). The MST's mass marches on Brasília, which by 1999 included more than 100,000 movement members, galvanized the public's attention on the inequality of land ownership in the countryside. Notably, women's autonomous rural unions and female leaders within CONTAG and the MST marched on the capital in 2000 to publicize the inequality of land ownership between the sexes.

Yet the effect on the legislative dimension of these mobilizations was modest. Actual and threatened land invasions often preceded limited concessions by the government to resettle tens of thousands of families. This factor contributed to the controversy surrounding the figures for the number of families settled by the government. According to the government, and despite President Cardoso's initial hesitation to pursue more extensive agrarian reform, 287,000 families were resettled through the national land reform program. The MST estimates that no more than 160,000 families were resettled, but they do not take into account the number of squatters already on seized land that received legal title (Pereira 2004: 104–5). Despite these differences, the actual number of resettled families pales in comparison to the total number of landless rural poor (between 10 and 16 million). Moreover, the capacity of land invasions to address the needs of this larger population is questionable. Perhaps because they were a successful tool of direct action, the Cardoso administration was obliged to make land invasions more difficult. In 2000, Cardoso issued an MP excluding land taken in invasions from disappropriation procedures. Coupled with landowners' escalating use of violence and police repression to counteract land invasions, the land reform debate became entangled with the problems of the inability of the Brazilian state to exercise order in the countryside. Left outside of the debate were the larger injustices produced by the patterns of conservative modernization of rural areas, a mode of development that neither the MST nor the Cardoso administration were inclined to change.

The MST's mixture of informality and direct action has an urban parallel in the new movement of people employed in the growing informal market. *Perueiros* (clandestine urban transport workers) and *camelôs* (street vendors) have organized their own move-

Table 5.2 MST land invasions and families participating, 1990–2001

Year	Invasions	Families
1990	119	12,805
1991	78	9,203
1992	149	20,596
1993	214	40,109
1994	125	24,590
1995	101	31,619
1996	250	42,682
1997	281	52,276
1998	388	62,864
1999	538	69,804
2000	555	73,066
2001	585	75,730

Source: MST.

ments in the major cities to defend their interests, often against formal sector workers and small businesses. While street vendors have been a presence in major cities for some time, a new population has emerged in recent years of unemployed industrial workers who utilize their severance benefits to purchase and then informally sell consumer products such as electronics, purses, and watches on sidewalks. These products are more valuable than the homemade trinkets normally sold by *camelôs* and they compete more directly with established storefront merchants. Illegal jitneys also compete against municipal bus services and private transport companies, whose workers are often the first to confront the *perueiros*. The resulting conflicts between these informal workers and formal sector actors have produced mass arrests, riots, and increasingly more frequent public demonstrations by organized *camelô* and *perueiro* groups. Organized labor has also struggled to come to terms with these factions as the CUT and the FS attempt to integrate more unemployed workers into their organizations. However, the labor unions cannot afford to lose the support of formal sector workers, many of whom see contradictions between the protection of flexible labor markets that *camelôs* and *perueiros* demand and the protection against increasing informality that formal sector workers require. This is yet another dimension on which the Brazilian labor movement will continue to fragment.

THE MIDDLE CLASS AND PROFESSIONALS

As unequal as Brazil clearly is, it has a relatively large middle class. The upper middle class is composed of university-trained white-collar workers who populate the middle and upper management of large and medium-sized firms and the major government agencies. This segment also includes academics, lawyers, doctors, journalists, engineers, and other technical workers. These highly educated elites compose 1.4 percent of the working population. Just under them are other professionals and small business owners, who represent 7.4 percent of the economically active population. If one adds lesser white-collar technicians with lower levels of education and fewer skills and the more advanced vocational and industrial workers, the Brazilian middle class composes approximately a quarter of the workforce. That is comparable to the more advanced economies in the region, including Mexico, Chile, and Venezuela (Portes and Hoffman 2003). In addition, some percentage of the middle class is in a reserve pool of labor that includes university students, self-employed artists, writers, and intellectuals, whose education if not their economic state places them in the middle class.

Its very heterogeneity makes the Brazilian middle class difficult to organize politically. No single association represents it, but several prominent organizations reflect the interests and sentiments of large segments of the middle class. For example, the Brazilian Bar Association (*Ordem dos Advogados do Brasil*, OAB), the Brazilian Press Association (*Associação Brasileira de Imprensa*, ABI), the Brazilian Medical Association (*Associação Médica Brasileira*, AMB), and the National Union of Students (*União Nacional dos Estudantes*, UNE) played key roles during the political liberalization period by representing the political views of their members. These organizations openly opposed the military's censorship laws and periodic crackdowns on academic freedom, and they condemned official violence (Alves 1985). Perhaps the most famous example was the concerted effort made by these and several other members of Brazil's grass-roots human rights movement to force the military government to admit in a civil suit brought in 1978 that it was responsible for the torture and death of a television news editor, Vladimir Herzog, in September 1975.

The middle class is a notable producer of ideas and leaders for urban social movements during the New Republic. Members of the Brazilian middle class are responsible for the creation of hundreds of environmental, feminist, neighborhood, and human rights organizations throughout the country (see chapter 6). Yet these groups tend to focus on particular issue areas, making the emergence of a larger, encompassing association that might articulate the specific interests of the middle class unlikely. Many observers doubt that the middle class could do more as a unified actor given its obvious diversity of interests, its distinct economic cleavages, and even its heterogeneous ideological perspectives (Weyland 1996: 66).

Business politics

Brazilian business associations played a key role in the twentieth-century politics of the country. Major business associations, particularly those based in the industrial heart of São Paulo state, helped the military come to power in 1964 and were instrumental in helping to end the twenty-one-year bureaucratic-authoritarian regime in 1985 (Payne 1994). Despite their importance, business interests in politics were never institutionalized in any consistent manner in Brazil. The corporatist legacy of the Vargas years did little to provide business with a stable set of institutions to represent their interests. This was partly owing to the dominance of the state rather than private industry in the strategy of economic development after 1945 (Evans 1979). But it was also the result of the design of corporatist institutions, beginning with the 1937 Consolidated Labor Laws (*Consolidação das Leis do Trabalho*, CLT), which divided business interests into distinct organizations (Diniz and Boschi 1979). It was also the outgrowth of the absence of either a unifying political organization, such as a business-oriented party, or a common threat to private property that would otherwise create a unified movement (Kingstone 2004: 169).

The corporatist system created a variety of business associations, including the National Confederation of Industry (CNI), the National Council for Commerce, and the National Council for Agriculture, with no single encompassing "peak association" of the type found in some of the advanced capitalist economies in Western Europe. The CNI, which was originally designed as a corporatist association for the national business class, was offset by the older and more powerful Federation of São Paulo Industries (*Federação das Indústrias do Estado de São Paulo*, FIESP), which guarded jealously its autonomy from the state and never trusted the CNI to represent its interests. FIESP has remained the key business association in Brazil through the present, but its focus on the industrial interests of its home state has failed to unite the business class throughout the country. Other state-based business associations, most notably FIRJAN (*Federação das Indústrias do Estado do Rio de Janeiro*) and FIEMG (*Federação das Indústrias do Estado de Minas Gerais*), are weak sister organizations to FIESP. They have a narrow, sectoral base that was historically linked inconsistently to the state corporatist system (Boschi 1978). These organizations have been either too dependent on the state to be autonomous representatives of the private business class or too focused on heavy industries to become truly representative of the full range of business interests (Weyland 1996: 53–4; Montero 2002).

The transition to democracy in the 1980s and the neoliberal reform agenda during the 1990s began to transform business's political role in Brazil, but democracy and freer markets also deepened many of the old problems that limited business representation. Pro-democracy industrialists during the long liberalization of the regime criticized the military government for its crackdowns on labor activism and they abandoned FIESP's resistance to labor's wage demands. Such open business opposition to the regime hurt the legitimacy of the authoritarian project at its core, since it came from the sector that the military's pro-growth policies were intended to promote (Payne 1994: 79–80). Entrepreneurial disillusionment with the state-led development program also prompted the formation of new business associations in response to FIESP's perceived accommodation of and dependence on public investments. After 1987, one of the most notable of these was the "National Thought of the Business Bases" (*Pensamento Nacional das Bases Empresariais*, PNBE), which opposed FIESP's near monopoly on business representation. Far from being a passive business association dependent on state resources, the PNBE campaigned for market-friendly reforms on behalf of its base of mostly small- and medium-sized firms (Gomes and Guimarães 2004). It was joined by another group that sprang from FIESP, the Institute for the Study of Industrial Development (*Instituto de Estudos para o Desenvolvimento Industrial*, IEDI), which articulated the pro-reform interests of big businesses. While these groups were generally supportive of fiscal reforms and market liberalization, they were critical of the absence of growth-enhancing industrial policies. Moreover, they advocated elements of the neoliberal agenda not out of an ideological conviction but out of a pragmatic concern for the failures and limitations of the ISI model (Kingstone 1999, 2004). Other business groups, notably the CNI and FIRJAN, provided more unqualified support for orthodox adjustment. These differences produced new ideas within the business sector, but they also deepened erstwhile rifts that existed across organizations of business actors. With the proliferation of new groups such as the PNBE and IEDI and the reluctance of older associations such as FIESP to embrace change, the transition to democracy failed to produce an encompassing system of business representation in Brazil (Weyland 1996: 65).

Some of the neoliberal reforms themselves produced divisions within the business class and between business and the government. For example, on the subject of regional integration as part of the Free Trade Area of the Americas, heavy industries opposed too quick a process while commercial and financial interests embraced the shortest time frames (see chapter 7). The subject of tax reform, long a sore spot for firms that complained about Brazil's multiple taxes at distinct points in production, distribution, and sale ("cascading taxes"), was continually supported by business. Yet the inability of the Cardoso administration to satisfy this demand for reform only frustrated entrepreneurs convinced that the government was not doing enough to improve their competitiveness.

Neoliberal reforms held the promise of altering the close, clientelistic relations between the state and big business that Cardoso (1975) once called "bureaucratic rings" and that he and other scholars identified as the core alliances of the developmentalist period (e.g., Evans 1979; Boschi 1978). Advocates of markets held that increased transparency of exchanges and clear competitive pressures would usher in a new accountability that would dissipate these bureaucratic rings. Yet the democratic-neoliberal period of the New Republic demonstrated that bureaucratic rings could survive the transition and that these ties would even be crucial for the implementation of neoliberal reform. As shown by numerous studies of privatization (e.g., Montero 1998), welfare reform (e.g., Weyland 1996), and other economic reforms requiring constitutional changes (e.g., Kingstone 1999; Schneider 2004), close business–state connections articulated through clientelistic exchange continued in Brazil. The modalities of privatization that had the state pay for the restructuring of firms, assume much of their debt before they were auctioned, and then subsidize private buyers with close links to the state are examples of how bureaucratic rings even made possible a major structural reform.

If big business generally benefited from neoliberal reform, small- and medium-sized enterprises did significantly worse. These firms suffered tremendously from the macroeconomic instability of the hyperinflationary years. Those that were not driven into bankruptcy before 1994 faced high financial costs once the Real Plan fixed real interest rates at a high level (often over 20 percent) in order to keep inflation down (Kingstone 2000: 200–2). The overvalued Real before the 1999 crisis also spurred imports that competed with domestic industries, which struggled to maintain their market shares at home. Although the Cardoso government sought to shield some of the larger industries such as automobiles from these pressures by offering limited tariff and non-tariff protection, smaller firms had to do without. Auto parts suppliers, for example, who proved effective in shaping the strategies of the car assemblers during the 1970s through cartels such as the National Syndicate for Producers of Auto Parts and Other Similars (*Sindipeças*), were unable to weather the influx of foreign imports and the associated pressure to modernize. Liberalization proved to be a "rude awakening" that broke the cartels and led many of the nationally owned firms to sell to foreign capitalists eager to begin or expand their operations in Brazil (Addis 1999). The cost and the scarcity of capital would continue to hamper the attempt of the remaining national firms in this and other industrial sectors to compete with imports and larger competitors.

It is within this context of neoliberal restructuring and a growing emphasis on competitiveness in international markets that businesses address Brazil's social disparities. Although entrepreneurs recognize the need to lift more Brazilians out of poverty, they do not embrace the concept of social redistribution. Instead, they point to bad policies and the weakness of economic growth as the causes of poverty (Reis 2000). Brazilian business prefers a focus on general education and professional skills development so that more Brazilians can become socially mobile. In this vein, the focus has been on the parapublic professional and vocational education institutions that train thousands of Brazilians in clerical, technical, and other skills. This so-called *Sistema S* is based on several institutions: the National Service for Commercial Training (*Serviço Nacional de Aprendizagem Comercial*, SENAC), the National Service of Industrial Training (*Serviço Nacional de Aprendizagem Industrial*, SENAI), the Social Service of Commerce (*Serviço Social do Comércio*, SESC), the Social Service of Industry (*Serviço Social da Indústria*, SESI), the National Service of Rural Training (*Serviço Nacional de Aprendizagem Rural*, SENAR), and the National Service of Transportation Training (*Serviço Nacional de Aprendizagem em Transportes*, SENAT). The IEDI and CNI have been active in mobilizing Brazilian business to support the *Sistema S*, which has become an international point of reference for other countries wishing to create a vocational training network (*Boletin Cinterfor* 1998: 98–9). The main coordinating and training body for the small- and medium-sized firms, the parapublic Brazilian Service of Support for Small- and Medium-Sized Firms (*Serviço Brasileiro de Apoio a Micro e Pequenas Empresas*, SEBRAE), has also played a role in using the *Sistema S* as a focus of its professional skills-development programs (Addis and Gomes 2001). Finally, the unions, led by the CUT, have gradually integrated calls for vocational and on-the-job training in their negotiations with industry. These efforts as a whole are important since they focus on the wage disparity–skills gap that is a central cause of poverty and inequality. Moreover, the *Sistema S* presents post-secondary education options for many poorer Brazilians who find themselves shut out of the university system.

CONCLUSIONS

The dynamics of poverty and inequality in Brazil are most certainly complex, as they involve fundamental aspects of the country's model of capitalist development and political change. Conceivably most of Brazil's social disparities are too firmly rooted in socio-economic structures and development patterns to change rapidly within even a generation. Add to that the weaknesses of the state since the 1980s (chapter 3) and the problems of inefficient political institutions (chapter 4), and the prospects for fundamental change in the near future seem ephemeral.

The story of social reform is not all negative, as some important changes have been consolidated in recent years. The Cardoso administration was able to implement substantial educational, health-care, and agrarian reforms, even in the face of intense opposition and burdened by tremendous fiscal and other macroeconomic constraints. Cardoso also started the process of social security reform, although he left it to his successor to carry out the most difficult aspects (see chapter 8). Nevertheless, Cardoso proved that welfare-enhancing reform is possible and that it can make a difference, even in a short period of time. As Lula consolidates these changes and aims more ambitiously to generate more social development, it is likely that inequalities in wages and land ownership will be reversed incrementally in the years to come.

Scholars of poverty and inequality in Brazil agree that the "democracy without equity" problem is at the heart of Brazil's political development and the contemporary reform agenda (Weyland 1996). The tension between social empowerment and political enfranchisement plays out in a variety of dimensions, including the aforementioned conflicts between business and labor, landless peasants and landowners, and urban marginals and formal sector workers and merchants. Yet these are only some of the axes upon which social cleavages and conflicts reflect the constant struggle of segments of civil society on behalf of social, economic, and political change. Chapter 6 will examine a broader range of social movements and non-governmental organizations that have sustained and deepened the struggle for democratic citizenship, the inclusion of all Brazilians in a society of civil and economic rights supported by the rule of law.

6

THE EMERGENCE OF A DEMOCRATIC CIVIL SOCIETY AS A FORCE FOR CHANGE

Brazil's history of political clientelism, oligarchical rule, state-led development, and social inequality and poverty places power in the hands of elites in the most basic way. The bureaucratic-authoritarian regime deepened these erstwhile tendencies by attempting to depoliticize civil society through co-optation, corporatism, and outright repression. It is therefore not surprising that political elites, and not grass-roots activists, shaped the main institutions of the transition to democracy and even that many of the same elites that supported the bureaucratic-authoritarian project became the leaders of the New Republic.

Yet the transition to democracy was also a time of growth and regeneration of Brazilian civil society. The *Diretas Já* campaign, the new union movement, and the Workers' Party were examples of how democratization was partly engineered by the autonomous mobilization of civil society. After the transition, however, the original energy that these movements sparked gave way to a more ordinary way of doing politics. *Fisiologismo* from Sarney to Lula has characterized Brazilian politics more than has social mobilization. Yet the New Republic has nonetheless experienced significant degrees of social activism by a wide range of political factions, grass-roots movements, and non-governmental organizations (Avritzer 2000). Distinct groups have collectively organized around not just economic and political interests, but also identities, common racial and gender categories, religion, environmental issues, neighborhoods, regional affiliations, and, of course, class. How effective these groups have been in expanding democratic citizenship is the focus of this chapter. This and other key lessons from the chapter are listed in **box 6.1**.

Below we first ask whether Brazil has a distinctive "political culture," a common, national identity based on enduring core beliefs, perceptions, and norms that shape the political behavior of all Brazilians. This question is fundamental to any discussion of civil society because it is at this level, on the dimension of how individual Brazilians think about politics, that civil societal organizations can most often engineer political change by responding to the views of regular people. How has Brazilian political culture evolved in the democratic period? Subsequently, we will

---

Box 6.1   The development of a democratic civil society

- Broad-based social and political mobilization has been weak in Brazil on account of the pervasive influence of clientelistic ties and organization. Only the mobilization of a democratic civil society during the democratic transition (especially *Diretas Já*) broke with this legacy.
- Social movements and non-governmental organizations (NGOs) are highly diverse actors that operate in multiple issue-areas. Yet their techniques of organization and action can be compared to provide insights about patterns and trends across Brazilian civil society.
- Periods of time (cycles of contention) can also be compared longitudinally. Movements and NGOs mobilized before 1985 to promote regime change, but after the period of transition they became more focused on expanding democratic citizenship.
- Urban social movements have shown great adaptability on a range of urban social issues by forming ties to church groups, informal sector workers, neighborhood associations, and even the official bureaucracy and the courts.
- The landless peasant movement tends to use direct action, but it also employs the techniques of NGOs in formal political processes to defend their claims to land and provide social services in the countryside.
- The women's movement pioneered and fed many other social movements. It has been responsible for some innovative social and urban programs. Yet the movement has not expanded the number of women in formal politics because of institutional impediments.
- Environmental movements are diverse national and local organizations. Conservation, democratic accountability, and promoting social activism domestically and internationally have been the concerns of these groups. Amazonian preservation reflects all of these aspects.
- Religious movements include some groups linked to the Catholic Church (CEBs and CPT) and others linked to charismatic churches. In recent years, Pentecostal movements have grown more rapidly and have moved into formal politics (e.g., the PL). All these religious movements attempt to organize the poor and work on behalf of social justice.
- Afro-Brazilian movements include nationalists and cultural groups that mobilize against racism and on behalf of efforts to recover black identity. It is ideologically diverse.
- The key challenge to Brazilian civil society is to find ways of institutionalizing its ideas and interests in good government at the local, state, and national levels.

---

examine the role that different civil societal groups played during and after the transition to democracy. What explains the success and failure of collective action of these various groups? Are there particular technologies of organization that have proven more effective than others in enhancing the political participation of these movements and organizations? We leave for the final section the more difficult task of assessing to what extent the activities of civil societal groups have expanded democratic citizenship.

POLITICAL CULTURE AND DEMOCRATIC CIVIL SOCIETY

The development of the state and the persistence of oligarchical rule as reflected in formal political institutions and economic structures have cultivated a political culture in Brazil that places personal and particularistic relationships above programmatic and universalistic identities. Scholars of Brazilian political culture such as the political anthropologist Roberto DaMatta (1979) and the Argentine sociologist Guillermo O'Donnell (1986) argue that most complex organizations in Brazil can be reduced to the existence of certain core personal networks. The glue that holds these networks together is a set of informal understandings. One manifestation of this is the clientelistic networks referred to in previous chapters. But the primacy of informal and personal ties in political culture is also a more widespread phenomenon. The popular suspension of formal rules to which all Brazilians have access through the informal mechanism known as the *jeito*, or the *jeitinho brasileiro*, is an example of how legal institutions and norms are less important than personal ties (Barbosa 1995). But does this mean that Brazilian political culture is "individualistic" or "anomic"?

The answer to this question can be found in a more focused examination of clientelism itself, which has always been a means for integrating important segments of civil society, including the poor, into politics. Bureaucratic rings and corporatist mobilization of workers, rural peasants, business and the middle class are mechanisms of social control that use clientelism to shape the political activity of these segments of civil society. Groups, more than individuals, are the agents in these networks. But at the same time the relationship clientelism requires is an unequal one. By pursuing clientelistic methods for addressing their concerns, civil societal actors run the risk of acquiring only ephemeral solutions to their problems. Scott Mainwaring (1999: 209) describes this tradeoff in the following way: "The system dampens issues of broad-based class entitlement. Politicians run favors and obtain resources for narrow categories more than broad groups or classes. Where representation is individualistic, party programs and class issues are undermined to the detriment of the popular sectors." So clientelism is two-faced in that it can incorporate many different groups into politics, but it does so in a way that favors some more than others, all the while limiting the autonomy of the weaker segments of civil society.

If this is the central and most enduring aspect of Brazilian political culture, it changed only during the long liberalization of the bureaucratic-authoritarian project and the transition to democracy. The autonomy of civil societal actors from the state and their capacity to articulate their own, broad-based interests as groups outside the corporatist formula was the essence of social mobilization during the democratizing period. That was most evident in the "new unionism" movement, which sought to create autonomous labor organizations that would no longer be under the constraints of the corporatist labor codes and their shop-floor enforcers, the *pelegos*. The CUT and the Workers' Party took the norm of autonomy and broadened it into a democratizing political movement during the 1980s that expanded representation and participation to more Brazilians. As the PT became a nationally viable party during the 1990s it broadened its original message, which reflected the interests of workers as a class, to include the middle classes, informal sector workers, and even business interests.

The story of the workers' struggle for organizational autonomy and democracy during the 1970s and 1980s found a corollary in a wide range of other movements during the *distensão* and *abertura* periods. Middle-class organizations such as the Brazilian Bar Association, church-based and evangelical movements, women's organizations, urban neighborhood associations, and scores of other groups mobilized extensively against the military regime alongside workers (Mainwaring and Viola 1984; Alves 1985; Doimo 1995). As Sonia Alvarez (1994: 19) observes: "though *distensão* did not generate political mobilization, it unquestionably fueled it." The *Diretas Já* campaign in 1984 represented the high point of this mobilization, as hundreds of thousands gathered in mass rallies throughout Brazil demanding direct elections for the presidency in 1985. These movements did more than participate in regime change, they also sought to deepen democracy in the years after the transition by calling for more spending on schools, public transport, rights for racial minorities, indigenous groups, women, and homosexuals. In this way, popular movements opened up new political spaces autonomous from the state corporatist system, but they also challenged the state to respond to a set of new demands posited by subaltern groups (Avritzer 2000; Cardoso 1992: 291–2).

It should be noted that the mobilization of Brazilian civil society during the transition was initiated in the 1970s and was catalyzed by institutional changes implemented by the authoritarian regime itself. Specifically, the opening of the political system to allow for an "official" opposition – the MDB – gave dissident groups a legitimate vehicle through which they could influence the gradual liberalization of the regime. At the same time, the MDB and its successor, the PMDB, remained a catch-all organization with no clear unifying method of opposition. This was bad for constructing a disciplined party later in the democratic period (see chapter 4), but it was good for social movements because it afforded them the political space of the official opposition to organize diverse kinds of representative and participatory forums, including neighborhood associations which were active at the municipal level. Elected and appointed local officials and their institutions had to adapt to these realities by finding ways of responding to the demands of neighborhood associations (Cardoso 1992: 293–4). So, as the national process of *abertura* progressed, a more localized experience of expanding participation and representation took place in major urban areas and towns throughout Brazil. These became the basis for the urban social movements and multiple other organizations that would emerge during and after the *Diretas Já* campaign peaked in the mid-1980s.

During the time that movements operated under the common umbrella of the MDB, tactical and substantive conflicts among them were subdued by the common agenda of moving the regime liberalization process forward. But once the military created the multiparty system in 1979, these conflicts came to the surface. Divisions emerged at this time, for example, between workers who supported politicians for the PT and those who backed the communists or representatives of the center-right parties. Other groups distanced themselves from party politics and focused on mobilizing particular societal groups such as women, Catholics, and Afro-Brazilians or issue-based actors such as environmentalists. These grass-roots movements concentrated on satisfying the social and political demands of their rank and file rather than supporting a particular party. The *Diretas Já* experience momentarily suspended the fragmenting effect of this pattern of grass-roots activity, but, once the issue of direct presidential elections was settled by Brazil's military and civilian elites, civil societal mobilization became noticeably fractious once again. The decision to hold indirect elections was in itself something that divided the movements, as some groups allied to the PMDB agreed to participate while other groups allied to the PT boycotted the election of the president by an electoral college.

The fragmentation of popular movements waxed and waned in subsequent years around moments of national mobilization. The two-year drafting of the 1988 constitution provided many movements with another opportunity to coordinate their actions. The drafting process allowed popular organizations to collect 30,000 signatures on behalf of their own amendments. About 168 of these popular amendments were submitted to the National Constituent Assembly and hundreds of movements and non-governmental organizations (NGOs) lobbied the convention on their behalf (Hochstetler 2000: 172). Then, in 1992, the United Nations' Earth Summit in Rio de Janeiro served as the culmination of a three-year period of eight meetings involving some 935 environmental NGOs. During the same year, mass protests calling for President Collor's impeachment recalled the street activism of the *Diretas Já* experience. Some of these events led to the creation of enduring partnerships and networks among movements and NGOs. For example, urban anti-violence and hunger groups enjoyed greater coordination after the Earth Summit, although that meeting was designed to focus on issues of the natural ecology.

Beyond these collaborative experiences, it was not clear how individual movements would transform Brazilian democracy. For many groups this transformative capacity was limited by the local and largely urban nature of the movements. As Ruth Cardoso (1992: 299) argues, groups that functioned at the neighborhood level failed to address the need for policy change at higher levels of public administration, especially the federal level. Local groups also competed among themselves for scarce resources, sometimes drowning each other out. The urban character of most of these groups limited what might have been more influential and tactical ties with rural groups. One prominent example of this tendency was the frictions that developed between the CUT and the MST in the organization of anti-corporatist worker groups (Sandoval 2004).

In the next chapter, we will examine Brazil's role in the world, but it is useful to mention here the extent to which much of the activation of Brazilian civil society incorporated the transnationalization of popular demands. Many of the social movements and NGOs analyzed below developed partnerships with organizations that operate at the international level. Perhaps the most studied has been the role that international environmental movements, particularly the World Wide Fund for Nature, played in working with rubber tappers, the PT, and Brazilian NGOs to change the Amazonian development strategies of the Brazilian state and the multilateral institutions (Keck 1995). Chico Mendes, the martyred union leader responsible for organizing the rubber tappers' ecological resistance to Amazonian development in the late 1980s, has since become an international symbol for environmentalists everywhere. International human rights NGOs such as Human Rights Watch and Amnesty

International have often worked in partnership with domestic NGOs on projects in defense of the rights of women, children, landless peasants, and racial and indigenous minorities (Sikkink 1996). Like the environmentalists and the human rights groups, the MST participates in international networks through the *Via Campesina* agrarian reform organization, which is composed of ninety peasant organizations in sixty different countries. The question of the extent to which Brazilian civil society is tied into wider international networks will be addressed more fully in the next chapter.

SOCIAL MOVEMENTS AND NON-GOVERNMENTAL ORGANIZATIONS

Any study of particular social movements and non-governmental organizations in Brazil must provide the qualification upfront that the lifecycle of any individual group or issue can be ephemeral. This is indicative of the complex organizational dynamics and the context affecting specific groups and not necessarily of the overall mobilization of civil society through cycles of protest (Hochstetler 2000: 163). Some groups sustain the original energies that brought them into being better than others, and some organizations evolve to take on a broader set of issues than the ones that first catalyzed them. The experience of any one movement or organization may say something more general about the techniques of mobilization and the evolution of agendas only when they are compared over time with other groups' experiences. With this in mind, this section will attempt to examine each group under issue areas and identity categories and then offer some comparative observations.

A couple of conceptual distinctions will help to clarify some of the questions raised in studies of Brazilian civil society. First, in Brazil, "social movements" are defined as short-term, mass-based protest activities that are sustained only through the voluntary commitments of their participants. "Non-governmental organizations," however, are longer-term and institutionalized entities with established and enduring leadership systems, financial and logistical functions, and a core set of ideological or otherwise normative principles that are used to sustain them. The pre-1985 groups that organized around the democratic transition were more often movements than NGOs proper, but some groups such as the Brazilian Bar Association (OAB) were NGOs. After 1985, scholarly attention came to focus more on NGOs since it was these groups that effectively institutionalized their strategies and agendas and became most relevant during the New Republic. This was particularly true during the Constituent Assembly, since NGOs were uniquely capable of monitoring legislation and lobbying over the two-year drafting period in an institutionalized setting (Hochstetler 2000: 178). Yet it is also the case that many NGOs employ direct actions and many movements include institutional actors within them. This ambiguity is sometimes difficult to cut through, especially when hybrid movements such as the environmentalists include the Green Party and more radical ecologists who do not agree on the usefulness of engaging in formal politics.

The previous section made the point that social movements in Brazil evolved under two different periods, or "cycles of contention" – the regime transition up to 1985 and then the post-1985 consolidation of democracy. It was in the latter phase that the unique qualities of each of these movements and NGOs became the focus of scholarly attention. Based on this work, one might speak of an expansive notion of "democratic citizenship" that sits at the core of the collective mobilization of Brazilian civil society. Democratic citizenship encompasses a call for greater social justice in a variety of areas: land ownership, economic opportunities, racial and sexual equality, reproductive rights, religious activism, freedom from police-sponsored violence, the elimination of hunger and disease, and the demand for affordable and adequate urban housing and public services (Jelin 1996; Caldeira 1998; Pinheiro 1997). Being a Brazilian citizen no longer meant voting and being a national of the country, it meant primarily having the right to basic human and communal dignities (Dimenstein 1996). To be sure, no single movement or NGO articulated all of these aspects of citizenship, but each embraced a piece of the whole concept.

Each group's experience was also different. Some employed the techniques of direct action, such as the MST's land invasions. Other groups used sustained lobbying and judicial actions to change official policy, such as the case of many women's organizations. Distinct groups also met with different levels of success. For example, some environmental NGOs were able to protect natural habitats in the face of plans to develop these areas for human use, while others failed to counteract these forces. But success can be measured in other terms. Kathryn Hochstetler (2000: 169) argues that an often neglected dimension of the experience of social movements and NGOs is that many of them can be incubators for the social change they would like to engineer in Brazil. Human rights, anti-hunger, and civil rights groups tend to include Brazilians from different walks of life, who would not meet each other but for the common opportunity they enjoy to work together on the same campaign. Below, we examine distinct types of movements and NGOs along all of these dimensions.

Urban social movements and NGOs

Members of urban social movements were among the most prolific activists during and just after the transition. The political decentralization of the authoritarian regime following the direct elections of governors and mayors in 1982 coincided with the growth of municipal-level activism. Many of these activists had experience organizing at the neighborhood level in church-based campaigns to help the poor during the 1970s and early 1980s (Mainwaring 1989). These progressive social workers gradually separated themselves from the Catholic Church's emphasis on providing support for existing communities in favor of more political projects to mobilize communities for new and better public services and social rights (Assies 1994: 84). NGOs were particularly well suited to these tasks since they were most interested in generating institutional changes, although many leaders spoke of these goals in more principled terms as generating "municipal democratization." As leftist parties came to power in some cities, progressive mayors and city councils created participatory policy-making institutions that regularly integrated the views of urban activists.

The range of activities and venues of urban NGOs is too diverse to detail here; however, some examples can be used to clarify what these groups do. For instance, NGOs active in the *favelas* of Rio have played an instrumental role in mediating levels of criminal and police violence. By publicizing acts of violence, bringing in international and national media attention, educating adolescents most likely to be drawn into criminal gangs, and mobilizing residents in denouncing violence, these groups have at times successfully reduced shantytown mayhem. NGOs have also undermined the patron–client ties between traffickers and many residents by distributing food and water and providing other services previously proffered by criminal kingpins (Arias 2004: 15–16). Providing services characterizes other urban social movements. For example, the São Paulo Union of Housing Movements, which includes some forty-five separate organizations, coordinates campaigns throughout Brazil on behalf of afford-able housing. Through sustained lobbying efforts and legal services, this movement helps to remove poor Brazilians from the informal housing market that drags many into the *favelas* in the first place.

Some of the most effective urban social movements have adapted strategically to the multiple venues in which they must operate. In large metropolitan areas, social prob-lems that emerge in one zone have an effect in other zones. The scourge of drug traf-ficking and violence in the *favelas*, for example, is intimately linked to drug demand and criminal assaults and robbery in richer areas. Consequently, urban social move-ments must coordinate diverse actors, including middle class anti-crime groups, law enforcement, and *favela* residents. These networks work best when they maintain secure and trustworthy channels of information among the various constituencies involved (Arias 2004). In this way, many urban social movements have evolved highly flexible techniques and strategies for dealing with interconnected problems. Activists operate in multiple arenas – the courts, municipal agencies, neighborhood associations, churches – and in alliance with other groups, including neighborhood watch commit-tees and women's NGOs focused on urban crime.

Urban social movements have emerged around groups that fall outside of the com-monly defined constituencies of other grass-roots movements such as the labor union movement. Urban popular groups have mobilized social actors typically seen as anomic or fragmented, largely unable to engage in collective action. The *perueiros* (clandestine urban transport workers) and *camelôs* (street vendors) mentioned in chapter 5 are examples that suggest that even informal market workers can engage in sustained protest and lobbying.

The landless peasant movement

Although we examined the MST along with agrarian reform in chapter 5, some of the organizational aspects of the movement should be discussed here. The landless peasant movement is one of Brazil's most sophisticated civil societal actors because it conducts its campaigns from multiple angles – in the courts, through direct action, through the media, and based on extensive and intensive grass-roots organization. Lawyers for the movement handle suits on behalf of squatters who seek legal title to occupied land even as the MST presses politicians and landowners through mass marches and land invasions. In virtually all cases, the MST surveys a target for occupation for some time, ascertains whether it is being used productively (since the law allows for squatters' rights only on unproductive land), and then moves clusters of families to the location. Relocated families are encouraged to farm the land while the movement's officials pursue formal recognition of squatters' rights through the Institute for Agrarian Reform (*Instituto Nacional de Colonização e Reforma Agrária*, INCRA). In some cases, the MST has been known to use direct action on INCRA itself through periodic occupations of the agency's buildings.

Direct actions can backfire and they sometimes do for the MST. Land invasions have often involved violent actions, although the MST does not officially employ violent confrontation as a preferred tactic. More typically, landowners' reactions to land invasions will be the catalyst for violence. Perhaps the most notable example occurred on 17 April 1996 in the Amazon (Eldorado do Carajás) when military police, at the behest of local landowners, broke up a roadblock of 2,000 protesting MST workers, killing nineteen and severely injuring fifty-one. Fear of such violence keeps many resettled families wrestling with the difficult choice of taking land, and suffering continued threats to their security by landowners and their hired gunmen, or remaining landless. While the number of resettled families increased during Cardoso's two terms and more recently under Lula's presidency, the degree of rural violence remains a problem.

Despite the pall of violence that some attribute to the MST, the movement's repertoire of action has evolved in recent years to integrate a variety of demands and techniques on behalf of land reform, social programs, and legal protections for rural peasants. First, it has broadened the justification for land invasions from the level of production on target land to holdings that employ slave labor (indentured servants) or simply do not respect labor law, farms that are linked to smuggling, narcotics or other illegal activities, and land that is being treated in an environmentally unsustainable fashion. Second, the MST has focused recently on deepening the state's fiscal commitment to land reform by protecting the Rural Territorial Tax (ITR) that finances expropriations. It also advocates the creation of credit programs to provide financial and technical assistance to settled families and to set up agricultural cooperatives, including those that use organic farming techniques. Expansion and service of rural infrastructure and education are two other major areas in which the MST demands more of a fiscal commitment by the state. Finally, the MST has become more active in the national human rights movement in Brazil. Given that local police are often corrupt or otherwise beholden to landowners, the MST favors investigations by the federal police of cases of rural violence.

The MST leadership sees the movement's actions as part of a wider campaign of "democratizing the land." This means that the group's tactics as well as its agenda are significant for other organizations. For example, members of the MST have transferred the movement's ideas and tactics in Rio Grande do Sul to the Homeless Urban Workers' Movement (*Movimento dos Trabalhadores Sem Teto Urbano*), which has emerged recently to employ MST-style action on behalf of the urban poor. This fact also underscores the degree to which the MST is now more of an established non-governmental organization than a peasant movement. Its leadership, surveying techniques, direct and judicial actions, and even its public relations functions are as sophisticated, particularly in the southern regions of Brazil, as those of any NGO, party, or other institutionalized political organization (Martins 2000). The MST receives funding from international donors, it manages a large budget of some US$35 million, and it maintains a permanent corps of "professional militants" ready to be called to action (Hochstetler 2000: 177). Moreover, the MST is itself today a source of social spending. The movement funds over 400 rural service associations and forty-nine agricultural cooperatives, including meat and dairy operations, throughout Brazil. It offers technical training in its settlements and, in partnership with UNESCO, 1,200 MST teachers are working in the countryside to reduce rates of illiteracy. More than 250 MST day-care centers, called *cirandas infantis*, and hundreds of other MST-sponsored schools serve about 150,000 children. In all of these ways, the MST reflects the complete evolutionary arc of a social movement, from protest actor to non-governmental organization to an institutionalized welfare system in the countryside.

Women's movements and NGOs

The Brazilian transition to democracy coincided with one of the most vibrant mobilizations of popular women's movements in Latin America. Soon after the bureaucratic-authoritarian regime initiated the *distensão* process, women working through the Brazilian Catholic Church's progressive initiatives in poor neighborhoods began to see social and political questions in gendered terms (Drogus 1999: 37). The plight of poor women, black women, and mothers catalyzed many of these largely middle-class militants to form organizations to focus more closely on the particular concerns of women (Alvarez 1994: 15–16; Bisilliat 1997). After the governors were directly elected in 1982, women's organizations in major urban centers pressed these newly autonomous leaders to institute legislative changes establishing centers to service the family planning, health, and day-care needs of women. Franco Montoro, São Paulo's governor, was the first to inaugurate an advisory Council on the Feminine Condition (*Conselho da Condição Feminina*) to give the leaders of women's organizations direct representation in the discussion of these new initiatives. Several other states followed this example, instituting not only state-level consultative councils but municipal councils and a federal National Council for the Rights of Women (*Conselho Nacional dos Direitos da Mulher*, CNDM). Feminist organizations continued to be the driving force in these institutions as they shaped the agenda and provided the grass-roots support needed to implement social change (Alvarez 1990, 1994). This organizational momentum carried over during the long process of drafting the constitution. Although only twenty-six of the 559 representatives in the constituent assembly were women, the National Council was effective in forming a lobbying group that extended numerous women's issues into the constituent debates. An umbrella group for 700 women's groups, the Women's Network (*Rede Mulher*), succeeded in getting passage of constitutional provisions protecting the equality of women and men and introducing maternity leave of 120 days, the right of divorce, and laws against domestic violence. The movement also prevented any attempt to make abortion illegal (Caldeira 1998: 78).

In the years following the transition, the women's movement grew into a wide array of different organizations. Many of these NGOs focused their attention, as environmental NGOs did before the Earth Summit, on the UN Women's Conference held in Beijing, China, in 1995. One women's organization, Brazilian Women's Articulation (*Articulação Mulheres Brasileiras*), coordinated women's NGOs throughout Brazil in preparation for the meeting. The collection included an assortment of organizations with the aim of providing legal advice, family planning and sex education, and NGOs that concentrated on the sensitivity training of law-enforcement personnel who deal with cases of female victims of violent crime. Teresa Caldeira (1998) argues that progress on these and other social questions relied on the NGOs more than on women's representation in formal politics. Not all parties or governors and presidents proved reliable or responsive to the official councils over time, so the activity of women's organizations remained fundamental to keeping the women's agenda vibrant.

One of the most innovative and sustained projects taken on by women's organizations was the creation of all-women's police stations (*Delegacias de Defesa da Mulher*, DDMs). This idea first emerged during the Montoro administration in São Paulo and as a result of the initiative of the Council on the Feminine Condition. Run by trained female law-enforcement officers, these stations specialize in crimes against women, including domestic violence and rape. As of 2000, there were 250 of these *delegacias* throughout Brazil (123 in São Paulo state alone). In theory, the DDMs affirmed in a powerful way the extent to which Brazil was becoming democratic, since these institutions were the embodiment of a public response against the oppression of women in the home as well as in the public domain (Nelson 1996). In practice, however, not all of the DDMs proved sensitive to women's concerns or even effective in enforcing laws designed to protect women. The low level of convictions of perpetrators of violence against women and the removal of feminist training of female police officers effectively made many of the DDMs as sexist as regular *delegacias* (Alvarez 1994: 46–7; Nelson 1996). Yet the fundamental idea of the DDMs and some of the better functioning ones remain a reflection of the most innovative aspects of women's advocacy politics in Brazil.

Other women's movements led to the creation of NGOs focused on protecting the rights of women to have safe access to abortion. Under the pressure of women's groups, public hospitals were required by law after 1985 to make this option available to women. Laws against sexual harassment, legislation extending health insurance coverage for reconstructive plastic surgery for women recovering from breast cancer, and maternity leave and benefits rights emerged similarly as a result of the mobilization of women's groups in subsequent years.

Despite the prominent role and success of women's groups during the transition and afterwards, the position of women in Brazilian formal politics has not changed much since 1985. As Mala Htun (2002) points out, "Brazil has the dubious distinction of being the Latin American country with the lowest level of women's representation in national politics." Only a negligible number of women (eleven) served in congress between 1950 and 1980. In 2002, only 6 percent of seats in the Chamber of Deputies and only 7 percent of seats in the Senate were held by women. The Latin American average is 15 percent for lower houses and 12 percent for upper houses. Women are represented more at the local level, but not by much. Only two of the twenty-seven governors in 2002 were women. Women held 10 percent of the seats in state legislatures, 6 percent of the mayoralties, and 12 percent of municipal council seats (Htun 2002: table 1). The 2004 municipal elections led to a slight increase in the number of female mayors, as 404 women were elected (7.32 percent of the total).

The low incidence of women in formal politics results primarily from institutional factors. Although a law passed in 1996 established a quota of seats for women in legislatures at all levels of government, the number of women holding seats in the federal congress *decreased* even as the new quota legislation increased the number of women in subnational office. Since the law required only that parties should reserve 30 percent of candidate slots for women, but not that they should distribute seats they win to women, the new legislation failed to empower women. Parties would nominate many more candidates than the number of seats available and then allocate the seats won by the party to men (Htun 2002). Furthermore, the strong tendencies in the Brazilian electoral system for politicians to cultivate a personal vote hurt women, who are at a disadvantage in a country with overwhelmingly masculine cults of personality (Htun and Jones 2002). Although some women have risen recently to prominent positions – Benedita da Silva (PT governor of Rio de Janeiro), Roseana Sarney (PFL governor of Maranhão and presidential candidate in 2002), Marta Suplicy (former PT mayor of São Paulo), and Luiza Erundina (former PT mayor of São Paulo) – many of them began their careers in the Workers' Party, which is one of the only programmatic parties. Personalism and the old (literally) boys' network of clientelist exchange tend to disadvantage the rise of women in politics.

In contrast to their situation in formal politics, women have made significant strides in the workplace. In 2003, over half of all women were in the workforce as compared with 73 percent of all men. Brazil also ranks second only to the US in the percentage of women in top management positions (44 percent to the US's 46 percent). The salaries of women have improved and are now growing at a faster rate than those of men and, as mentioned in chapter 5, girls now complete on average slightly more schooling than boys. Consequently the wage-skill gap between the sexes is closing. These socio-economic outcomes are important, and they seem to be at least partially indicative of the vibrant role that women's movements and NGOs have played in addressing the social and economic structures that have tended to disadvantage Brazilian women.

Women play key roles in other movements and non-governmental organizations not necessarily focused on family or women's issues. For instance, ten of the twenty-two top leaders of the MST are women. This reflects the movement's increasing concerns with the gender inequalities in land titling and the MST's broader commitment to empowering mothers and young girls through the provision of *cirandas infantis* and other aid, so they may work and become more active in the movement. Middle-class feminists have also played key roles in leading urban social movements, including church-based groups and advocacy networks on behalf of schools, affordable housing, and proper sanitation services. In this sense, then, the Brazilian women's movement is larger than the organizations that focus on gender-specific issues.

Environmental movements and NGOs

Like the women's movement in Brazil, the environmental movement first evolved during the bureaucratic-authoritarian regime on the local level, and it rapidly expanded to include over a thousand non-governmental organizations and less-institutionalized activist groups. The movement is multifaceted, with some of its segments, such as the Green Party (*Partido Verde*, PV) and the many ecological activists that are part of the PT, engaged in formal representative politics and some of its grass-roots sections focused on local activism. However, one can speak of a *national* environmental movement engaged in politics only since the late 1980s when ecological groups mobilized throughout Brazil at various national forums, including the Constituent Assembly in 1987–8 and at the Earth Summit in 1992 (Hochstetler 1997). Yet most environmental organizations remain small and local, as NGOs more engaged with the particular ecological problems of a single area.

National environmental policy emerged earlier than the national movement. The military created an environmental ministry soon after the 1972 UN Conference on the Human Environment. Non-governmental organizations were included in the first advisory National Environmental Council (CONAMA) in 1981. Other parts of the environmental protection bureaucracy emerged after the regime transition, with the federal Brazilian Institute of Environment and of Renewable Natural Resources (*Instituto Brasileiro do Meio Ambiente e Recursos Naturais Renováveis*, IBAMA) in 1989 and Itamar Franco's decision in 1994 to make the Secretariat of the Environment a cabinet-level office. During the 1980s, many of the Brazilian states created their own environmental protection agencies and advisory councils, in some cases as a result of sustained movement lobbying and activism. This multilevel environmental bureaucracy soon suffered from inefficiencies of overlapping functions and jurisdictional conflicts, which typically draw in other agencies such as INCRA, energy regulators, and state utility companies (Ames and Keck 1997–8: 5–6).

The goals of Brazilian environmental movements are as varied as the organizations, but they revolve around several consistent themes that were apparent during the drafting of the constitution. First, reflecting the movement's conservationist origins during the 1970s, Brazilian environmentalists call for the protection of natural habitats, parks, resources, and indigenous communities. Second, environmentalists followed the examples of other movements during the 1980s in calling for the deepening of democratic citizenship, the expansion and protection of civil rights, and the inclusion of more voices in political decision-making at all levels of the Brazilian polity. Third, environmentalists sought to coordinate the activism of other social movements. This was a new function for the movement, since before the early 1990s most of these groups remained localized and isolated from one another (Hochstetler 1997). But, in preparation for the 1992 Earth Summit, ecological NGOs held national and subnational summits of their own to plan the activism of a wide array of citizen groups and urban social, gender- and race-based movements and organizations. Given the environmental movement's own long history of broad-based mobilization on behalf of democratic citizenship, it is not entirely surprising that environmentalists would be among the chief coordinators of encompassing movements on behalf of social justice concerns.

Like the MST, environmental organizations are simultaneously concerned with local politics. This reflects the fact that the movement first emerged through subnational conservationist organizations such as Rio Grande do Sul's Gaucho Association for Protection of the Natural Environment (AGAPAN). At this level, diverse environmental organizations engage in representative politics by electing their members onto city commissions or otherwise getting them on state task forces focused on environmental issues. Some organizations, such as AGAPAN, coordinate their activities with political parties (e.g., PT) while others cultivate ties with other movements (e.g., MST). The diverse experiences of these politics at the state level are too varied to summarize here, but several recent studies have shown that domestic and international environmental NGOs, state and local politicians, and even bureaucrats can sometimes form alliances that reinforce old or establish new environmental protections (e.g., Ames and Keck 1997–8). Outcomes depend on the nature of state politics, particularly the extent to which clientelistic exchange and the influence of private developers impinge on politicians' behavior. These factors make the job of environmental NGOs more difficult as they navigate the typically dense bureaucracies of many states. In such cases, the activism of local NGOs with a good understanding of state and municipal politics offers the best chance of shaping policy results.

Perhaps in no other area of Brazil has the influence of the environmental movement been more apparent than in the management of Amazonian development. Despite the evident interest that environmental movements would have for protecting Brazil's single greatest ecosystem, ecological organizations became active in the Amazon basin only after the transition to democracy (Hochstetler 1997: 211). The military and public industries took an interest in developing the region decades before, when massive projects such as the Vale do Rio Doce Company's Carajás mining facility were touted by the generals as the forerunners to Brazil's emergence as an economic and regional superpower. Strategic concerns also remained central to the thinking of the armed forces years after the regime transition as the Amazonian satellite surveillance system (SIVAM) project extended the military's responsibility for guarding Brazil's porous and unprotected Amazonian borders (Martins Filho and Zirker 2000; Wittkoff 2003). But environmentalists were somewhat late to become more involved in the Amazon, in part on account of lingering nationalist resentments that these groups would open Brazil's greatest natural resource to foreign "interlopers" (Hochstetler 1997). The oft-quoted popular dictum "A amazona é nossa!" ("the Amazon is ours!") survived beyond the jingoistic propaganda of the authoritarian period to become a norm commonly accepted throughout Brazilian society.

Even so, a variety of environmental protection networks that include both international and domestic actors have played important roles in Amazonian policy-making since the regime transition (Rodrigues 2000). The preservation of certain natural resources such as rare and expensive mahogany trees has pitted the timber industry and developers against the environmental movements and international organizations concerned with the dwindling numbers of particular species. Excessive deforestation caused by "slash and burn" agriculture and the pollution of rivers from illegal mining continue as major problems as well. In short, there is virtually no limit to the number of unsustainable practices in the Amazon that will continue to elicit the attention of environmental activists. The Amazon's sheer size and its importance as the "green lung of the planet" will also keep international ecological organizations involved.

Finally, it should be noted that other movements and organizations regularly engage in environmental activism although it is not their core focus. For example, the MST's National Collective on the Environment (Equipe do Meio Ambiente, EMA) coordinates the movement's initiatives in organic agriculture. The EMA produces and disseminates studies on environmental problems and farming and other solutions. It also engages directly in organic production of coffee in the state of Espírito Santo and rice in Rio Grande do Sul, and directs reforestation projects in the Pontal do Paranapanema (São Paulo state).

Religious movements

Popular religious movements were the source of many of the social movements that emerged during the *distensão* and *abertura* periods. Thousands of religious groups engaged in grass-roots activism as members of the Catholic Church, which during the 1980s was Brazil's most important protector of the poor (Della Cava 1989: 143). The most noteworthy were the Ecclesiastical Base Community movements (*comunidades eclesais de base*, CEBs), Bible-study groups and parishes that engaged in social justice activism in rural areas and in urban shantytowns during the 1970s and 1980s. Many of the early militants in the rural and the urban women's movements were trained in social mobilization within the CEBs (Deere 2004: 179–80; Drogus 1999). The intense focus of these groups on linking social justice concerns and the religious principles of the Catholic Church made the CEBs articulators of liberation theology. This diverse set of ideas, borrowing heavily from Marxism, called on church pastors and Catholic priests to recognize and work to change systems of social and political inequality through direct action (Berryman 1987). Liberation theology, which had distinct strands in different areas of Latin America, fueled the mobilization of thousands of Brazilian groups concerned with problems ranging from public services and violent crime in the cities to agrarian reform in the countryside. The CEBs and their members thus overlapped with urban social movements, women's groups, and the landless peasant movement. The last of these produced one of the most vibrant elements of the larger movement, the Church's pastoral land commission (*Comissão Pastoral da Terra*, CPT). The CPT publicized human rights abuses in rural areas and *favelas*, it campaigned on behalf of agrarian reform, it coordinated its social services with the MST's settlements, and it lobbied for the recognition of peasants' legitimate rights to land titles.

Another strand of religious activism emerged from the Pentecostal movement in Brazil, the growth of evangelical churches springing from Protestant missionaries and their ministries in North America and other Latin American countries. The Pentecostal movement in many parts of Brazil took up the functions of the CEBs beginning in the late 1980s and early 1990s. Many of the CEBs by that time had become inactive. The decline of the CEBs and the rise of evangelical movements was the result of several factors. First, religious pluralism increased in Brazil after 1986. Poor Brazilians in particular, who were mostly nominally Catholic but not faithful practitioners, became more religiously active in the Pentecostal churches. Charismatic evangelical ministers proliferated in poor neighborhoods and their ministries prospered as millions became more disillusioned with the Church's inability to bring about the extensive social change it had long promised (Berryman 1996). Presently, evangelicals account for 15 percent of the population (Monclaire 2004: 82). Second, after the regime transition, the Catholic Church reduced the role of the popular church and de-emphasized liberationist practice. Although a large percentage of Brazilian clergy remained liberationists, the official Church led by the staunchly anti-communist Pope John Paul II launched a conservative retrenchment that turned it away from progressive and mobilizational strategies during the late 1980s (Serbin 2000: 148). Finally, the role of the CEBs declined as the number of competitors in Brazil's "religious market" increased. Popular church groups did not compete just with the Pentecostals, they also competed with various alternative religious strands within Protestantism, the Afro-Brazilian religions, and even New Age movements (Vázquez 1999).

Pluralistic forces in the religious market made the evolution of politics and religion in Brazil during the 1990s complex and difficult to gauge. Pentecostalism seemed to be the big winner, but the movement was itself disparate in theology and structure, so it is difficult to make out a particular strand or organization as predominant. Much of the charismatic tradition emphasizes social mobility along with emotional spirituality based on the Bible and the figure of Christ in particular, but, unlike the Catholic Church, it does not offer a unified set of principles to coordinate social action nationally. This difference in theology allowed the Church to retain a national perspective as a "moral watchdog" in the new democracy, although at the local level more Brazilians turned to evangelicals to deal with their everyday problems.

Pentecostal churches easily moved into politics by electing evangelicals directly to the Constituent Assembly in 1986 and thereafter to the congress. The evangelical base in parties such as the PL is large and influential, and it has defended its interests by playing, often with expert precision, the *fisiologista* politics of Brazil (Serbin 2000). In response, Catholic interests have been slow to mobilize in formal politics, but the National Conference of the Bishops of Brazil and the remaining CEBs still play a role at the national and local levels, and increasingly they act in cooperation with Pentecostal ministries. For instance, CEB community organizers and activists in evangelical organizations in the *favelas* routinely mediate between residents and drug traffickers (Arias 2004). CPT leaders also collaborate with evangelicals in rural communities as organizers of settlements. Women's Catholic groups enjoy a particularly vibrant networking role since they are very experienced in collective activism throughout Brazil. These and other areas will encourage ecumenical alliances as a dimension of the future growth of base community movements. This seems more likely as Pentecostals continue to appropriate aspects of the liberationist discourse while Catholic organizers become more open to cooperation in the same communities with evangelicals.

Afro-Brazilian movements and NGOs

Since the abolition of slavery in Brazil, differences of race have tended to be either ignored or encompassed by competing concepts such as class in discussions of the problems facing Brazilian society. As a country of mixed cultural and racial heritage, Brazil sees itself as a *mestizo* civilization. But unlike other multi-ethnic societies where racial strife is common, Brazilians believe that their country has escaped these problems by forging an enduring "racial democracy" (Guimarães 2003). This term describes an exceptionalist norm in Brazilian society that ignores the need to address real social and economic differences between blacks and whites. Consequently, "racial democracy" has been a mindset that black empowerment movements have mobilized against, but at the same time this widespread norm has been an impediment to generating racial political consciousness among blacks (Hanchard 1994). At the heart of the concept is the challenge for black movements to articulate an agenda that is unique to Afro-Brazilians and cannot be incorporated or co-opted by alternative classifications such as class, region, and profession or by the corporatist traditions of the state (Lamounier 1968).

Black power movements have a long history in Brazil despite the otherwise demo-bilizing effects of the "racial democracy" norm. These movements have been ideo-logically diverse, including right-wing fascist groups during the 1930s and revolutionary leftist groups during the late 1970s and early 1980s. However, their focus on the common problems of racial discrimination and prejudice and their effects on the social mobility and political enfranchisement of Afro-Brazilians allow them to be studied as a common phenomenon. No other organization within the black move-ment experience directed as much attention to these political questions as the United Black Movement (*Movimento Negro Unificado*, MNU). The MNU emerged in 1978 alongside other urban social and women's movements and the "new unionism." Black militants were part of the same mobilizing dynamic during the *distensão* and *abertura* periods that led to an explosion of civil societal activism. And, like several of these other movements, the MNU was divided between a core leadership that focused on the fight for democracy and civil rights within formal institutions and a more radical, cultural leadership and base that embraced fundamental critiques of Brazil's social structures and polity (Barcelos 1999: 161–3). The latter group mixed revolutionary Marxism with an Afro-centrist nationalism that saw Afro-Brazilians as African descen-dants first and not simply as people of the black race, a phenotype without a national identity. Black nationalism easily tied into the long history of separate black settlements and civilizations (*quilombos*) made up of runaway slaves during the colonial and impe-rial periods. Zumbi, the leader of the most famous *quilombo*, Palmares (1695), was elevated by the black movement as the first of a series of national heroes. And Afro-Brazilian religion and spirituality, which in many parts of Brazil survived for centuries alongside the Catholic liturgical tradition, became more visible than ever. MNU leaders and other black power groups used these symbols to rally Afro-Brazilians around an alternative political consciousness that could counteract the ideas of racial democracy and fight racism.

More than any of the other movements compared here, the black power movement in Brazil relies upon constructing (or retrieving old) identities in the fight to expand democratic citizenship. But the focus is still on many of the same things that concern urban social movements, women's groups, environmentalists, and religious move-ments. The MNU has been successful in securing both legislative changes recognizing the need to eliminate racial discrimination and intellectual exclusion from the entire education system and laws designating racially motivated crimes, with police stations specially designed for Afro-Brazilians. Affirmative action (racial preferences) is still in its infancy in Brazil, but the MNU has been a staunch defender of the need to imple-ment it fully for the hiring of public sector workers. The movement has also been successful in gaining national recognition for its symbols. Zumbi's Day (20 November) is a national holiday. The drafting of the 1988 constitution provided several opportu-nities for making enduring changes in Brazilian law. Millions of blacks were enfran-chised by the constitution's extension of the right to vote to illiterates. Racism was also designated a crime not subject to bail or a statute of limitations. And, while the number of blacks who run for office in Brazil is small and the number with seats in the congress never surpassed twenty for both houses during the 1990s, these politicians nonetheless proved key actors in advocating legislation to fight racism and discrimina-tion (Johnson 1998).

From this core example of mobilization through the MNU, the black power movement has since become more diverse, linking with distinct parties and forming non-governmental organizations that work with a range of allied groups and on non-race issues. **Table 6.1** lists some of the largest Afro-Brazilian organizations. What is notable about these groups is that they are not exclusively political or social movements, but cultural and educational as well, and they are ideologically diverse. This fact underscores one of the enduring aspects of the black power movement in Brazil, that it has not created a single racial consciousness linking all organizations (Hanchard 1994: 78).

One of the distinguishing cleavages within the larger Afro-Brazilian movement is the mobilization of black women. Women's organizations were catalyzed by the growing availability of socio-economic data demonstrating the particularly parlous condition of black women (Caldeira 1998: 82). Over time these groups have grown to encompass a wide range of women's and family issues, as well as racial concerns.

Conclusions: a new democratic citizenship?

Any survey of Brazilian social movements will show that the extensive mobilization of civil society during the democratic transition evolved into a more diverse array of organizations over time. Despite the continuation of traditional elites in power, grass-roots activists continued to play a key role in deepening democratic citizenship and enforcing accountability (Avritzer 2000). In this way, social movements and NGOs acted in much the same manner in which Scott Mainwaring (1989: 197) once predicted they would: "[these movements] are likely to continue acting as the 'conscience' of the society, placing on the agenda issues of socio-economic justice, rights for the popular classes and minority groups, and popular participation."

One method for assessing the enduring impact of social mobilization in Brazil is to focus on the lessons learned from the rise and fall of different movements. Are there particular organizational techniques and strategies that have proven effective? Borrowing from Sidney Tarrow (1998: 30–1), a prominent theorist of contentious movement politics, are there identifiable "repertoires of contention" in democratic Brazil? That is, are there established mobilizational actions that groups take in which they are particularly expert and to which others, including elites, understand and respond as movements expect? The full array of Brazilian social movements and NGOs offer a wide variety of organizational strategies that range from the direct actions of the MST, to the focus on reclaiming cultural symbols of the MNU, to the establishment of new institutions such as the women's movement's DDMs. Many more could be listed, but it is clear that repertoires of contention in democratic Brazil are as varied as the movements and NGOs themselves. At the same time, there is ample evidence of the ability of many of these groups to evolve and to forge strategic alliances with each other. Sustained networking is associated with some of the most powerful forms of mobilization. And in many of these cases, the organizational specialties of one group can be used alongside those of another. Thus the MST's land invasions coincide with the CPT's moral denunciation of violence against landless peasants and the social activism of women's groups on settled land.

Table 6.1 Major Afro-Brazilian movements and NGOs

Organization	Target population	Type
Movimento Negro Unificado	Afro-Brazilians	Political
Sociedade Afrosergipiana de Estudos e Cidadania	Afro-Brazilians and Women	Political
Center for Articulation for Marginalized Peoples	Afro-Brazilians	Political
Fundação Cultural Palmares	Afro-Brazilians	Political/ educational
National Council of Black Entities	Afro-Brazilians	Political/ cultural
Partido Popular Poder para a Maioria	Afro-Brazilians	Political
SOS Racismo	Afro-Brazilians	Political
National Commission of Blacks (CUT)	Afro-Brazilians and Women	Political
Instituto Cultural Steven Biko	Afro-Brazilians	Educational
Grupo Cultural Olodum	Afro-Brazilians	Cultural/ educational
Ile Aiye	Afro-Brazilians	Cultural/ educational
Djumbay	Afro-Brazilians	Political/ cultural/ educational
Casa Dandara	Afro-Brazilians	Cultural
Afrobras	Afro-Brazilians	Educational
Coletivo de Empresários e Empreendedores Afro-Brasileiros de Triângulo Mineiro	Afro-Brazilians	Educational
Instituto Africa America	Afro-Brazilians	Cultural
Núcleo de Estudos do Negro	Afro-Brazilians	Educational
Centro de Referência do Material Didático Afro-Brasileiro	Afro-Brazilians	Educational
Centro de Estudos das Relações do Trabalho e Desigualdades	Afro-Brazilians	Educational
União de Negros Pela Igualdade	Afro-Brazilians	Political
Trabalhos Estudos Zumbi	Afro-Brazilians	Cultural/ educational
Thema Educação	Afro-Brazilians	Educational
Geledes Instituto da Mulher Negra	Afro-Brazilian women	Political
CRIOLA	Afro-Brazilian women	Political
Fala Preta!	Afro-Brazilian women	Political/ health/ educational
Maria Mulher	Afro-Brazilian women	Political
Casa de Cultura da Mulher Negra	Afro-Brazilian women	Cultural/ political
Associação Cultural de Mulheres Negras	Afro-Brazilian women	Educational

Source: Compiled for the author by Lesley Warner.

Establishing general observations about such a diverse set of civil societal actors is always difficult. Yet some overarching conclusions are possible. For example, the national lifecycle of Brazilian movements during the New Republic can be divided into pre- and post-transition analysis (Hochstetler 2000). Before the regime transition, movements were engaged with the Brazilian state more as an opposition than as a demand-oriented set of actors. After 1985, however, movements and non-governmental organizations became part of the network of policy-making that included proposing reform, lobbying for legislative changes, and enacting policy. Far from there being an opposed, arm's-length relationship between state and civil society, Kathryn Hochstetler argues that movements and NGOs remain an active part of the deepening of democracy in the New Republic.

But frictions and inefficiencies have developed, particularly as the interests of different movements and NGOs have come into conflict with one another. Money is at the heart of some of these problems. Some NGOs wield greater financial influence than others, sparking criticisms by less well-endowed groups that they are "selling out" or protecting elite interests or simply being conservative with the management of resources. NGO–movement linkages are another area of conflict, as movement participants often expect NGOs to provide all of their technical and lobbying support and NGO leaders expect the rank and file of movements to exert pressure and publicize issues as the organization prefers. Differences in viewpoint on the specifics are bound to emerge in these contexts. And it should be said that many NGOs and movement leaders are subject to the classic Brazilian tendencies to engage in clientelistic exchange and even outright corruption in some cases. Therefore, the proliferation of NGOs and movements and even the greater interaction of these actors in Brazilian civil society may not be a reliable indicator of the growing vitality of social mobilization or the deepening of democratic citizenship.

An alternative indicator of the changes made by a more active civil society is the extent to which the public sector responds by changing the way political decisions are made. Throughout Brazil, the transition to democracy opened new political spaces for social movements and NGOs to participate in policy-making. During the 1980s, the most prominent examples were the government councils at the national and at the state and municipal levels that invited popular associations to participate in designing policy in a range of thematic areas – education, environment, women's issues, etc. Above we mentioned the National Council on the Environment and the National Council on Women's Rights, both of which played some role in shaping federal policy in these areas. Nevertheless, these experiences included their own dangers in that politicians on the councils often subjugated the movements' demands to their own partisan interests (Hochstetler 2000: 174–5; Alvarez 1990). While some of the government councils succeeded in hammering out meaningful policy proposals that were subsequently implemented, most failed to produce much of real substance. This fact underscores one of the most important limitations of social mobilization as a method for deepening democracy: how do empowering ideas get institutionalized and develop into part of the democratic order without becoming watered down by clientelistic interests? This was the essential conflict of social movements during and just after the transition to democracy when the initial energy that fueled movement action against the authoritarian regime could not be sustained during the subsequent consolidation of the New Republic.

Brazil does have some prominent examples of ideas that have become institutionalized in a way that encourages popular participation. These experiences provide some ideas as to how social mobilization and political institutionalization may coincide. At the state and municipal levels, the experience of participatory budgeting opened whole new possibilities for integrating popular demands into the design of annual municipal and state budgets (Abers 1998). Starting with the 1988 mayoral elections, the Workers' Party significantly increased the number of municipal governments its members ran (see table 4.3). These governments began to challenge the hold of traditional elites by instituting new ways of including popular sector groups in policy-making. PT mayors and city councils wanted to decentralize power and improve government accountability to the people. Participatory budgeting would do that by using representatives of neighborhood groups to elect popular councils that would compose the details of municipal budgets. This would move budgetary priorities away from highly centralized public works that traditionally benefited large construction companies rather than residents. The more profound effect of the participatory budgets would be to undermine the closed system of clientelistic exchange and municipal patronage that typically included only neighborhood leaders, politicians on city councils, and influential contractors (Abers 1996: 39). The popular councils would also serve as mechanisms for institutionalizing the agenda of urban social movements and other groups whose priorities were projects to enhance city services, counteract violent crime, and expand participation in municipal planning. Over the course of the 1990s, the participatory budgeting councils spread throughout Brazil to encompass state governments and cities not under the direct management of the PT, although the councils functioned best in PT-run states and cities and particularly in the south, where Rio Grande do Sul and its main city, Porto Alegre, managed the most extensive participatory budgeting experience.

Participatory budgeting has produced generally good results if one examines the quality of public services and the fiscal performance of states and cities using this model (popular councils do not tend to be spendthrifts). More controversial, however, has been the idea of many advocates that the participatory budget experience would expand participation itself, include a wider array of social movements and NGOs, and lead to a more profound articulation of democratic citizenship. In his studies of participatory budgets in Minas Gerais and Rio Grande do Sul, William Nylen (2002) demonstrates that the experience has not led to a linear increase in popular participation in policy-making, although states and cities with participatory budgets are generally more accountable to their citizens and more transparent in their decision-making than states and cities without participatory budgeting. One of the core reasons why the experience has not been a catalyst for wider social mobilization is that, owing to fiscal constraints, budgetary processes by their nature exclude ideas. The interests and governing styles of mayors and municipal councils also influence how popular views are ultimately translated into policy results (Wampler 2004). Citizens become disillusioned and their attendance at council meetings declines as they see little relation between their participation and policy outcomes (Abers 1996: 42–3).

The case of participatory budgeting demonstrates once again the dilemma of institutionalizing social mobilization as part of a project for deepening democracy. Conceivably one might ask if the extensive mobilization of Brazilian civil society *by itself* is enough to produce a deeper appreciation for democracy. One relevant measure comes from surveys of how Brazilians regard democracy. What these studies reveal is troubling, since they show consistently that Brazilians' support for democracy has declined markedly in the last few years despite sustained social mobilization, NGO activities, and experiences such as participatory budgeting. While 50 percent of those polled by *Latinobarómetro* in 1996 and 1997 expressed the view that democracy is preferable to any alternatives, in 2002 only 37 percent of Brazilians agreed (Hunter 2003: 156). The good news is that mass action against democracy is less likely today than it was in the early 1960s when democracy broke down. A solid majority of those polled do not see authoritarianism as an option. More than anything, surveys of the Brazilian polity tend to reveal a deepening cynicism that is based on a profound distrust of public institutions. In part, this is a product of a highly heterogeneous society, one in which geographic and social differences, ideological fragmentation, modest social reform, and the tendency to channel political disaffection into informality or criminality deflate mass activism. Marginal and disaffected groups also have less incentive to take to the streets or engage in anti-system violence because the electoral system maintains low thresholds for these actors to elect their own representatives. Ironically, it is these features of "low-quality democracy" that keep the regime from collapsing.

7

Forging an Identity in a Globalized World: Brazil in the International Political Economy

Brazil's current position in the global structure of trade, production, finance, and security is mired in a profound identity crisis. Brazil is "neither fish nor fowl" when it comes to determining whether it is a liberal market economy or a protectionist state. It is not clear if the country is committed to becoming a competitive producer and exporter in the global marketplace or if it is more interested in avoiding competition. Brazil's love–hate relationship with regional integration and bilateral trade pacts bespeaks an uncertainty about the direction of its own economic diplomacy. Is it a leader of Latin America on the issue of regional commercial integration or an island looking out for its own interests? It is also not clear that Brazil sees itself primarily as a major international economic power because it is a significant agricultural and commodity goods exporter, because it is an industrialized goods manufacturer, or because it is Latin America's largest domestic market. Its national security policy reflects this identity crisis as well. Does Brazil seek a permanent seat on the United Nations Security Council because it has ideas to offer, or because it wants the international prestige that comes with such a visible position? Does the country even have a clear image concerning its own national security following the 11 September 2001 terrorist attacks?

For most of the twentieth century, and certainly since the end of World War II, Brazil's foreign policy has focused on the country's economic development. Its relationship with the United States in particular was shaped by expectations, following its involvement on behalf of the Allies, that the country would receive Marshall Plan monies for post-war development. These unrequited hopes spurred a deepening suspicion of American motives and general skepticism that the two countries could maintain a special relationship in the world. This ambivalence in Brazil's relations with the US became more apparent during the bureaucratic-authoritarian period, when the intense industrialization of the country brought it into conflict with American efforts to slow or stop the transfer of technology to countries, like Brazil, that preferred to retain their political independence from the US and the Soviets during the Cold War. The military government pursued a policy of "responsible pragmatism" that sought to diversify

Brazil's foreign commitments and to use them on behalf of a concentrated project of economic modernization.

Since economic development remained the most important focus of Brazilian foreign policy, the country's economic goals and self-image fundamentally shaped its interactions with the world. But Brazil's economic identity was never so certain, adding to its "neither fish nor fowl" problem. It is a mistake to see the Brazilian economy as strictly protectionist or even autarkic, since the country's economic modernization during the ISI period coincided with a growth in agricultural exports, industrial goods imports, and manufactured goods exports. It is also a mistake to believe that Brazil entertained integrating itself further into world markets during the 1980s and 1990s simply because it was pushed by a growing fiscal crisis. During the ISI era and the debt crisis, Brazilian producers and the state looked for ways to promote exports. Export promotion was central to the bureaucratic-authoritarian regime's efforts to pay for the public subsidies that went to ISI industries during the 1960s and early 1970s. During the early 1980s, well before the brunt of the debt crisis was to be felt in Brazil, major business groups, led by the National Development Bank, embraced the need to improve the competitiveness of industry in the global marketplace. Industrialists and economic policy-makers gathered under the principle of "competitive integration," an idea that represented neither a dogmatic embrace of free markets nor a halfway approach to liberalization. Brazilian business believed that it was time to abandon the most fiscally onerous forms of import-substitution and complete a process started earlier in the bureaucratic-authoritarian period to produce manufactured goods and commodities for export and to begin to empower Brazilian firms to compete with imported goods and multinational corporations (Kingstone 2004: 164–5). The result of these developments made Brazil's economy a mixed one, neither exclusively liberal nor strictly protectionist.

Export promotion and competitive integration, however, did not represent a full embrace of the free market principles being championed by economists and some governments around the world in the latter half of the twentieth century. Brazil remained a relatively closed economy. Even today, imports and exports each represent just over 7 percent of GDP. That is the same level as before the period of sustained market liberalization in the 1980s, although the value of trade has expanded in absolute terms. Moreover, foreign investors still regard Brazil as a place to invest for its large domestic market, not for the skills of its workers or its other assets that could otherwise make it a production, assembly, or export platform like India and China (Kingstone 2004: 174). As Brazilian companies come into closer and more intense competition with the enterprises of these other large developing countries, Brazil may be forced to deepen its erstwhile commitment to "competitive integration."

Assuming the ideas are there, Brazil has a fine corps of highly professional diplomats to articulate and defend its policies. The Foreign Ministry, known for the name of the stately building in which it was once housed in the old national capital of Rio de Janeiro, Itamaraty, is one of the Brazilian state's few "pockets of efficiency." Itamaraty's expert cadre of statesmen is capable of designing and implementing all major aspects of Brazil's diplomatic relations with the world without much input from politicians or civil society. Because of its relative autonomy, Itamaraty has developed a heightened sense of its own vision for Brazil, which is sometimes grandiose. The foreign policy establishment sees this continent-sized country as destined to claim its rightful place among the most influential countries in the world as befits its geographic size and economic importance. In this way, Itamaraty has used economic diplomacy, most recently through the process of regional integration, to expand Brazil's international influence in the world.

Other parts of the Brazilian state – the armed forces, the economic bureaucracy (e.g., the Finance Ministry, the National Development Bank), and the state governments – embrace the idea that Brazil is a great power that deserves to have more globally competitive industries and greater influence in the world's major diplomatic institutions. Like Itamaraty, these groups passionately advocate for Brazil's unique role in the world and they jealously guard the country's autonomy from the command of other powers, and particularly the United States.

Nationalism, sustained developmentalism ("competitive integration"), and a fierce and highly effective diplomatic articulation of Brazil's interests combine to make it one of the most significant of the middle-income countries on the world stage. Yet what Brazil wishes to say in the world and what it wants to become remain altogether uncertain. This chapter will examine the Brazilian role in the world by outlining the country's position in global markets, its place in regional and hemispheric integration, its approach to multilateral organizations, and other major dimensions of its foreign policy, such as security affairs and counter-narcotics. **Box 7.1** summarizes the major findings.

The challenge of globalization

One cause of Brazil's uncertain identity in the world is its leadership's love–hate relationship with the global integration of markets many call "globalization." Lula da Silva's visits to the World Social Forum in Porto Alegre and his subsequent jaunts to the World Economic Forum in Davos, Switzerland, represent either a commitment to marrying market-friendly capitalism with a vibrant social justice agenda or a somewhat inconsistent and perhaps contradictory set of tendencies. Lula, like his predecessor, Fernando Henrique Cardoso, insists that social justice and capitalism are not mutually exclusive and that globalization does not necessarily undermine equity. He has tended to embrace liberal market policies as president, although his political career before his election was based on almost two decades of keen and sometimes acidic criticisms of these policies. Lula's critics insist that the president still holds these views and that they will eventually become more evident during a prolonged presidency with a second term. More probable, say many observers of Brazilian politics, is that Lula is a pragmatic leader who realizes that Brazil has become a more open economy and must operate in a competitive world in which powerful investors will punish major moves away from liberal market principles.

Brazil's integration into global markets has both constrained and empowered its economy. Based on 2002 figures, Brazil was the eleventh destination for foreign direct investment in the world, the second behind China in the developing world, and the first in the Latin American region. As **table 7.1** demonstrates, Brazil was a primary destination during the global investment boom before 2002, and its share of foreign

Box 7.1 Major findings regarding Brazil's role in the international
political economy

- The size and nature of its economy, its increased role in international diplomacy and global trade negotiations, and its professional diplomatic corps equip Brazil well to play a bigger role in the world, especially among developing countries. But it lacks a clear and consistent self-identity of what it wishes to do in world politics.
- Economic liberalization, privatization, macroeconomic stabilization, the growth of exports and the importance of the domestic market to foreign direct investors have enabled Brazil to have a bigger voice in regional and global trade negotiations.
- Mercosul has evolved inconsistently, but, given the growing importance of trade to the Brazilian economy and the benefits of negotiating with the US and the European Union (EU) as a bloc, the country may be entering a new period of bolstering the regional trade group.
- Disagreements with its regional trade partners, and primarily the US, have slowed progress on the FTAA and conflicts over agriculture have impeded talks with the EU.
- Brazil participates in a wide variety of international organizations (e.g., UN, OAS) and regimes (e.g., human rights, nuclear non-proliferation), and has aspirations of gaining a permanent seat on the UN Security Council.
- Under Lula, Brazil has pursued a strategy of "benign restraint" in the face of the American superpower. Yet this has not translated into a consistent set of policies on a diverse range of issues, including the drug war and Amazonian defense.
- The bilateral relationship with Argentina has weathered several crises and now seems stronger. Yet it is the bilateral relationship with the US that is most important. Brazil remains more cooperative than conflictual in its ties to Washington, despite periodic trade-related and security-policy conflicts.

direct capital fell as the markets cooled in subsequent years. Trade made up for part of this decline after 2001 as Brazil posted its first trade surpluses in a decade. Taken together with the importance of the exchange rate, foreign capital flows and trade make up the primary means through which the Brazilian economy is tied to the fortunes of global markets and the interests of foreign economic actors. Decisions made at the World Trade Organization (WTO), an international organization that enforces open-market rules, and in the boardrooms of major multinational enterprises such as the American auto assemblers General Motors and Ford, have a direct impact on the Brazilian economy. Likewise, decisions made by government agencies, including Brazil's own Central Bank, and the presidency, but also regulatory bodies in Europe and the US, can swiftly alter the performance of the Brazilian economy.

How Brazil became increasingly constrained by global markets and liberal international organizations such as the WTO is a story that begins most clearly with the debt

Table 7.1 Foreign direct investment flows into Brazil and other countries, 1997–2003 (US$ billion)

	1997	1998	1999	2000	2001	2002	2003	Average % of total 1997–2003
Developed countries	270	472	825	1,120	589	460	467	73.0
European Union	128	250	475	684	389	374	342	46.0
US	103	174	283	314	144	30	87	19.6
Developing countries	193	191	229	246	209	162	156	24.0
Asia	109	100	109	142	107	95	99	13.2
China	44	44	40	41	47	53	57	5.6
Africa	11	9	12	8	19	11	14	1.5
Latin America	73	82	108	95	84	56	42	9.4
Argentina	9	7	24	12	3	1	0.3	1.0
Brazil	19	29	29	33	22	17	10	2.8
Mexico	14	12	13	15	25	14	10	1.8

Source: Investe Brasil.

crisis that swept Latin America during the 1980s. During this time, Brazilian foreign economic policy became immobilized by a deepening domestic fiscal crisis that prompted the first presidents of the New Republic to move toward more open-market policies (Hirst 1996: 201). Average nominal tariffs fell by half or more across the most important industrial sectors (Amann and Nixson 1999: 62). Along with privatization, this had a substantial effect on the performance of several industries in Brazil, sometimes for the better. For example, in the steel sector the adjustments required by the combined effects of privatization and trade liberalization boosted labor productivity, sales, and international competitiveness throughout the 1990s.

Macroeconomic stabilization, and particularly inflation control, was another priority of Brazilian governments in the post-debt crisis period. Although successful reform came only with the Real Plan in 1994 and a substantial adjustment following the January 1999 currency crisis, inflation control became another pillar of Brazil's more open market economy. The Brazilian Central Bank during the 1990s became particularly cautious about using interest rates as a means for subsidizing industrial development, a key policy mechanism during the heyday of ISI. The bank embraced a policy of monetary austerity by maintaining high, real interest rates to keep inflation at bay. Following the 1999 crisis of the Real it moved to a strategy of allowing market mechanisms to establish the value of the currency, although it retained the option of intervening selectively in the money markets to encourage modest adjustments.

Liberalization, privatization, and macroeconomic stabilization were also the products of Brazil's interactions with the multilateral financial institutions, and particularly the International Monetary Fund (IMF). Although the IMF did not play a primary role in reform efforts during the Sarney, Collor, and Franco administrations, the multilateral agency became far more important to Brazil in the wake of several financial crises during the late 1990s in Asia (1997), Russia (1998), and Argentina (2001). Nervous international investors already stung by these crises fled the Brazilian market in 1998, causing President Cardoso to negotiate a standby agreement with the IMF in the fall of that year. Brazil would receive several billion dollars in short-term multilateral loans from the fund in return for fiscal reform. Still, that agreement could not head off Brazil's own currency crisis in January 1999. Cardoso had to turn once again to the IMF for another substantial tranche of multilateral financing to stem the tide of financial outflows. His government signed a letter of intent for a $35 billion IMF loan, the largest ever to a developing country. In return, the IMF required Cardoso and Lula to restrain public spending and reduce gaping fiscal and trade deficits. Both presidents agreed to produce budgetary surpluses at a level that would meet or exceed targets set by the IMF.

It is in this context of domestic fiscal adjustment that other multilateral international institutions have become important to Brazil. Given Brazil's efforts to improve the competitive position of its industries, its economic foreign policy establishment has contested changes in global trading rules that consolidate the advantages of the rich countries. During the multi-year trade round in Uruguay during the 1990s of the General Agreement on Tariffs and Trade (GATT, WTO's predecessor), Brazil consistently opposed the wishes of the United States and Europe to protect intellectual property and rich-country subsidies for industry and agriculture. When the WTO was created at the beginning of Cardoso's first term, Brazil continued its opposition to environmental regulations and information technology accords, in part because the Brazilians believed they burdened developing countries unfairly (Guilhon Albuquerque 2003: 285).

Presently, the multilateral Doha round of WTO-sponsored trade talks is the focus of attention for Brazil's trade policy. And, as is the case with much of the country's diplomacy, Brazilian leaders evince a mixed self-image of their role in the Doha talks. As part of this round, Brazil and other developing countries are pressing for much greater access for their agricultural products to the markets of the rich countries. Before the WTO talks in the fall of 2003, Brazil proposed a free trade agreement among twenty-one developing countries, also known as the G-21. As ringleader, Lula appeared as an organizer of developing countries against the interests of richer states, particularly on the issue of phasing out agricultural subsidies. This position clashed most acrimoniously with the interests of the United States and the European Union in the WTO talks at Cancún, Mexico. After days of embittered finger-pointing, the talks broke down when the ministers of major developing countries walked out of the meeting.

Brazil's recent reliance on export-driven growth makes achieving breakthroughs in the Doha round all the more important. By December 2004, the country had turned a record current account deficit of $33 billion into a surplus of $33 billion. Trade has grown with developing countries such as China and India as fast as it has with Europe and the United States. But these countries are also competitors in the sale of manufactured goods, so the potential for growth in Brazilian trade will continue to focus on advanced economies. Exports to the US are clearly one of the primary areas for future trade growth, since commerce between the US and Latin America as a whole has increased notably in recent years. US exports to the region went from 17 percent of total exports in 1992 to 21 percent in 1998. More impressive has been the increase in US foreign direct investment in the region, which more than doubled from $71 billion in 1990 to $172 billion in 1997; that is 20 percent of all US direct investment abroad (Feinberg 2002: 132). Therefore, ironing out agreements during the Doha talks with the United States and the Europeans is in the interests of the Brazilian economy.

Another corollary of Brazil's current integration into global trade and investment trends is that the benefits of regional integration are more obvious now than ever before. Trade among Latin American states has expanded even as trade between Latin America and the US has increased. If the economies of the Americas have progressively become more interdependent, then it stands to reason that they would benefit from institutions that would reduce the costs of trade and investment and thereby encourage further growth in these trends. Lower tariffs, fewer regulations on foreign investment, and the elimination of subsidies and other non-tariff barriers to trade should stimulate economic exchange among the countries of the region. Yet ultimate intentions do not guarantee the means for arriving at cooperative outcomes in trade policy. The countries of the region know far too well that how the rules of regional integration are written will benefit some countries more than others. Therefore, conflicts over the details of regional integration treaties have slowed the process considerably.

Another obstacle to greater globalization and regional integration of the Brazilian economy is that these trends do not guarantee that the benefits of growth will be equally shared within the country. Indeed, the social gains from Brazil's boom of primary and commodity product exports are likely to be meager. Since the country has a relative surplus of labor and because the wages paid to primary export workers are lower than in the industrial sector, the surplus from the growing export sector will not trickle down to laborers (Skidmore 2004: 135–6). More important, the mode of production in most of the agro-industrial and mining sectors is capital-intensive, so growth in these areas will not even necessarily lead to a boom in employment over time. And, following the points raised in chapter 5, the many structural causes of income inequality in Brazil will continue to water down the welfare-enhancing effects of economic growth.

The environmental costs of a Brazilian export model based on agricultural, mining, and other commodity goods is another area for caution. The extraction of iron ore has already razed large tracts of land in the Amazon and other areas, setting the stage for environmental disasters. This is one of the reasons why some transnational environmental NGOs and domestic movements and organizations have joined the ranks of globalization's critics. Although some progress has been made in Mercosul to address some of these concerns, environmental issues remain too much on the back burner in other regional integration processes. Moreover, the US's renunciation of the Kyoto Protocol creates additional obstacles to writing major environmental protections into global trade accords.

MERCOSUL AND THE FREE TRADE AREA OF THE AMERICAS (FTAA)

As a result of the global and domestic pressures forcing the Brazilian economy toward openness, regional integration of the country's economy with its Latin American and

North American neighbors became a major pillar of structural reform. With the collapse of foreign credit to the region during the "lost decade" of the 1980s, the large economies of South America were compelled to export to promote higher growth rates. Regional integration emerged as part of the process of facilitating export growth only when Mexico announced soon after the election in 1988 of President Carlos Salinas de Gortari that it would pursue a trade pact with the United States and Canada, which already had their own bilateral free trade agreement (Feinberg 1997). Two years after the North American Free Trade Agreement (NAFTA) was born, the East European economies began to open to foreign investors. Starved for capital and eager not to be left behind as other countries in Latin America and around the world positioned themselves in an increasingly more competitive global economy, Brazil began to conceive its own regional integration strategy. These were the forces that shaped the creation of the Common Market of the South (*Mercado Comum do Sul* – Mercosul – in Portuguese; *Mercado Comun del Sur* – Mercosur – in Spanish), which was set up by Brazil, Argentina, Paraguay, and Uruguay, with Bolivia and Chile as associate members. Created through the Treaty of Asunción on 26 March 1991 and started in January 1995, Mercosul is designed to reduce all tariffs among the signatories and set common external tariffs for most goods imported into the common market. In relation to the world trading system, Mercosul is the globe's third largest trading bloc, behind the EU and NAFTA, with an aggregate GNP of US$1 trillion (Carranza 2003: 68).

The actual evolution of Mercosul from its initiation in 1995 to its tenth year in 2005 was nothing short of tortuous. First, the consolidation of the common market was periodically upset by differences in the macroeconomic policies of the two largest members. Argentina's strict peg of the peso to the dollar overvalued the country's currency, and that allowed Brazilian imports to flood its market. At times the Brazilian government aggravated these differences when it pursued tariffs on imports of Argentine goods such as cars and auto parts in 1995 in an attempt to keep foreign car assemblers in the country, a direct affront to Mercosul's new trade regulations for automobiles (Cason 2000b: 30–3). Second, macroeconomic crises deepened these problems, sometimes overnight. When the Brazilian currency crisis hit in January 1999, the devaluation of the Real hurt Argentine exports to its trading partner and led to the dumping of cheaper Brazilian goods on the Argentine domestic market. Then it was Argentina's turn, following its own currency and financial collapse in December 2001 and a steep devaluation of the peso in January 2002. These convulsive episodes thwarted all attempts to forge a closer and linear consolidation of Mercosul (Carranza 2003). After 2001, virtually all press and scholarly accounts of Mercosul focused on the common market's moribund status or how it might be revived (e.g., Phillips 2001). Only in 2004, with Argentina's posting of 8 percent growth rates and expanding Brazilian trade surpluses, did commentators begin to claim that the prospects for Mercosul were rosy once again.

Part of the dilemma facing Mercosul is the fact that its members are so dependent on trade with one another that even slight deviations in macroeconomic policy have an effect on their trade balances. To be sure, the members are not equally dependent. Uruguay and Paraguay are far more reliant on access to the two larger economies. Yet even Argentina, which sends one-third of its exports to Brazil, is sensitive to shifts in the Brazilian Central Bank's strategy. Moreover, both countries have weathered a litany of trade disputes recently. Just in the last five years, the two countries have had public trade conflicts involving Brazilian frozen poultry, textiles, shoes, appliances, autos and steel, and Argentine dairy products and low Argentine tariffs on imports of machine goods. While Argentina enjoyed substantial trade surpluses with Brazil in 1995–2003, Brazil began to post large surpluses after this period, inhibiting the ability of the Argentine economy to grow out of its financial crisis. Usually these trade conflicts involved one or both nations applying unilateral restrictions on imports from their Mercosul partner in the form of new licensing regulations or quotas. These non-tariff barriers and the occasional retaliatory tariff against "dumping" by the rival have added to the already difficult complications facing the trade accord. Brazil tends to prevail in many of these disputes, if only because its stakes in the bloc are comparatively smaller. Only 2.3 percent of Brazilian exports go to Argentina. As **figure 7.1** indicates, even Brazil's trade with China is larger than its trade with Mercosul.

Closeness and mutual dependence have not cultivated more collaborative relations between Argentine and Brazilian business. Each still eyes the other as a rival. Brazilian business remains skeptical of the more ideological commitment of Argentine industry to market liberalization, while Argentine entrepreneurs fear that Brazilian industry will revert to protectionist instincts at the next crisis (Carranza 2003: 78–9). And there is much recent history to support these views. Brazilian automobile assemblers supported protective tariffs during crises, while Argentine industries have suffered from the over-valuation of the peso based largely on President Menem's dogma that forceful liberal-

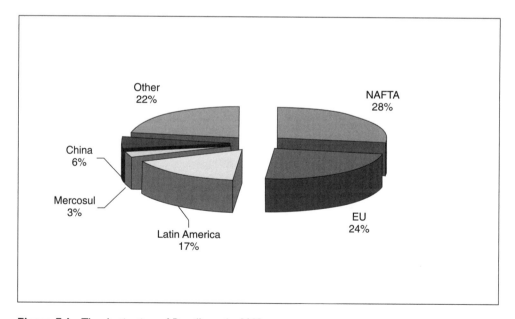

Figure 7.1   The destination of Brazil's trade, 2003
Source: The Economist, 5 February 2004, and Investe Brasil.

ization combined with a pegged exchange rate would promote growth with stability. Such distrust made it that much easier for the business sectors in both countries to accept the death of Mercosul following the financial meltdown in Argentina in 2001–2.

Nevertheless, news of the death of trade pacts in an age of globalization can often be exaggerated, and that might well be true of Mercosul. Recent months have demonstrated that the trade bloc still has some life in it, although its future will be determined largely by the commitments of the members to building supranational institutions. Just before the Argentine financial crisis, the signatories of Mercosul agreed in October 2001 to work toward the coordination of their macroeconomic policies, thereby allowing members temporarily to adjust to currency shifts. Then, in February 2002, the Mercosul countries agreed to form a permanent tribunal of five arbitrators to guard against the excessive and abusive use of tariffs during or just after currency crises. Such institutional changes offer a rudimentary structure for systematically handling trade disputes that have slowed the progress of regional integration. Harmonization in other areas such as exchange-rate regimes and industrial policy will likely be easier because of the existence of these more robust dispute-resolution mechanisms (Carranza 2003).

Other recent institutional developments in Mercosul involve some of the important political dimensions of the trade bloc. For example, Mercosul's environmental protection components have made some progress. By 2001, the four members signed and ratified all of the major multilateral conventions on species depletion, climate change, toxic waste, and other ecological questions, and signed the environmental framework agreement for Mercosul. Although these regulations are relatively weaker than national regulations available in Brazil, they reflect an incremental improvement nonetheless (Hochstetler 2003). The "democracy clause," which was signed by the Mercosul signatories in 1996, represents another major political development. Under this principle, the Mercosul signatories have agreed that the failure of constitutional democracy in any member justifies that country's expulsion from the accord. This provision has already played a role in bolstering democracy in the weakest member, Paraguay (Feinberg 2002: 142). Taken together, the institutionalization of these diverse economic and political principles are indicators that Mercosul will continue to evolve and will not become an irrelevance any time soon.

To be sure, if Mercosul were to become extinct, cooperation between the two largest members would still be possible and advantageous to both. The leaders of Brazil and Argentina agree that good mutual relations strengthen their nascent democracies (Cason 2000a: 207). Given a long history of economic and political rivalry, the pursuit of diplomatic and economic ties represents a significant turn in Brazilian–Argentine relations (Hirst 1996: 211). From the signing of the Itaipu-Corpus Treaty in 1979, establishing a cooperative hydroelectric project, to economic and nuclear cooperation after 1985, the bilateral relationship has never been stronger, despite recent rough times. And it should also be said that the strengthening of democracy in both countries has itself been a catalyst for finding a way to reinforce economic cooperation, not for turning inward (Remmer 1998). So even if Mercosul were to fail, both countries would still pursue regional integration and perhaps in the form of the Free Trade Area of the Americas (FTAA).

THE FTAA

NAFTA and Mercosul were part of a larger hemispheric integration process catalyzed in large part by the United States. During the George H. W. Bush administration (1989–93), Washington unveiled the Enterprise for the Americas Initiative (EAI), which foresaw the creation of a free trade area throughout the region. Yet the actual diplomacy during the 1990s to make this vision a reality was more forcefully advanced by Latin American governments than by the US (Feinberg 1997). The leaders of the hemisphere, excluding Cuba's Fidel Castro, began the process at the first Summit of the Americas in December 1994 in Miami. This meeting laid out a general outline of how regional trade integration would be negotiated through 2005, beginning with formal talks in 1998. But the Mexican peso crisis weakened already skeptical American interests in the FTAA, and President Clinton's lack of "fast-track" authority to negotiate an agreement without waiting for congressional amendments slowed the process considerably (Cason 2000b). Then, the election of George W. Bush in the US in 2000, the return of the president's fast-track authority in 2002, and President Bush's re-election in 2004 signaled a renewed commitment to free market principles in Washington (Feinberg 2002). So, as Brazil and the US prepared to be joint chairs of the FTAA in 2005, talks heated up again.

However, the process remained tortuous as differences in principle and interest kept the two largest economies apart. First, the US favors making rapid progress on an FTAA while Brazil prefers a go-slow approach. The Brazilian view is shaped by the concerns of many of its domestic businesses, which fear an influx of foreign goods will crowd them out of the domestic market. A slow FTAA process reflects their preferences for caution and perhaps the watering down of any agreement. Washington, on the other hand, sees a rapid consolidation of the FTAA as part of a larger strategy of moving quickly to reinforce the global trading and investment regime. As the Americans see it, progress on thorny North–South issues such as intellectual property rights and agricultural subsidies cannot be made unless the US elicits the support of more developing countries for free trade principles. Second, the Brazilians and most of the other Latin American countries distrust the extent to which the US will forgo agricultural subsidies and other non-tariff protection of its domestic market. Washington removed discussion of agricultural supports from the FTAA process, leaving this contentious issue to the WTO round at Doha. Finally, the Americans insist, since the US is the largest and most open market in the hemisphere, that it is the Latin Americans who need to shed protectionist tendencies. They point to an exclusionary service sector and government procurement policies in Latin America, and Brazil in particular, that serve as counter-incentives to foreign investment and trade. Differences on these and other issues listed above have led to continued stalemate in talks on the FTAA. For example, the working agreement made in Miami in November 2003 proved toothless on the key issues of US reductions of tariff and non-tariff protections. The 34-country agreement included modest tariff reductions and the adoption of several common standards but not much more. In this way, the acrimony of Cancún is afflicting the FTAA process and presenting major stumbling blocks.

When not disagreeing on matters of principle, the two largest economies in the FTAA disagree on specific policies involving head-to-head conflicts of interest. Brazil and the United States have recently grappled with one another on a whole series of trade conflicts, some of which have been played out before the World Trade Organization. The steel conflict of 2003–4 is the most famous. In March 2003, President Bush slapped 30 percent tariffs on imports into the US of steel, a major Brazilian export. Brazil took the matter to the WTO, and, with EU pressure, the Americans abandoned the new tariff regime months later. Other trade rows in US–Brazilian relations have involved WTO cases on soy, orange juice, cotton, and sugar, making for a litigious bilateral relationship between the two countries.

Putting aside its reactions to American trade policy, there is much ambiguity regarding how Brazil sees its role in the FTAA process. At times, the governments of Cardoso and especially Lula have mused about forming a South American bloc within the FTAA as a counterweight to the US. The National Development Bank has even used about US$382 million of its development assistance monies to support "regional cohesion" initiatives involving cross-border infrastructure and utility projects in Venezuela and Argentina. Other initiatives have focused on the Andean Group countries, with which Mercosul signed a framework agreement in 1998. Yet in no way have these ties developed into a coherent or consistent effort to bring together the major South American economies within the FTAA process.

Part of the problem is that Brazil is itself not a credible articulator of a common trade policy for Latin America. Other Latin American countries view Brazil's trade policy orientation as intensely protectionist, and with good reason. In seeking the best trade position for itself, Brazil has often undermined the integration agenda (Cason 2000b). Even its Mercosul neighbors routinely accuse Brasília of using environmental and other regulations as non-tariff barriers to trade (Hochstetler 2003: 14), although all the members employ such protection egregiously (Nogués 2003). Other Latin American countries disdain Brasília's efforts to water down any FTAA. Smaller economies in particular, such as Ecuador and the Central American states, became frustrated with Brazil's handling of the WTO meeting at Cancún and later with Brasília's wrangling with the Americans on the FTAA without having much to show for it. Colombia, Peru, Costa Rica, and several other countries showed their displeasure by walking away from Brazil's G-21 group. Many of these countries subsequently started talks with Washington on their own bilateral free trade accords.

Ever since the inauguration of Mercosul in 1995, talks between the regional trading bloc and the European Union, the members' chief external trade partner outside the Americas, have proceeded on a number of fronts. Formal negotiations on a framework agreement for constructing a permanent free trade accord between the two customs unions began but thereafter proceeded slowly. This inter-common market agreement would be the first of its kind in the world, but significant domestic political differences across the two regions have stalled negotiations at several points. The EU's Council of Ministers, the executive body of ministers from the EU-15 (now EU-25), has prevented progress on a number of concerns in the agricultural and fishing areas (Bulmer-Thomas 2000). National agriculture ministries, and particularly the French, have set up barriers to Mercosul's attempts to gain greater access for the common market's agricultural exports to Europe. EU members with important domestic agricultural sectors see imports from Latin America as a threat to the elaborate subsidy system underwritten by the Common Agricultural Policy (CAP). Such steadfast opposition helped to keep Mercosul exports to the EU stagnant during the 1990s, even while the EU concentrated its exports on Mercosul, which provides more than half of its export sales in Latin America and is home to 66 percent of its foreign direct investment in the region. On the Mercosul side, it is unlikely that the members, and Brazil in particular, maintain a strong interest in concluding an agreement with the EU before finishing negotiations on the FTAA. After all, as figure 7.1 indicates, Brazil exports more to NAFTA than to the EU. Any accord with the Europeans would likely undermine the strategy of keeping a broad range of issues on the table during the FTAA process. If anything, Mercosul's intermittent talks with the EU are a bargaining tool for placing pressure on Washington as the bloc positions itself for the best deal with the North Americans (e.g., Bulmer-Thomas 2000: 3).

The very problems that have impeded the Mercosul members from concluding the FTAA afflict negotiations with other large trading blocs such as the EU. So it is unlikely that much will be accomplished with either the FTAA or the EU until Mercosul's members, if not the bloc as a whole, deal with the weakness of macroeconomic harmonization and inconsistent use of dispute resolution mechanisms. Brazil can play a leadership role in this process by forging close working bilateral commercial relations with the US, Argentina, and the EU. What is certain, in any case, is that Brazil and the Mercosul countries are not likely to turn inward in the future. Since these countries are the exporters of the most protected products in the world – agro-industrial and commodity goods – the longer these countries are shut out of free trade blocs in the Americas and Europe, the longer their own economies will suffer (Nogués 2003). While these countries agree on the goals of free trade, forging an agreement is all about the details, and that is where the Devil is.

INTERNATIONAL ORGANIZATIONS

Brazil's position in international organizations is shaped by its emerging role in the world. Brasília believes in multilateralism and in collaborating on common defense and security projects, but it sees its particular contribution as distinctive. Brazil's leaders claim that they speak for much of the developing world, a self-image that is reflected in Brazil's attempt to build a G-21 as a counterweight to the US and the EU. And yet, despite Brazil's actions at the "disaster in Cancún," Brasília also cultivates friendship with more advanced economies, especially when it is in its interests to do so. The positions that Brazil stands for in international organizations are often more likely to be those of the US and the EU. For example, Brazil has worked through the Organization of American States (OAS), Latin America's pre-eminent multilateral instrument, as well as Mercosul and the United Nations (UN), to strengthen nascent democracies around the region and in the world. Brazilian peacekeeping troops are in Haiti and were an important presence in East Timor during peace negotiations.

Other basic principles of Brazilian foreign policy embrace the founding ideas behind the United Nations charter: peaceful mediation of conflicts, self-determination of nations, non-intervention in the domestic affairs of other states, and respect for international law (Guilhon Albuquerque 2003: 268). Furthermore, Brazil is a signatory to all of the major international conventions and treaties governing the treatment of individuals by states. In the area of human rights, it is a signatory of the International Covenant on Civil and Political Rights, the International Covenant on Economic, Social and Cultural Rights, the Inter-American Convention on Human Rights, the Convention on the Rights of the Child, the Convention Against Torture and Other Cruel, Inhuman, or Degrading Treatment or Punishment, and the Inter-American Convention to Prevent and Punish Torture. Brazil is also governed by the United Nations' Universal Declaration of Human Rights, which forms the legal basis for most of the international human rights conventions. Additionally, Brazil recognizes the competence and authority of the Inter-American Court on Human Rights.

While Brazil's embrace of international human rights and governance principles and its actions on behalf of multilateralism show the country to be a fine citizen of the world, its foreign policy goals are most often shaped by self-interest. Its interactions with the US and Europe in the Doha rounds and concerning regional integration demonstrate that the country holds its own economic interests above larger principles such as the efficiency of global markets. Nationalism, a constant theme in Brazilian foreign policy, also makes its diplomatic establishment wary of following the dictates of the US too closely, and that includes Brazil's participation in international bodies such as the UN (Guilhon Albuquerque 2003).

In recent years Brazil has had some success in cultivating at least rhetorical support for its claim to a permanent seat on the UN Security Council. Brazil has coordinated its campaign with South Africa and India, two other countries vying to get permanent seats on the council. And while expanding the Security Council to reflect the interests of large developing countries makes the body more representative of the world, it cannot be forgotten that the five permanent members (the US, Britain, France, China, and Russia) hold vetoes and have few incentives to give other countries the same right. In order to get the seat, Brazil's diplomats will need to temper their opposition to rich-country interests and be willing to accept a vetoless permanent seat if that is the only alternative to having no seat at all.

Another area of Brazil's interaction with international organizations involves the fact that it is a nuclear country. Its three major nuclear plants, Angra I (active), II (off-line), and III (still under construction), supply a small portion of the country's electrical energy. Brazil has the fifth largest reserve of uranium in the world, which makes it a major exporter of uranium oxide, the key ingredient in nuclear energy production. Although Brazil has uranium enrichment capacities, it is a signatory of the Non-Proliferation Treaty (1998) and it regularly cooperates with the International Atomic Energy Agency (IAEA) in allowing inspections of its nuclear facilities, including the uranium enrichment plant at Resende, Rio de Janeiro. These facilities are controlled by the National Nuclear Energy Commission (CNEN), which also maintains four energy research institutes. The main issue these capacities raise is the potential that Brazil may soon be capable of producing weapons-grade nuclear fuel that it might sell along with its own enrichment technology. This has brought Brazil under some US pressure to allow more extensive IAEA inspections, and Brasília has tended to cooperate – although, to Washington's consternation, in 2004 it resisted inspections. Yet Brazil's non-proliferation credentials are solid nonetheless. The country halted its nuclear weapons program in 1994 and has standing agreements with Argentina to control nuclear technologies in the Southern Cone. Additionally, the Lula government has reduced some security fears by cutting the nuclear budget by 20 percent, an indication that Brazil will not seek to expand its nuclear capabilities any time soon.

ISSUES IN BRAZILIAN FOREIGN POLICY

Brazilian foreign policy has in recent years been pulled in two very different directions. One of these directions is based on the interests of large export-oriented businesses, politicians, economists, and the international financial institutions that embrace free market principles. These groups are delighted with any progress on the FTAA and Brazil's development in a more globally competitive position. These interests view Mercosul as merely an integrative mechanism, a common market to be linked to others such as the Andean Pact and the EU. The US is a competitor but also a guarantor of the consolidation of neoliberal principles in the global financial and trade institutions, principally the WTO. Hence, greater cooperation with the US, including in security affairs, is positive. Meanwhile, other interests emanating from the Brazilian armed forces, import-competing businesses, labor unions, and social movements pull Brazilian foreign policy in a decidedly different direction. These groups prefer that Brazil retain its independence from the United States. If Brazil engages in international security and trade agreements, it should design its own approach and not allow Washington to tell it what to do. Regional integration, both economic and in cooperative security, is positive only under these conditions.

These partially contradictory tendencies in Brazilian foreign policy during the democratic period help to explain the uncertain complexion of the country's relationship with its neighbors, the world, and the United States in particular. As we argued above, the presence of distinct constituencies in Brazil that support and oppose further engagement with the world produce an identity crisis in the country's foreign policy. The result in practice is that Brazil does not always act consistently in its relationships with other countries. The United States is a case in point. Celso Amorim, Lula's foreign minister, inaugurated a policy of "benign restraint" regarding the US, in which Brazil seeks to challenge the hegemonic power in the world on particular positions such as the war in Iraq, but generally cooperates with the Americans on issues such as the drug war and the war against terrorism. On the one hand, Brazil argues that it speaks for the G-21 developing countries, but, on the other hand, it has sneakily negotiated side deals with Washington to get what it wants in the FTAA process.

The identity crisis in Brazilian foreign policy is difficult to untangle given the wide array of distinct policy areas that Itamaraty, the armed forces, and other actors within the Brazilian state regard as important. These different segments of the state have interacted with foreign governments and non-governmental organizations in distinct ways. Further study of particular issues such as the drug war in South America, Amazonian defense, and security cooperation reveal some consistent patterns, but they do not represent a coherent foreign policy or a clear self-image of Brazil's global role.

Regarding the drug war in South America, the Brazilian government has consistently focused on interdiction, as has the United States. But changes in the development of the drug business have challenged the effectiveness of these efforts. Brazil is not a primary cocaine-producing country, but it does serve as an important distribution and trans-shipment country. That means that cocaine flows through Brazil only at the rate and degree that it is produced in the major source countries of Colombia, Bolivia, and Peru. Cocaine distribution, however, is important to criminal syndicates in urban centers such as Rio, from the top money operators in organized crime to the low-level traffickers and dealers (Leeds 1996: 56–7). In-country consumption fuels the trade, as Brazil is the world's second largest consumer market for cocaine (Wittkoff 2003: 548). Given the domestic availability of many of the chemicals needed to process coca paste, it is conceivable that much of the refining activities in cocaine production will shift in the future to Brazil as anti-narcotics officials in Colombia prove more successful in breaking up cocaine processing there. That makes the task of interdiction efforts in Brazil even more complicated. Efforts to eradicate domestic use will have to coincide with stepped-up efforts against corruption and organized crime, and that will involve greater cooperation with the Andean countries and Colombia, where many of the transnational drug syndicates are based.

Brazil's security policies in the area of Amazonian defense are relevant to the drug war. According to President Cardoso's National Military Defense Strategy, Amazonian surveillance and defense are at the core of regional security, including the drug war (Martins Filho and Zirker 2000). Brazil's concern in this area focuses on Colombia, where the stepped-up efforts to counteract drug trafficking and illegal harvesting of expensive mahogany trees have led to numerous incursions by the cartels into the Brazilian Amazon. This has caused the Brazilian armed forces to shift troop levels from the secure borders of the south to the Amazon, substantially militarizing Brazil's borders with Peru, Colombia, and Venezuela (Wittkoff 2003: 545–6). These concerns have increased during Lula's presidency, as President Álvaro Uribe of Colombia expands the war against the largest guerrilla group, the FARC, and Peru under Alejandro Toledo experiences the return of the Shining Path (*Sendero Luminoso*) guerrillas. All of these tendencies underlie a general militarization of the Amazon as the air force's SIVAM project, the federal police, and the Brazilian army increase their presence. The sharing of SIVAM data, which covers 300 kilometers of southern Colombia, and cooperation between the Brazilian federal police and Colombia's anti-narcotics special forces will effectively bring Brazil more closely into its neighbor's many internal conflicts.

How Brasília chooses to negotiate the details of its security policy with its neighbors and the US will largely determine the effectiveness of its overall approach to cooperative security, including in the area of Amazonian defense. Already some aspects of the current security policy have produced frictions with Brazil's international partners. For example, Brazil passed a shoot-down law in 1998 that allows the air force to track and down planes flying illegally, presumably because these flights involve narcotics shipments and other criminal activities. While the Colombian and Brazilian governments agree that a shoot-down law is necessary to fight narco- and other forms of "terrorism," the US has opposed the Brazilian law because it fears that innocent pilots and their passengers will be targeted. The Americans point to the wrongful downing of a plane containing an American missionary family in Peru in 2002, but the Lula government remains intent on implementing the shoot-down law nonetheless (Wittkoff 2003: 553). Such differences will continue to prove nettlesome as the US, Brazil, and other South American countries agree on the general principles of fighting drug trafficking and securing the Amazon, but disagree on the best way to achieve these goals.

Brazil's bilateral relationship with Argentina has also involved the security dimension, but the emphasis in this case has been on using international security cooperation as a means of consolidating civilian control over the armed forces in both countries. Soon after their respective transitions to democracy in the 1980s, both countries engaged in a series of cooperative agreements, beginning with the one renouncing the development of nuclear weapons in 1990, which was signed by presidents Fernando Collor and Carlos Menem (Resende-Santos 2002). Brazil and Argentina also agreed to collaborate in the peaceful uses of nuclear energy. These actions by civilian presidents effectively demilitarized the most dangerous weapons technology in the Southern Cone (Hurrell 1998). They also shifted these and other key areas of security policy from the armed forces to the foreign ministries, thereby heightening civilian management of security policy (Sotomayor Velázquez 2004: 32). Moreover, Brazil's cultivation of close and secure ties with Argentina is a main pillar of the National Military Defense Strategy, which calls for a shifting of military assets from the southern border to the under-patrolled Amazon (Pion-Berlin 2000: 52–3). So cooperation with Argentina will remain a linchpin of Brazil's larger strategy for dealing with regional security threats.

Even accounting for Argentina, it is the bilateral relationship with the United States that remains Brazil's most important. And, despite the many points of friction between the two largest countries in the hemisphere, Brasília and Washington agree more often than they disagree. It should be remembered that Lula was the first president of a country that opposed US involvement in Iraq to be invited to the White House after Saddam Hussein was toppled in 2003. On security matters, Brazil has agreed to share data gathered through SIVAM to help the US in its regional anti-narcotics and anti-terrorism efforts. The Brazilian air force could also use more regular access to data from the US radar installation in Puerto Rico, which can monitor tree-high flights throughout the Amazon, information that they are likely to get. That cooperation is part and parcel of a largely collaborative and mutually supportive relationship. Even with substantial disagreements with the Americans on the FTAA and the war in Iraq, Brazilian diplomats readily note the consistent support their country has received from the US in backing IMF loans and in respecting Brazil's point of view on an array of economic and security issues in their bilateral relationship.

Conclusions

Brazil's economy, the diplomatic expertise of Itamaraty, the geographic and strategic values of the Brazilian state, and the Brazilian nation's own heightened sense of its importance in the world make this middle-income country a significant presence on the global stage. Brazil's rising importance is reflected in the way that it has shaped the regional integration debate in the Americas as well as the larger negotiations between advanced capitalist states and developing countries at WTO-sponsored trade rounds. Amazonian defense, the national nuclear program, and the central role that

Brazil plays in the hemispheric war against drug trafficking are other areas in which the country exerts tremendous influence.

Yet, as this chapter has argued, it is not Brazil's importance in the world that is in dispute, but rather its purpose. While domestic economic development remains the overriding priority of foreign policy, it is not clear which route Brazil advocates to achieve high growth with social distribution. The country maintains a love–hate relationship with international markets and global financial interests and corporations. On the one hand, Brazil supports the process of regional integration, but it fights to keep many of the tariff and non-tariff protections it believes shield its domestic producers from foreign competition. On the other hand, Brazil has not been reticent about the need for rich countries to eliminate their own impediments to free markets. Brazilian–US relations in particular are shaped by these tendencies, as Brazilian presidents of different ideological stripes such as Collor, Cardoso, and Lula have all tenaciously defended the independence of the country's foreign policy from the undue influences of Washington.

What Brazil wants in the world and what it gets can also diverge. This validates contrary points of view on existing foreign policy, perhaps even causing governments to shift directions entirely. The effects of globalization on Brazilian development are contested in this way. While some business interests wish to integrate the country's markets even further into global trade, production, and investment, nationalists decry the loss of control over the national development pathway that these choices require. Yet shifting sovereignty to organizations such as the WTO or locking in market-friendly policies with bilateral and multilateral free trade agreements calm the nerves of foreign investors and make Brazil more likely to receive consistent and much-needed capital investment.

The effects of Brazil's increased insertion into global markets has had only ambiguous implications for deepening democracy. At first glance, neither globalization nor regional integration has reinforced democracy clearly in Brazil. Trade, macroeconomic, and fiscal policy-making remain the products of elite and often just executive design. This "democratic deficit," as Jeffrey Cason (2002a: 205) argues, is intentional, since the politicians and technocrats that make foreign economic policy, including the elites in Itamaraty, see the influence of societal actors as something akin to "political meddling." On the other hand, a more comprehensive understanding of the results of Brazil's integration into multilateral trade and collective security arrangements in the Americas reveals that these have reinforced democratic institutions more profoundly. Brazil's commitments to international human rights, to the democracy clause of the Mercosul and the FTAA, to the regional security apparatus of South America, and to OAS and UN peacekeeping operations in the hemisphere and around the world have all strengthened its dedication to democratic rule in principle and in practice at home.

Brazil understands that it is the pre-eminent Latin American power in the region, the indispensable state without which neither economic integration nor collective security is possible. If the country's leaders succeed in composing a clear vision of the country's role in the world in the near future, Brazil will be able to develop a clear direction in its foreign policy that is commensurate with its global importance.

8

THE LULA GOVERNMENT: AN EXPERIMENT IN SOCIAL DEMOCRACY?

The second-round presidential election victory of Luiz Inácio "Lula" da Silva on 27 October 2002, with 61.3 percent of valid votes, represented a fundamental change in the office of the Brazilian presidency as the first individual not representing the country's social and economic elite took the presidential sash (Monclaire 2004: 81). Unlike his elected predecessors such as Fernando Collor, Lula did not come from a monied, landowning family. He was not affiliated with the former military regime like José Sarney. And the new president did not enjoy anything like the international academic acclaim heaped upon Fernando Henrique Cardoso before he became a leader of the PSDB. Lula's modest rural family background and his own working-class experience as a lathe operator make him stand out sharply against the array of landowners, military officers, business people, and leaders of political machines that have dominated the presidency since the proclamation of the republic in 1889. During the 2002 campaign, Lula used his humble background to connect to the Brazilian everyman. As candidate Lula repeated on numerous occasions, "I know where I came from, who my true friends are from yesterday, from today. I have a vivid awareness that, in life as in death, we always return to the place from where we came."[1]

That Lula was finally elected was itself a watershed in the maturation of Brazilian democracy. Elements of the political right who predicted chaos in 1989, when the PT almost beat out Fernando Collor, accepted Lula's 2002 election with nary a comment about the health of Brazilian democracy (Hunter 2003: 153). Public approval of Lula's government when he took office stood at an unprecedented 84 percent. This is notable in comparison to Cardoso's situation during his first months in office. Cardoso had high approval ratings, although not as high as Lula's during the first 100 days, and he also had the Real Plan, which increased average incomes by 30 percent over the previous year. Average incomes were *down* by 13 percent when Lula took office, which makes more evident the uniquely *personal* support he received (Sola 2004). Moreover, 64 percent of those polled believed that Lula would carry

---

1 As quoted in the *Los Angeles Times*, 25 January 2005.

out his campaign promises, indicating a notable groundswell of popular trust in his administration.

Lula's Workers' Party also changed. As late as December 2001, at the PT party congress in Recife, party leaders embraced a declaration of principles that reflected a sustained criticism of neoliberal reform, a position the party had held since the mid-1980s. But in May 2002, several months before the decisive election and while polls had Lula ahead of his competitors, the party's leaders released a "Letter to the Brazilian People" that embraced practical political alliances and the liberal market principles of efficiency and protection of property rights. Sensing that the responsibilities of government would soon be upon the PT, Lula dispatched key economic advisors to soothe the fears of investors in New York City that a Lula presidency would break with Cardoso's eight-year commitment to free market reform.

Lula's government can be evaluated in terms of how it addressed and generated progress on the main persisting economic, social, and political problems identified in this book. At the time of writing, the first two years of Lula's first term can be assessed on these grounds and reasonable projections can be discussed based on stated intentions and accomplishments. First, we might consider how Lula attempted to ameliorate social and economic inequality. This issue, more than any other, was the centerpiece of his presidential campaign in 2002. Second, Lula and the PT presented a "new way of doing politics" in Brazil, so the extent to which his governing style changed the nature of political representation should figure prominently as a litmus test of progress. Finally, the Lula presidency should be evaluated in terms of how it transformed the Brazilian state. Federalism, public agencies, the judiciary, the problem of bureaucratic corruption, and other issue areas are closely associated with the development of Brazilian democracy and any attempt to address problems of social inequality. Economic reform might be considered a fourth area, but, given the close relationship between the economic reform agenda and the three areas of social inequality, political representation, and state reform, progress on this front necessarily involves improvement in these other dimensions. The same might be said of Brazil's position in the world, which relies as much on the success of the domestic reform agenda as it does on the constraints that international investors and foreign governments place on Lula's range of choices.

POVERTY AND INEQUALITY

There is no doubt that Lula fundamentally believes that poverty is the number one problem facing Brazil. The Brazilian president has even become a global spokesperson on the ravages of poverty and inequality. During a May 2004 trip to China to attend a World Bank conference on poverty in Shanghai, Lula asserted that poverty was the most devastating "weapon of mass destruction." He berated the US and the European Union for spending the average of $2 a day in farm subsidies for each cow while most people in the world survive on less than half that amount daily.[2] Along with other world leaders, such as French president Jacques Chirac, Lula has even called for the creation of a global tax on financial transactions to pay for a stepped-up global

2   Quoted in *Brazil Focus*, 22–8 May (2004): 4.

program to alleviate world hunger.[3] Regarding poverty in Brazil, Lula came to power on a PT platform that held that social development is a central aspect of economic development (Partido dos Trabalhadores 2002). So his election to the presidency was regarded as the beginning of a Brazilian government that would aggressively redress the country's social inequities.

Some of Lula's bold social reforms captured headlines, but they were modest once put into practice. The PT's "Zero Hunger" (*Fome Zero*) program, which focused on eliminating hunger in Brazil through the distribution of monthly cash disbursements to qualified families and other measures, captured the popular imagination as a centerpiece of Lula's presidential campaign. Yet the first stage of the program was limited to a few municipalities in the north. And even this modest implementation ran into multiple problems, including corruption and bureaucratic inefficiencies. Zero Hunger also lost resources as Lula was forced to cut social spending to stay within IMF-approved fiscal surplus targets. By comparison, the government's "Zero Illiteracy" program seemed more successful. This program promises to wipe out functional illiteracy by 2006. Its implementation in 1,768 municipalities and the recruitment of 56,000 "literacy agents" including university students is a good sign of the government's commitment. Yet the program currently covers fewer than half of all municipalities, and funding cuts will likely make the target date unrealistic.

Such targeted public social expenditures have had a progressive impact on poverty in Brazil, but the most effective programs must address the core cause of inequality – the wage disparity–education link – in order to reduce poverty levels for the long haul (World Bank 2003). The most important reforms must focus on expanding access to primary and secondary education to place more high school diplomas in the hands of young people entering the labor market. The *Bolsa Escola* program, which began under Cardoso in 1995 and expanded in 2001, channels cash assistance to families with school-age children. This program pays for school supplies per child and rewards families for consistent school attendance. Other existing programs to reduce chronic repetition, expand summer and night school, and increase the number of innovative rural schools (*escolas ativas*) that use pedagogical techniques more suited to these children, as well as the use of accreditation exams to evaluate performance, must all be expanded, as must the FUNDEF program (Larach 2001). Cardoso's 1996 National Education Law, which was named after the late famous anthropologist Darcy Ribeiro, empowered municipalities with new resources and authorities to develop pedagogical quality. More resources, however, must be devolved to towns and cities to extend the successes of the Darcy Ribeiro Law into the secondary levels of the public schools (Draibe 2004a). This is the focus of Lula's own education reforms, which hope to increase the FUNDEF program to 20 percent of all subnational tax revenues (Hall 2003: 278). But time is of the essence, since the current population of school-aged children represents a demographic high point. If more is not done to expand this cohort's access to education, the declining skill set of the population will drop precipitously and, with it, wages will fall more quickly. Commensurate with these efforts, the federal and state governments must expand post-secondary vocational and other education opportunities to train under-skilled workers. Pouring more resources into

3 See *Le Monde*, 20 September 2004.

the *Sistema S* institutions (e.g., SENAC, SENAI, etc.) and encouraging more Brazilian businesses to become involved is a good start. With all of this in mind, Lula's government enjoys a wealth of useful ideas and active programs on the ground. The remaining questions concern the sufficiency of resources and the political will to focus them where they are needed most.

In the area of pension and social security reform, the Lula government scored some important early victories in the fall of 2003 by passing the first phase of social security reform. The approved legislation raised the minimum retirement age, placed stricter limits on benefit ceilings, reduced survivor benefits, and taxed pensions and benefits for those receiving more than R$1,440 per month. Issues including the taxation of social security benefits for judges and military officers and the reduction of survivor benefits for the latter group were stumbling blocks in cross-party negotiations. These and other issues became the basis for government concessions, among them reducing proposed cuts so that the total annual saving produced by the reform was less than half of the original target. Larger and more expensive questions such as the expansion of pension benefits to take in the large unprotected population of workers were left for a future reform effort. Still, the first phase of reform laid the basis for the first real cut in Brazil's exploding pension deficit.

Pension and social security reform are intimately tied to the Lula government's efforts to address Brazil's social disparities. Without freeing up the disproportionate share of fiscal resources that these programs represent, redistributive programs will likely fall short of sufficient resources (World Bank 2003). The political obstacles to social security reform remain formidable (see below), but the Lula government has already demonstrated a capacity for some progress on this front. What should also be underscored is that social reform means much more than adjusting the pension and social security systems. Housing, sanitation, and the quality and reliability of public transportation also sit at the top of the social reform list as perennially neglected areas that will require much more attention than the Cardoso administration was apt to give them (Draibe 2004a: 72). And, despite Cardoso's good record on improving the health-care system, 70 to 80 million Brazilians still do not have adequate access to quality basic care either in the public or in the private sector.

Addressing these and other equity-enhancing reforms must also coincide with or follow a profound reorganization of Brazil's regressive tax structure. By far the most regressive aspect of the tax system is the growing weight of indirect taxes that falls on all income levels, but more heavily on the poor. These taxes occur on all personal expenses, food, purchases of clothing, medication and health services, and they represent two-thirds of the total tax burden. The most important example is the increase after 1998 in the rate of the COFINS (social security) tax, which was established by the constitution in 1988 at 0.5 percent and then raised during the 1990s to 3 percent. Along with the state VAT (ICMS) and other indirect taxes, the increase in the COFINS rate accounts for most of the increase in federal tax shares vis-à-vis the states and cities after 1996. If the Lula government could shift more of this tax burden away from personal expenses and onto private vehicles, housing, and leisure/luxury goods, many of the most regressive aspects of indirect taxation in Brazil would be ameliorated. Of course, such a reform would require the government to resist the lobbying of the large auto companies and luxury goods importers.

Agrarian reform

Lula confronts the most intractable contradictions between Brazil's fiscal situation and its social needs in agrarian reform. If he adheres too closely to Cardoso's tendency to protect commercial agriculture's interests and avoids substantial land reform, he risks energizing the landless peasant movement in the way his predecessor did. At the same time, Lula cannot pursue the level of land deconcentration and redistribution preferred by the MST, which, if taken at face value, means prohibiting the ownership of singular land holdings larger than 1,000 hectares (Pereira 2004: 106). Inevitably, these parameters have set the stage for prolonged conflict.

Perhaps sensing that the Lula government would be more sympathetic, the MST dramatically increased the rate of land invasions in 2003–4, especially those by the more militant branch of the movement in the north. According to the MST's own numbers, over 147,000 families have organized or are preparing to organize invasions during the current administration. Lula promised to resettle 430,000 families according to the MST, but budgetary realities made actual redistributions fall well short of this target (60,000 in the first two years of his administration). Therefore it is inevitable that the expectations of landless peasants and the government's own fiscal capacities will make the situation in the countryside more unstable. MST rhetoric and direct action will continue to escalate tensions and test the Lula government's commitment to fiscal austerity and modest social reform.

International social partnerships

Despite initial fears that a Lula presidency would defy the international financial institutions, his government has developed a solid working partnership with these organizations. In return, the international financial institutions have become more sensitive to the Brazilian government's social priorities. During his first year as president, Lula signed agreements with the World Bank and the Inter-American Development Bank to create and fund new social assistance programs. Following on the Zero Hunger experience, new family stipend programs will funnel some US$2 billion to 11 million families by 2006. More of these innovative partnerships between the government and the global financial community will go a long way to reducing the fiscal constraints on Lula's bold social initiatives. In this way, Lula's government has united the ideas of Davos and Porto Alegre.

Even with these new social initiatives, Brazil's problems of poverty and inequality are seemingly too big for the finite resources of the Brazilian state and the multilateral agencies. President Cardoso realized this early on in his presidency when he declared at a press conference soon after his inauguration in 1995 that his administration could only help that percentage of the population falling from the working class into the ranks of the poor. It could not lift the majority of the poor out of their poverty. Some observers called this assessment pragmatic, a realistic view of the capacities of the Brazilian state. Others decried Cardoso's position as blithe and too dismissive of the real potential for change. Lula might end up doing better than his predecessor, but it is all too likely that Brazil's problem of "democracy without equity" will continue after he leaves the presidential palace.

POLITICAL REPRESENTATION

Pragmatism as a style of governing has created serious paradoxes for the Lula presidency. Despite his criticism of Cardoso's tendency to kowtow to clientelistic interests, many of them in the conservative parties and in the poorest regions of Brazil where opposition to agrarian reform and social distribution is strongest, Lula has also depended upon the support of some of these forces to pass reform legislation. While Lula has not gone to the expensive extents Cardoso did in buying the support of governors and political machines in congress, his reforms have suffered the watering-down effect that comes with making politically expedient concessions to secure passage. And, like his predecessor, Lula has done little to reinforce the discipline of political parties or reduce the fragmentation of the legislature. The expulsion of rebel members of the PT demonstrates his commitment to partisan discipline in his own party, but the absence of electoral reform reinforces Lula's pragmatic realization that his party must work with much less disciplined allies on the center-left and center-right.

Lula's rise to power has changed some aspects of the dominant alliance patterns, but some fundamental problems with legislative coherence continue. Lula's PT has forged a somewhat stable congressional alliance including parties on the right and center-right (PL, PTB, PMDB) and on the left (PSB, PPS, PCdoB) in favor of his reform agenda. For example, the passage of the first phases of social security reform in 2003 reflected relatively coherent support among the "pro-government" parties during the roll-call votes on these reform packages. Even the fractious PMDB, which increased its interests in acquiring cabinet positions and working with Lula in congress, voted for the government's policies. This makes the PMDB arguably the most important single party in Lula's "coalition" outside of his own PT. These votes also reflected the weakness of the opposition parties. Over 43 percent of the opposition PFL and PSDB deputies voted for the social security reforms.

Yet Lula's first "victories" also underscored the Achilles heel of relying on the support of undisciplined parties. Defections from the government parties, including four notable PT members who were expelled from the party in December 2003, made congressional support unreliable. For example, the roll-call votes on the first phase of social security reform in the Chamber suffered nearly sixty defections out of approximately 350 deputies from the "government coalition" parties. The reforms would not have passed the required three-fifths majority threshold without votes from the PFL and PSDB, parties that nominally are not allied to the government. Later, in mid-2004, the government suffered an embarrassing loss when its bill to increase the minimum wage went down in the Senate as a result in part of the opposition of three PT senators.

The Workers' Party itself may be the key to Lula's continued attempts to forge ties to other parties. Going against its own historic tendency to avoid alliances, the PT's core leadership, *Articulação*, has accepted and actively sought out these alliances and has brought dissident factions within the party along (Lacerda 2002). The internal discipline of the PT will continue to be a factor as the leaders strip "rebel members" in congress of their committee privileges or expel them altogether.

The vote-buying corruption scandal that erupted midway through 2005 holds the real potential to be a turning point in Lula's presidency and in the evolution of the

Workers' Party. If the allegations against top PT leaders stick but the scandal does not spread to the president himself, or to other top officials, then Lula may use the crisis to reinforce his command over the organization. Another wave of internal reform will no doubt strengthen the party's substantial oversight and auditing agencies. Yet currying the support of allied parties for reform will still require the president to negotiate patronage agreements, which may be more difficult now that some transactions of this type have been linked to graft. If the crisis broadens and tarnishes Lula personally – at the time of writing he still enjoys appreciable (albeit somewhat reduced) popular support – both his government and his chances for re-election will be severely disrupted. The PT itself may splinter into factions that not even *Articulação* will be able to keep tied to a common organizational mission. Popular revulsion against the system of politics-as-usual may open the door to rogue populist leaders as it did in 1989–90 when Fernando Collor briefly enjoyed strong public support for his aggressive yet ill-fated reforms.

The vote-buying corruption scandal of 2005 might also generate renewed support for a more wholesale political reform. Given that so many of Brazil's problems are worsened by the inefficient political system, it would be logical to reform it. Undoubtedly the first target for reform should be the open-list PR electoral system, which creates strong incentives for federal and state deputies to cultivate personal votes. Yet any reform in this area faces the problem that the foxes (politicians) will not wish to lock the chicken coop of patronage and throw away the key (Lessa 1997: 135). Surveys of federal legislators show that a substantial majority of them (65.2 percent) support a change, but just as large a majority (64.5 percent) favor a new system in which parties *will not* determine candidate placement on the ballot (Power 2000a: 27). Legislators like the mixed-member system made popular through the German example in which ballots are split between PR and single-member districts. But if the Brazilian version integrated open-list PR on the PR side of the ballot, that would only continue the highly individualistic nature of campaigns and elections. Moreover, it is unlikely that the many small parties will agree to a German-style 5 percent threshold, since they would lose the few seats they currently hold in the Chamber of Deputies.

Cardoso introduced electoral reform legislation during his second term, but this initiative did not go very far during the second half of his lame-duck presidency. Emboldened by popular support for anti-corruption efforts in the legislature, Lula may stake his re-election and the success of a second term on making demonstrable headway in this area. If and when Lula acts on political reform, he will get the most success from legislation that would implement the German mixed-member ballot with closed-list PR and a threshold of around 5 percent. To be sure, such a change would not guarantee the immediate creation of program-oriented rather than individualistic campaigns and party organizations, as the Russian application of the German system attests. A more substantial reform would call upon Lula to alter the electoral system while simultaneously changing the powers of the presidency and elevating the autonomy of the legislature from the executive's current dominance over policy initiation (Power 2000a: 34–5). This sounds like a gargantuan task, but in a certain sense Lula is uniquely placed to do this. It would be logical for the head of the PT, the most programmatic party in Brazil, to favor a changed system that would reward the party's strong internal discipline. Without these changes, many of the most perverse aspects of Brazil's "democracy without representation" will continue.

STATE AND ECONOMIC REFORM

From the middle of 2002 on through the election, Lula was the focus of much hand-wringing in global financial circles. Investors wondered which Lula and PT would come to power in Brazil: the Lula and the party that for so long advocated a rupture with the neoliberal reform agenda or a reform-minded leader and organization that would take up where Fernando Henrique Cardoso left off. So, from the beginning, Lula suffered a credibility gap on market and state reform even as he enjoyed soaring popularity within Brazil after taking office (Sola 2004).

The new president proceeded during his first eighteen months in office with caution, placing emphasis on a continuation of Cardoso's commitment to fiscal prudence and incremental structural reform. Lula's macroeconomic policies sustained his predecessor's dedication to meeting and exceeding IMF deficit targets. Whereas Cardoso maintained a primary budget surplus of 3.8 percent of GDP, Lula announced his target would be 4.3 percent, and he reached it during the first year of his administration (Amann and Baer 2004: 3). The government achieved fiscal prudence the traditional way by limiting public expenditures and raising tax revenues. Benchmark interest rates remained on average high, at 17 percent, to keep inflationary pressures low, a practice that coincided with the Central Bank's use of inflation targets to mitigate expectations about price increases in the future.

Lula's other international commitments also reassured nervous investors. The president's strategic but nonetheless positive engagement with the United States on trade issues indicated that he would not move toward a permanent conflictual relationship with Washington in the way that Venezuela's Hugo Chávez entertained early in his presidency. US–Brazilian trade relations continued to suffer from numerous problems over American tariffs on Brazilian steel, soy, and orange juice exports, but both countries agreed in November 2003 to ease the way toward an implementation of the FTAA in 2005. Brazil won an important concession in having the US negotiate directly with Mercosul in 2004. Nevertheless, there is still time for the PT's radical base to push Lula to a more aggressive position on the FTAA, particularly on political components encompassing environmental and labor standards (Hochstetler 2003: 24). Given Mercosul's own underdeveloped political conventions, Lula cannot push Washington too far on this ground for fear of losing the backing of his Mercosul allies, who remain cool on developing these aspects of the common market.

The partnering of Brazil's new social policies with the resources of multilateral agencies has provided a strong testament to Lula's belief that Brazil's path to equity with growth would be paved through engagement in the global marketplace rather than a turn from it. In this sense, Lula's commitment to attend the World Economic Forum in Davos after visiting the World Social Forum in Porto Alegre signaled his government's commitment to finding ways of bridging the two goals of social justice and market-oriented growth strategies.

Despite its embrace of fiscal prudence, regional integration, and globalization, Lula's government did not generate substantial macroeconomic improvements. First, annual growth rates were either negative (in 2003) or very low (in 2004), too low for a developing country competing for markets with the likes of China, Mexico, Malaysia, Argentina, and India, all of which had substantial growth rates during the same period. Second, inflation did not explode but remained too high to loosen monetary policy with a reduction of high interest rates. Consequently, the high cost of borrowing will remain a factor hindering private investment and economic growth. Third, in part as a result of a slowdown in markets elsewhere, foreign direct and portfolio investment continued their decline from the beginning of Cardoso's second term. The fall of foreign direct investment by more than half after 2001 was the more hurtful of these trends, since this had been one of the salient sources of capital in the economy for much of the 1990s. Finally, and most alarmingly, the public debt continued its steady upward climb. In 2004, the total external debt stood at US$216 billion, with 60 percent of it coming due over the next three years and at average annual amortization payments of US$43 billion (Amann and Baer 2004: 9).

On the positive side, the government's commitment to tight fiscal and monetary policy caused imports to decline at a time that exports soared, thus continuing the reversal of trade deficits during the last year of Cardoso's second term and the con-solidation of a trade surplus of over US$33 billion by the end of 2004. Foreign reserves also expanded, to US$50 billion, giving the Central Bank additional resources. In addition, quarterly growth rates at the end of 2004 showed some signs of the begin-ning of a turnaround, as the economy grew 6 percent and industrial production picked up. If Brazil's trade surplus continues to grow, foreign direct investors may return in the next few years. Argentina's recent recovery from the financial crisis of 2001–2 has added to the trading prowess of Mercosul, which will likely see increases in foreign direct investment in its members over time. This may lead to a turnaround on the FTAA. Brazil's growing trade surplus and more positive prospects for Mercosul's per-formance will both improve much faster if the Brazilians secure greater access to the American marketplace.

To be sure, Brazil will need these trends to continue, but the going will remain tough as amortization payments on the debt combined with the decline of foreign investment constrain Lula's bold social agenda and put even more of a premium on maintaining large and growing surpluses on the trade and fiscal accounts. Testament to the bind that Lula's government is in is the fact that growth, unemployment, and wage rates are all moving in undesirable directions. Real incomes continue their decline as the Gini coefficient for Brazil remains high and shows signs of increasing even more. Moreover, the tight fiscal policies demanded by the IMF will severely hinder Lula's plans for expanding spending on targeted social entitlement programs. As mentioned above, *Fome Zero*, education, and health-care spending will remain priorities for the government but their expansion will be limited by these fiscal realities. This all puts more of a premium on reforming existing imbalances in the fiscal and social security systems, the former being the mother of all reform in that it can potentially free up additional resources for social entitlements.

Fiscal reform

Lula's government introduced a tax reform soon after his inauguration that included all of the major provisions of Cardoso's multiple tax reform drafts: the simplification and unification of the states' value-added tax (ICMS), reductions in the overall tax burden on business (currently 35 percent), the elimination of state tax incentive schemes that spark wasteful fiscal competition among the states, and the permanence of the CPMF, the financial transactions tax. Lula even worked with the governors to guarantee them compensation for the federal government's suspension of taxes they impose on exporters. Yet none of these items on the legislative agenda saw the kind of progress that social security reform enjoyed. Most were postponed. Other aspects of tax reform that require attention were left unaddressed entirely by proposed legislation. For example, tax evasion, which is estimated at some US$70 billion per year in lost revenues, continues to be a problem. Regressive aspects of the tax system, such as sales levies that collect more than the income tax but fall more heavily on the poor, remained unaddressed as well. Lula's tax reforms also suffered from some fundamental internal contradictions. For example, attempts to eliminate the "cascading effect" of multiple taxes were stymied by the realization that these revenues needed to be substituted by monies from another source. The concern for tax evasion also hindered action against the cascading tax system, since the existing system reliably prevents entrepreneurs from hiding taxable value and income (Cardoso 2004: 50).

Lula skillfully used the promise of new tax receipts, compensation for taxes lost on exports, and the removal of federal earmarks on the states' current revenues to buy the support of the governors. He met with the twenty-seven governors repeatedly during 2003 and 2004 to work out the details of fiscal reform. Although this improved on Cardoso's often bitter relations with the governors, the accomplishment proved a double-edged sword. The price of the governors' support for tax reform involved substantial concessions of tax revenue shares to the states and the unearmarking of state revenues that might otherwise have been used to control spending and reduce the mounting federal debt. The governors succeeded in protecting their share of most discretionary spending. If fiscal reform is to go forward, Lula will need to make such concessions, but, following the example of social security reform, these side payments might water down tax reform legislation, offering few substantial fiscal benefits.

The judiciary and fighting corruption

Perhaps no area of state reform embroiled Lula's government in more trouble than the attempt to reduce corruption and reform the judiciary. Top officials in Lula's government were implicated in major corruption cases. The most notorious was undoubtedly the vote-buying scandal of 2005, but this was not the first case implicating the Lula presidency. The year before, Waldomiro Diniz, who maintained suspicious relations with organized crime interests linked to the bingo-gambling sector in Rio de Janeiro, was caught on videotape offering favors in return for campaign finance. The scandal ruined Diniz's reputation and led to his firing. In the ensuing uproar, Diniz's close relations with party chief José Genoino terribly marred the PT itself.[4] The scandal brought the light of public attention on the PT's shady ties to the illegal numbers racket (*jogo do bicho*) in Rio de Janeiro. Several numbers-game bosses were "outed" by PT whistle-blowers as key contributors to the party. Time will tell whether this and the 2005 vote-buying scandal form the tip or the entirety of the iceberg of PT-related corruption.

The most corruption-infested part of the state remains the judiciary and law enforcement. The federal police initiated "Operation Anaconda" in São Paulo in 2003 to root out corrupt judges who sold writs of habeus corpus and other "services" to defendants. The operation exposed a crime ring implicating eleven federal judges, police and other agents of the court system. Such events, coupled with pension reforms that seek to limit the benefits that retired judges can claim, escalated tensions between the presidency and the judiciary. Yet, for now, Lula has the benefit of popular support, as surveys show that the judiciary is considered the most corrupt and least reliable of institutions in Brazil. These views add to the already widespread belief among Brazilians that they continue to live in a "democracy without citizenship."

Security and the war against terrorism

As Cardoso warned during the final year of his presidency, Brazil must guard against the trend that, in the post-11 September world, issues of security will outpace matters of equity and development. Lula's government is committed to fighting terrorism but it is unwilling to ignore social injustice or to bend to the security policies of the US. The fact that in 2003 the Brazilians began to fingerprint Americans traveling to the country in response to the Bush administration's policy of doing the same to foreigners with visas traveling through American airports is evidence that the Lula government retains its autonomy and initiative. How the administration handles American objections to Brazil's shoot-down law over the Amazon will also be a test of Brasília's independence. Lula will need to retain Brazil's security policy autonomy while at the same time to speak, as Cardoso did, about keeping social justice issues at the forefront of the global discussion. Lula's statement that poverty is the world's most devastating weapon of mass destruction indicates that he is doing so, if with some hyperbolic flair.

However US–Brazilian relations evolve on security matters, it is clear that Brazil's bilateral relationships with Colombia and Argentina will remain central to the country's strategies against terrorism, including narco-terrorism. President Álvaro Uribe's success in fighting the FARC, disarming the paramilitaries, and expanding the extradition of drug traffickers is a two-edged sword. On the one hand, the reduction of violence in Colombia will help Brazil control the flow of drugs into the country. On the other hand, the stepped-up government offensive in Colombia might trigger a larger flow of narco-traffickers and Colombian guerrillas to the Brazilian side of the Amazonian border. Lula has clearly opted to support President Uribe and to strengthen Brazil's ties with Colombia, despite Itamaraty's deep suspicions concerning US involvement in the drug war in this neighboring country.

4 For more on these scandals, see Larry Rohter, "Brazil Party Threatened by Videotape Showing Graft," *New York Times*, 16 February 2004.

On the southern border, sustained cooperation with Argentina will help to stem the flow of arms smuggling, a major worry of American anti-terrorism experts, who see the Iguaçu area with its large Muslim immigrant population as a potential base for armed fundamentalists. More significant for the security of democracy, nuclear cooperation with Argentina will keep major international security questions in the hands of civilians in each country's foreign ministry and away from the manipulative hands of the armed forces.

As memories of 9/11 fade in the years to come, security affairs will shift back to the primary concern of the drug war. Brazil has already received the US's attention on this matter. The US State Department reported in March 2004 that Brazil is not only a "jurisdiction of primary concern" for money laundering but it represents the largest single money-laundering venue in the world (US Department of State 2004). Most of this involves the proceeds of drug trafficking, so Brazilian–US security relations will increasingly focus there. In the short term, however, the link between money-laundering activities tied to terrorist groups will remain on the table as a subject of concern in the bilateral relationship. Lula will have to tread around these questions carefully so as not to help the Americans conflate the larger and more immediate problem for Brazil of the drug war with the global war on terrorism.

Despite his leftist credentials and Brazil's fiercely autonomous foreign policy, Lula will likely keep US–Brazilian relations mutually respectful. This will continue as long as Lula engages Washington concerning its own security and economic concerns. Recent history shows that maintaining open lines of communication and listening have been crucial in the rare instances in which Latin American governments and the United States have maintained mutually supportive relations that have respected the autonomy of the weaker country (Pastor 2001). The US–Brazil relationship enjoys those conditions now, and so Lula's task is to keep listening and to make sure that the Americans do not stop listening.

CONCLUSIONS

Two years after his post-election cross-Atlantic sprint from Porto Alegre to Davos, Lula da Silva appeared for a third time as Brazilian president at the World Social Forum in January 2005. This time around, however, he received more jeers from the assembled throng of activists, non-governmental organization leaders, and landless peasant groups than ever before. Some said the ex-labor leader had sold out to global investors while others lamented his conservative embrace of Cardoso's reform agenda. The 2005 WSF thus represented a turning point in Lula's presidency, as his followers made choices about whether they could support their leader's pragmatism or whether they should abandon him and pursue more fundamental change through direct action and sustained opposition. All realized that having a progressive voice in the most powerful office in Brazil could not guarantee the social justice revolution many at the WSF long for.

The Lula presidency's mixture of modest social reform with a sustained commitment to fiscal probity and open markets will continue to build on Cardoso's accomplishments, but, like his predecessor, Lula will not be able to generate vast social and political structural change. Indeed, his presidency's record thus far on state and economic reform reflects all of the problems identified by the themes in this book. Brazil is a democracy but a "democracy without . . ." First, it is a "democracy without a strong state." Once the leaders of the Brazilian state were capable of transforming Brazilian society with industrialization, investment, technological progress, and corporatist governance. Now, merely reforming small parts of the state requires a Herculean political effort. The Brazilian state remains big, but, as many scholars have observed, it is like a Gulliver tied down by thousands of particular (Lilliputian) interests. Clientelism, patronage politics, and even Lula's own use of *fisiologismo* perpetuate enduring inefficiencies in the logic of the Brazilian state. Ironically, there is not a major problem the country faces that will not need a sustained effort by state agencies and fiscal resources to address. So if Brazil remains a "democracy without a strong state" it will be condemned to be an ineffective political system.

"Democracy without representation" adds to and even guarantees the continued ineffectiveness of the Brazilian state. Without the best efforts of a coherent, disciplined, and reform-minded political class, the wishes and demands of most Brazilians will never be fully represented. Oligarchical interests have always shaped the functioning of political institutions in Brazil, and these continue to subvert the realization of democratic possibilities. Only disciplined parties, efficient legislative procedures, and programmatic government can generate the kinds of reforms the Brazilian state, economy, and society will need to make full use of democratic government.

The seemingly intractable problems of poverty and inequality present the biggest obstacles to progress. Yet, ironically, these problems persist not because of the lack of resources but as a result of the failure of politics. To be sure, fiscal limits will continue to bear down on the capacity of even a reform-minded president like Lula to make "zero hunger, zero poverty" a reality. But even the modest social reforms generated under Cardoso and Lula suggest that a little can go a long way in changing the lives of millions of poor Brazilians, especially the young. A renewed and vibrant democratic politics can free resources now tied into the clientelistic and sometimes corrupt practices of the political elite. The pathway to a solution to the "democracy without equity" problem is paved with more and better democracy.

Part of the formula for a new democratic politics in Brazil must depend not only on reform-minded elites. It is also incumbent upon leaders in civil society to generate new ideas and pressure for social and political change, as much of Brazilian civil society did during the transition to democracy. Lula and the PT were, after all, products of these forces, so the politics of democratic citizenship can go far indeed in Brazil. Making progress on environmental issues, racial and gender rights, social disparity, and violence will require a second if not a third "resurgence of civil society" to stimulate Brazilian democracy back to life again.

Brazil's own identity in the world will be transformed by these changes. Even as Lula's presidency struggles with defining a role for this country of 170 million people, how Brazilian foreign and security policy evolve will send signals to the US, Europe, Latin America, and other areas of the world. Will others continue to see an economic giant coming to life and fully aware of its growing responsibilities at home and abroad, or will they see a petulant upstart, unsure what it wants but eager to receive the respect it believes it deserves by dint of its size? Undoubtedly, few Brazilianists might think of many other leaders more respected and universally liked than Lula to lead Brazil at this juncture in its history. So it will fall to this former lathe operator to engineer a new role for his country in the world that not only reflects the maturity of its own democracy but also helps to consolidate that democracy for the twenty-first century.

REFERENCES

Abers, Rebecca. 1996. "From Ideas to Practice: The Partido dos Trabalhadores and Participatory Governance in Brazil." *Latin American Perspectives* 23:4: 35–53.
——. 1998. "From Clientelism to Cooperation: Local Government, Participatory Policy, and Civic Organizing in Porto Alegre, Brazil." *Politics and Society* 26: 511–37.
Abranches, Sergio. 1978. "The Divided Leviathan: State and Economic Policy Formation in Authoritarian Brazil." PhD diss., Cornell University.
Abrúcio, Fernando Luiz. 1998. *Os Barões da Federação: Os Governadores e a Redemocratização no Brasil*. São Paulo: Editora Hucitec.
Addis, Caren. 1999. *Taking the Wheel: Auto Parts Firms and the Political Economy of Industrialization in Brazil*. University Park: Pennsylvania State University Press.
Addis, Caren, and Eduardo R. Gomes. 2001. "Um Outro Lado da Liberalização: Impactos Sociais Transformadores do Apoio do Sebrae às Micro e Pequenas Empresas." In *Competitividade e Desenvolvimento: Atores e Instituições Locais*, ed. Nadya Araujo Guimarães and Scott Martin. São Paulo: Editora SENAC.
Afonso, José Roberto Rodrigues. 1996. "Descentralizar e Depois Estabilizar: A Complexa Experiência Brasileira." *Revista do BNDES* 3 (June): 31–62.
Almeida, Maria Hermínia Tavares de. 2004. "Privatization: Reform Through Negotiation." In *Reforming Brazil*, ed. Mauricio A. Font and Anthony Peter Spanakos. Lanham, MD: Lexington Books.
Almeida, Maria Hermínia Tavares de, and Maurício Moya. 1997. "A Reforma Negociada: O Congresso e a Política de Privatização." *Revista Brasileira de Ciências Sociais* 12:34: 119–32.
Alvarez, Sonia E. 1990. *Engendering Democracy in Brazil: Women's Movements in Transition Politics*. Princeton, NJ: Princeton University Press.
——. 1994. "The (Trans)formation of Feminism(s) and Gender Politics in Democratizing Brazil." In *The Women's Movement in Latin America: Participation and Democracy*, ed. Jane S. Jaquette. 2nd edn, Boulder, CO: Westview Press.
Alves, Maria Helena Moreira. 1985. *State and Opposition in Military Brazil*. Austin: University of Texas Press.
Amann, Edmund, and Werner Baer. 2004. "Rhetoric and Reality: The Economic Consequences for Brazil of President Lula's First 18 Months in Office." Paper presented at the 25th Congress of the Latin American Studies Association, Las Vegas, 7–9 October.

Amann, Edmund, and F. Nixson. 1999. "Globalisation and the Brazilian Steel Industry: 1988–97." *Journal of Development Studies* 35:6: 59–88.

Ames, Barry. 1995. "Electoral Strategy under Open-List Proportional Representation." *American Journal of Political Science* 39: 406–33.

——. 2001. *The Deadlock of Democracy in Brazil*. Ann Arbor: University of Michigan Press.

——. 2002. "Party Discipline in the Chamber of Deputies." In *Legislative Politics in Latin America*, ed. Scott Morgenstern and Benito Nacif. New York: Cambridge University Press.

Ames, Barry, and Margaret E. Keck. 1997–8. "The Politics of Sustainable Development: Environmental Policy Making in Four Brazilian States." *Journal of Interamerican Studies and World Affairs* 39:4: 1–40.

Amorim Neto, Octavio. 2002. "Presidential Cabinets, Electoral Cycles, and Coalition Discipline in Brazil." In *Legislative Politics in Latin America*, ed. Scott Morgenstern and Benito Nacif. New York: Cambridge University Press.

Amorim Neto, Octavio, Gary W. Cox, and Matthew D. McCubbins. 2003. "Agenda Power in Brazil's Câmara dos Deputados 1989–98." *World Politics* 55: 550–78.

Andrews, George Reid. 1991. *Blacks and Whites in São Paulo, Brazil, 1888–1988*. Madison: University of Wisconsin Press.

Arbix, Glauco. 2000. "Guerra Fiscal e Competição Intermunicipal por Novos Investimentos no Setor Automotivo Brasileiro." *Dados – Revista de Ciências Sociais* 43.

Arias, Enrique Desmond. 2004. "Faith in our Neighbors: Networks and Social Order in Three Brazilian Favelas." *Latin American Politics and Society* 46:1: 1–38.

Arretche, Marta. 2004. "Toward a Unified and More Equitable System: Health Reform in Brazil." In *Crucial Needs, Weak Incentives: Social Sector Reform, Democratization, and Globalization in Latin America*, ed. Robert R. Kaufman and Joan M. Nelson. Baltimore: Johns Hopkins University Press.

Assies, William. 1994. "Urban Social Movements in Brazil: A Debate and its Dynamics." *Latin American Perspectives* 21:2: 81–105.

Avritzer, Leonardo. 2000. "Democratization and Changes in the Pattern of Association in Brazil." *Journal of Interamerican Studies and World Affairs* 42:3: 59–76.

Azevedo, Clovis Bueno de. 1995. *A Estrela Partida ao Meio: Ambigüdades do Pensamento Petista*. São Paulo: Entrelinhas.

Baer, Werner. 1965. *Industrialization and Economic Development in Brazil*. Homewood, IL: Richard D. Irwin.

——. 2001. *The Brazilian Economy: Growth and Development*. 5th edn, New York: Praeger.

Barbosa, Lívia Neves de H. 1995. "The Brazilian Jeitinho: An Exercise in National Identity." In *The Brazilian Puzzle: Culture on the Borderlands of the Western World*, ed. David J. Hess and Roberto A. DaMatta. New York: Columbia University Press.

Barbosa, Rubens Antônio, ed. 2002. *O Brasil dos Brasilianistas: Um Guia dos Estudos sobre o Brasil nos Estados Unidos, 1945–2000*. São Paulo: Paz e Terra.

Barcelos, Luiz Claudio. 1999. "Struggling in Paradise: Racial Mobilization and the Contemporary Black Movement in Brazil." In *From Indifference to Inequality: Race in Contemporary Brazil*, ed. Rebecca Reichmann. University Park: Pennsylvania State University Press.

Barros, R. P., R. Henriques, and R. Mendonça. 2000. "Pelo fim das Décadas Perdidas: Educação e Desenvolvimento Sustentado no Brazil." In *Desigualdade e Pobreza no Brasil*, ed. Ricardo Henriques. Rio de Janeiro: Instituto de Pesquisa Econômica Aplicada.

Barros de Castro, Antônio. 1994. "Renegade Development: Rise and Demise of State-Led Development in Brazil." In *Democracy, Markets, and Structural Reform in Latin America*, ed. William C. Smith, Carlos H. Acuña, and Eduardo A. Gamarra. New Brunswick, NJ: Transaction Publishers.

Berryman, Philip. 1987. *Liberation Theology*. Philadelphia: Temple University Press.

——. 1996. *Religion in the Megacity: Catholic and Protestant Portraits from Latin America*. Maryknoll, NY: Orbis Books.

Bisilliat, Jeanne. 1997. "La participation des femmes aux politiques publiques: un exemple contemporain au Bresil." *Recherches Feministes* 10:2: 91–111.

Boletin Cinterfor. 1998. "Sindicatos de Brasil: La Novedad en el Frente se Llama Capacitación." September–December: 87–107.

Boschi, Renato R. 1978. *Empresariado Nacional e Estado no Brasil*. Rio de Janeiro: Forense Universitária.

Bulmer-Thomas, Victor. 2000. "The European Union and MERCOSUR: Prospects for a Free Trade Agreement." *Journal of Interamerican Studies and World Affairs* 42:1: 1–22.

Caldeira, Teresa P. R. 1998. "Justice and Individual Rights: Challenges for Women's Movements and Democratization in Brazil." In *Women and Democracy: Latin America and Central and Eastern Europe*, ed. Jane S. Jaquette and Sharon L. Wolchik. Baltimore: Johns Hopkins University Press.

Cano, Ignacio. 1997. *The Use of Lethal Force by Police in Rio de Janeiro*. Rio de Janeiro: ISER.

Cardoso, Eliana. 2004. "Monetary and Fiscal Reforms." In *Reforming Brazil*, ed. Mauricio A. Font and Anthony Peter Spanakos. Lanham, MD: Lexington Books.

Cardoso, Fernando Henrique. 1975. *Autoritarismo e Democratização*. 3rd edn, Rio de Janeiro: Paz e Terra.

Cardoso, Ruth Corrêa Leite. 1992. "Popular Movements in the Context of the Consolidation of Democracy in Brazil." In *The Making of Social Movements in Latin America: Identity, Strategy, and Democracy*, ed. Arturo Escobar and Sonia E. Alvarez. Boulder, CO: Westview Press.

Carey, John M., and Matthew Soberg Shugart. 1995. "Incentives to Cultivate a Personal Vote: A Rank Ordering of Electoral Formulas." *Electoral Studies* 14:4: 417–39.

Carneiro, Leandro Piquet. 2003. "Democratic Consolidation and Civil Rights: Brazil in Comparative Perspective." In *Brazil Since 1985: Politics, Economy and Society*, ed. Maria D'Alva Kinzo and James Dunkerley. London: Institute of Latin American Studies.

Carranza, Mario E. 2003. "Can Mercosur Survive? Domestic and International Constraints on Mercosur." *Latin American Politics and Society* 45:2: 67–103.

Cason, Jeffrey. 2000a. "Democracy Looks South: Mercosul and the Politics of Brazilian Trade Strategy." In *Democratic Brazil: Actors, Institutions and Processes*, ed. Peter R. Kingstone and Timothy J. Power. Pittsburgh: University of Pittsburgh Press.

——. 2000b. "On the Road to Southern Cone Economic Integration." *Journal of Interamerican Studies and World Affairs* 42:1: 23–42.

Castro, Cláudio de Moura. 2000. "Education: Way Behind but Trying to Catch Up." *Dædalus* 129:2: 291–314.

Cavalcanti, Carlos Eduardo G., and Sérgio Prado. 1998. *Aspectos da Guerra Fiscal no Brasil*. Brasília: IPEA.

Conca, Ken. 1997. *Manufacturing Insecurity: The Rise and Fall of Brazil's Military-Industrial Complex*. Boulder, CO: Lynne Rienner.

Couto, Cláudio Gonçalves. 1998. "A Longa Constituinte: Reforma do Estado e Fluidez Institucional no Brasil." *Dados – Revista de Ciências Sociais* 41: 51–86.

Cox, Gary W. 1990. "Centripetal and Centrifugal Incentives in Electoral Systems." *American Journal of Political Science* 34:4: 903–35.

Dain, Sulamis. 1995. "Federalismo e Reforma Tributária." In *A Federação em Perspectiva: Ensaios Selecionados*, ed. Rui de Britto Álvares Affonso and Pedro Luiz Barros Silva. São Paulo: FUNDAP.

DaMatta, Roberto. 1979. *Carnavais, Malandros e Heróis: Para uma Sociologia do Dilema Brasileiro.* Rio de Janeiro: Zahar.

Deere, Carmen Diana. 2004. "Os Directos da Mulher à Terra e os Movimentos Sociais Rurais na Reforma Agrária Brasileira." *Estudos Feministas* 12:1: 175–204.

Deininger, Klaus, and Lyn Squire. 1996. "A New Data Set Measuring Income Inequality." *World Bank Economic Review* 10:3: 565–91.

Della Cava, Ralph. 1989. "The 'People's Church,' the Vatican, and *Abertura.*" In *Democratizing Brazil: Problems of Transition and Consolidation,* ed. Alfred Stepan. New York: Oxford University Press.

DIEESE (Departamento Intersindical de Estatística e Estudos Sócio-Econômicos). 2002. *Anuário dos Trabalhadores 2000–2001.* São Paulo: DIEESE.

Dimenstein, Gilberto. 1996. *Democracia em Pedaços: Direitos Humanos no Brasil.* São Paulo: Companhia das Letras.

Diniz, Eli, and Renato Boschi. 1979. *Agregação e Representação de Interesses do Empresariado Industrial: Sindicatos e Associações de Classes.* Rio de Janeiro: Edições IUPERJ.

Dix, Robert H. 1989. "Cleavage Structures and Party Systems in Latin America." *Comparative Politics* 22:1: 23–37.

——. 1992. "Democratization and the Institutionalization of Latin American Political Parties." *Comparative Political Studies* 24: 488–511.

Doimo, Ana Maria. 1995. *A Vez e a Voz do Popular: Movimentos Sociais e Participação Política no Brasil pós-70.* Rio de Janeiro: Relume-Duman.

Draibe, Sônia. 2004a. "Social Policy Reform." In *Reforming Brazil,* ed. Mauricio A. Font and Anthony Peter Spanakos. Lanham, MD: Lexington Books.

——. 2004b. "Federal Leverage in a Decentralized System: Education Reform in Brazil." In *Crucial Needs, Weak Incentives: Social Sector Reform, Democratization, and Globalization in Latin America,* ed. Robert R. Kaufman and Joan M. Nelson. Baltimore: Johns Hopkins University Press.

Drogus, Carol Ann. 1999. "No Land of Milk and Honey: Women CEB Activists in Posttransition Brazil." *Journal of Interamerican Studies and World Affairs* 41:4: 35–51.

The Economist. 2004. "Democracy's Low-Level Equilibrium." 12 August.

Evans, Peter B. 1979. *Dependent Development: The Alliance of Multinational, State, and Local Capital in Brazil.* Princeton, NJ: Princeton University Press.

——. 1989. "Predatory, Developmental, and other Apparatuses: A Comparative Political Economy Perspective on the Third World State." *Sociological Forum* 4: 561–87.

Feinberg, Richard E. 1997. *Summitry in the Americas.* Washington, DC: Institute for International Economics.

——. 2002. "Regionalism and Domestic Politics: US–Latin American Trade Policy in the Bush Era." *Latin American Politics and Society* 44:4: 127–51.

Figueiredo, Argelina, and Fernando Limongi. 1995. "Partidos Políticos na Câmara dos Deputados: 1989–1994." *Dados – Revista de Ciências Sociais* 38: 497–525.

Fleischer, David. 2004. "Political Reform: The 'Missing Link'." In *Reforming Brazil,* ed. Mauricio A. Font and Anthony Peter Spanakos. Lanham, MD: Lexington Books.

Frieden, Jeffry A. 1991. *Debt, Development, and Democracy: Modern Political Economy and Latin America, 1965–1985.* Princeton, NJ: Princeton University Press.

Giambiagi, Fabio, and Marcio Ronci. 2004. "Fiscal Policy and Debt Sustainability: Cardoso's Brazil, 1995–2002." *IMF Working Paper* 4:156: 27–39.

Gomes, Eduardo Rodrigues, and Fabrícia C. Guimarães. 2004. "Entrepreneurs: The PNBE." In *Reforming Brazil,* ed. Mauricio A. Font and Anthony Peter Spanakos. Lanham, MD: Lexington Books.

Guilhon Albuquerque, José Augusto. 2003. "Brazil: From Dependency to Globalization." In

Latin American and Caribbean Foreign Policy, ed. Frank O. Mora and Jeanne A. K. Hey. Lanham, MD: Rowman & Littlefield.

Guimarães, Antonio Sérgio Alfredo. 2003. "The Race Issue in Brazilian Politics." In *Brazil Since 1985: Politics, Economy and Society*, ed. Maria D'Alva Kinzo and James Dunkerley. London: Institute of Latin American Studies.

Guimarães, Nadya Araujo, Álvaro A. Comin, and Márcia de Paula Leite. 2001. "Por um Jogo de Soma Positiva: Conciliando Competitividade e Proteção ao Emprego em Experiências Inovadoras de Negociação no Brasil." In *Competitividade e Desenvolvimento: Atores e Instituições Locais*, ed. Nadya Araujo Guimarães and Scott Martin. São Paulo: Editora SENAC.

Hagopian, Frances. 1996. *Traditional Politics and Regime Change in Brazil*. New York: Cambridge University Press.

Hall, Anthony. 2003. "Education Reform in Brazil under Democracy." In *Brazil Since 1985: Politics, Economy and Society*, ed. Maria D'Alva Kinzo and James Dunkerley. London: Institute of Latin American Studies.

Hanchard, Michael George. 1994. *Orpheus and Power: The Movimento Negro of Rio de Janeiro and São Paulo, Brazil, 1945–1988*. Princeton, NJ: Princeton University Press.

Hirst, Monica. 1996. "The Foreign Policy of Brazil: From the Democratic Transition to its Consolidation." In *Latin American Nations in World Politics*, ed. Heraldo Muñoz and Joseph Tulchin. 2nd edn, Boulder, CO: Westview Press.

Hochstetler, Kathryn. 1997. "The Evolution of the Brazilian Environmental Movement and its Political Roles." In *The New Politics of Inequality in Latin America: Rethinking Participation and Representation*, ed. Douglas A. Chalmers, Carlos M. Vilas, Katherine Hite, Scott B. Martin, Kerianne Piester, and Monique Segarra. New York: Oxford University Press.

——. 2000. "Democratizing Pressures from Below? Social Movements in the New Brazilian Democracy." In *Democratic Brazil: Actors, Institutions and Processes*, ed. Peter R. Kingstone and Timothy J. Power. Pittsburgh: University of Pittsburgh Press.

——. 2003. "Fading Green? Environmental Politics in the Mercosur Free Trade Agreement." *Latin American Politics and Society* 45:4: 1–32.

Htun, Mala. 2002. "Puzzle of Women's Rights in Brazil." *Social Research* 69:3.

Htun, Mala, and Mark Jones. 2002. "Engendering the Right to Participate in Decision-Making: Electoral Quotas and Women's Leadership in Latin America." In *Gender and the Politics of Rights and Democracy in Latin America*, ed. Nikki Craske and Maxine Molyneux. London: Palgrave.

Human Rights Watch. 1997. *Police Brutality in Urban Brazil*. New York: Human Rights Watch.

——. 2004. *Behind Bars in Brazil*. URL: www.hrw.org/reports98/brazil/Brazil.htm (accessed 5 December).

Hunter, Wendy. 1997. *Eroding Military Influence in Brazil: Politicians against Soldiers*. Chapel Hill: University of North Carolina Press.

——. 2000. "Assessing Civil–Military Relations in Postauthoritarian Brazil." In *Democratic Brazil: Actors, Institutions and Processes*, ed. Peter R. Kingstone and Timothy J. Power. Pittsburgh: University of Pittsburgh Press.

——. 2003. "Brazil's New Direction." *Journal of Democracy* 14:2: 151–62.

Hurrell, Andrew. 1998. "Security in Latin America." *International Affairs* 74: 210–33.

Inglehart, Ronald. 1999. "Trust, Well-Being and Democracy." In *Democracy and Trust*, ed. Mark Warren. New York: Cambridge University Press.

IBGE (Instituto Brasileiro de Geografia e Estatística). 2004. *Síntese de Indicadores Sociais Abril 2004*. URL: http://www.ibge.gov.br/home/presidencia/noticias/13042004sintese2003html.shtm (accessed 24 May).

Jelin, Elizabeth. 1996. "Citizenship Revisited: Solidarity, Responsibility, and Rights." In *Constructing Democracy: Human Rights, Citizenship, and Society in Latin America*, ed. Elizabeth Jelin and Eric Hershberg. Boulder, CO: Westview Press.

Johnson, Ollie E. 1998. "Racial Representation and Brazilian Politics: Black Members of the National Congress, 1983–1999." *Journal of Interamerican Studies and World Affairs* 40:4: 97–118.

Keck, Margaret E. 1992. *The Workers' Party and Democratization in Brazil*. New Haven, CT: Yale University Press.

——. 1995. "Social Equity and Environmental Politics in Brazil: Lessons from the Rubber Tappers of Acre." *Comparative Politics* 27: 409–24.

Kingstone, Peter R. 1999. *Crafting Coalitions for Reform: Business Preferences, Political Institutions, and Neoliberal Reform in Brazil*. University Park: Pennsylvania State University Press.

——. 2000. "Muddling Through Gridlock: Economic Policy Performance, Business Responses, and Democratic Sustainability." In *Democratic Brazil: Actors, Institutions and Processes*, ed. Peter R. Kingstone and Timothy J. Power. Pittsburgh: University of Pittsburgh Press.

——. 2004. "Industrialists and Liberalization." In *Reforming Brazil*, ed. Mauricio A. Font and Anthony Peter Spanakos. Lanham, MD: Lexington Books.

Knack, Stephen, and Philip Keefer. 1997. "Does Social Capital Have an Economic Payoff? A Cross-Country Investigation." *Quarterly Journal of Economics* November: 1251–88.

Laakso, Marku, and Rein Taagepera. 1979. "Effective Number of Parties: A Measure with Application to West Europe." *Comparative Political Studies* 12: 3–27.

Lacerda, Alan Daniel Freire de. 2002. "O PT e a Unidade Partidária como Problema." *Dados – Revista de Ciências Sociais* 45:1: 39–76.

Lagos, Marta. 2001. "Between Stability and Crisis in Latin America." *Journal of Democracy* 12:1: 137–45.

Lamounier, Bolívar. 1968. "Raça e Classe na Política Brasileira." *Cadernos Brasileiros* 47: 39–50.

——. 2003. "Brazil: An Assessment of the Cardoso Administration." In *Constructing Democratic Governance in Latin America*, ed. Jorge I. Domínguez and Michael Shifter. 2nd edn, Baltimore: Johns Hopkins University Press.

Lamounier, Bolívar, and Rachel Meneguello. 1986. *Partidos Políticos e Consolidação Democrática*. São Paulo: Brasiliense.

Larach, Linda. 2001. "Brazil: Secondary Education Profile: A Summary of 'Secondary Education': Time to Move Forward." *Secondary Education Series no. 24555*. Washington, DC: World Bank.

Leeds, Elizabeth. 1996. "Cocaine and Parallel Polities in the Brazil Urban Periphery: Constraints on Local-Level Democratization." *Latin American Research Review* 31:3: 47–83.

Lessa, Renato. 1997. "A Política da Reforma Eleitoral: Considerações a Partir do Caso Brasileiro." In *Reforma do Estado e Democracia no Brasil*, ed. Eli Diniz and Sérgio de Azevedo. Brasília: Editora UnB.

Lisboa, M., and M. Viegas. 2000. "Desesperança de Vida: Homicidio em Minas Gerais, Rio de Janeiro e São Paulo, 1981–1997." *Ensaios Econômicos* 383: 1–53.

Lovell, Peggy A. 1994. "Race, Gender, and Development in Brazil." *Latin American Research Review* 29:3: 7–35.

Macaulay, Fiona. 2003. "Democratisation and the Judiciary: Competing Reform Agendas." In *Brazil Since 1985: Politics, Economy and Society*, ed. Maria D'Alva Kinzo and James Dunkerley. London: Institute of Latin American Studies.

McGuire, James W. 2001. "Democracy, Social Policy, and Mortality Decline in Brazil." Paper presented at the 23rd International Congress of the Latin American Studies Association, Washington, DC, 6–8 September.

Madrid, Raúl L. 2003. *Retiring the State: The Politics of Pension Privatization in Latin America and Beyond.* Stanford, CA: Stanford University Press.

Mainwaring, Scott. 1989. "Grassroots Popular Movements and the Struggle for Democracy: Nova Iguaçu." In *Democratizing Brazil: Problems of Transition and Consolidation,* ed. Alfred Stepan. New York: Oxford University Press.

———. 1993. "Presidentialism, Multipartism, and Democracy: The Difficult Combination." *Comparative Political Studies* 26: 198–228.

———. 1995. "Brazil: Weak Parties, Feckless Democracy." In *Building Democratic Institutions: Party Systems in Latin America,* ed. Scott Mainwaring and Timothy R. Scully. Stanford, CA: Stanford University Press.

———. 1997. "Multipartism, Robust Federalism, and Presidentialism in Brazil." In *Presidentialism and Democracy in Latin America,* ed. Scott Mainwaring and Matthew Soberg Shugart. New York: Cambridge University Press.

———. 1999. *Rethinking Party Systems in the Third Wave of Democratization: The Case of Brazil.* Stanford, CA: Stanford University Press.

Mainwaring, Scott, and Aníbal Pérez-Liñán. 1997. "Party Discipline in the Brazilian Constitutional Congress." *Legislative Studies Quarterly* 22: 453–83.

Mainwaring, Scott, and Eduardo Viola. 1984. "New Social Movements, Political Culture, and Democracy: Brazil and Argentina in the 1980s." *Telos* 61: 17–52.

Martin, Scott B. 2001. "Globalização e Imbricamento da Flexibilidade do Trabalho: Perspectivas Contemporâneas da Indústria Automobilística nas Américas (Brasil, México e Estados Unidos)." In *Competitividade e Desenvolvimento: Atores e Instituições Locais,* ed. Nadya Araujo Guimarães and Scott Martin. São Paulo: Editora SENAC.

Martínez-Lara, Javier. 1996. *Building Democracy in Brazil: The Politics of Constitutional Change, 1985–95.* New York: St Martin's Press.

Martins, Monica Diaz. 2000. "The MST Challenge to Neoliberalism." *Latin American Perspectives* 27:5: 33–45.

Martins Filho, João R., and Daniel Zirker. 2000. "Nationalism, National Security, and Amazonia: Military Perceptions and Attitudes in Contemporary Brazil." *Armed Forces and Society* 27:1: 105–29.

Maybury-Lewis, Bjorn. 1996. *The Politics of the Possible: The Brazilian Rural Workers' Trade Union Movement, 1964–1985.* Philadelphia: Temple University Press.

Melo, Marcus André. 1997. "O Jogo das Regras: A Política da Reforma Constitucional de 1993/96." *Revista Brasileira de Ciências Sociais* 33 (February): 63–85.

Meneguello, Rachel. 1989. *PT: A Formação de um Partido, 1979–1982.* São Paulo: Paz e Terra.

———. 1994. "Partidos e Tendências de Comportamento: O Cenário Político em 1994." In *Anos 90: Política e Sociedade no Brasil,* ed. Evelina Dagnino. São Paulo: Brasiliense.

Mesquita Neto, Paulo de, and Adriana Loche. 2003. "Police–Community Partnerships in Brazil." In *Crime and Violence in Latin America: Citizen Security, Democracy, and the State,* ed. Hugo Frühling, Joseph Tulchin, and Heather A. Holding. Baltimore: Johns Hopkins University Press.

Monclaire, Stephane. 2004. "Lula le pragmatique." *Politique Internationale* 102 (winter): 79–96.

Montero, Alfred P. 1998. "State Interests and the New Industrial Policy in Brazil: The Case of the Privatization of Steel, 1990–1994." *Journal of Interamerican Studies and World Affairs* 40:3: 27–62.

———. 2000. "Devolving Democracy? Political Decentralization and the New Brazilian Federalism." In *Democratic Brazil: Actors, Institutions and Processes,* ed. Peter R. Kingstone and Timothy J. Power. Pittsburgh: University of Pittsburgh Press.

——. 2002. *Shifting States in Global Markets: Subnational Industrial Policy in Contemporary Brazil and Spain.* University Park: Pennsylvania State University Press.

——. 2004. "Competitive Federalism and Distributive Conflict." In *Reforming Brazil*, ed. Mauricio A. Font and Anthony Peter Spanakos. Lanham, MD: Lexington Books.

Morgenstern, Scott. 2004. *Patterns of Legislative Politics: Roll-Call Voting in Latin America and the United States.* New York: Cambridge University Press.

Nelson, Sara. 1996. "Constructing and Negotiating Gender in Women's Police Stations in Brazil." *Latin American Perspectives* 23:1: 131–48.

Nicolau, Jairo Marconi. 1992. "A Representação Política e a Questão da Desproporcionalidade no Brasil." *Novos Estudos* 33 (July): 222–35.

Nogués, Julio J. 2003. "MERCOSUR's Labyrinth and World Regionalism." *Cuadernos de Economía* 40:121: 452–9.

Nunes Leal, Victor. 1976. *Coronelismo, Enxada e Voto: O Município e o Regime Representativo no Brasil.* São Paulo: Editora Alfa-Omega.

Nylen, William R. 1997. "Reconstructing the Workers' Party (PT): Lessons from North-Eastern Brazil." In *The New Politics of Inequality in Latin America: Rethinking Participation and Representation*, ed. Douglas A. Chalmers, Carlos M. Vilas, Katherine Hite, Scott B. Martin, Kerianne Piester, and Monique Segarra. New York: Oxford University Press.

——. 2000. "The Making of a Loyal Opposition: The Workers' Party (PT) and the Consolidation of Democracy in Brazil." In *Democratic Brazil: Actors, Institutions and Processes*, ed. Peter R. Kingstone and Timothy J. Power. Pittsburgh: University of Pittsburgh Press.

——. 2002. "Testing the Empowerment Thesis: The Participatory Budget in Belo Horizonte and Betim, Brazil." *Comparative Politics* 34 (January): 127–45.

O'Donnell, Guillermo. 1986. *Contrapontos: Autoritarismo e Democratização.* São Paulo: Vértice.

Oliveira, Francisco de. 2003. "The Duckbilled Platypus." *New Left Review* 24 (November–December): 40–57.

Palermo, Vicente. 2004. "Brasil, El Gobierno de Lula y el PT." *Nueva Sociedad* 192 (July–August): 4–11.

Partido dos Trabalhadores (PT). 2002. *Programa do Governo, 2002.* São Paulo: Partido dos Trabalhadores.

——. 2004. *PT Eleições 2004.* São Paulo: Partido dos Trabalhadores.

Pastor, Robert. 2001. *Exiting the Whirlpool: US Foreign Policy Toward Latin America and the Caribbean.* Boulder, CO: Westview Press.

Payne, Leigh. 1994. *Brazilian Industrialists and Democratic Change.* Baltimore: Johns Hopkins University Press.

Pereira, Anthony W. 1997. *The End of the Peasantry: The Rural Labor Movement in Northeast Brazil, 1961–1988.* Pittsburgh: University of Pittsburgh Press.

——. 1998. "Persecution and Farce: The Origins and Transformation of Brazil's Political Trials, 1964–1979." *Latin American Research Review* 33:1: 43–66.

——. 2000. "An Ugly Democracy? State Violence and the Rule of Law in Postauthoritarian Brazil." In *Democratic Brazil: Actors, Institutions and Processes*, ed. Peter R. Kingstone and Timothy J. Power. Pittsburgh: University of Pittsburgh Press.

——. 2004. "Agrarian Reform." In *Reforming Brazil*, ed. Mauricio A. Font and Anthony Peter Spanakos. Lanham, MD: Lexington Books.

Pereira, Anthony, and Mark Ungar. 2004. "The Persistence of the 'Mano Dura': Authoritarian Legacies and Policing in Brazil and the Southern Cone." Paper presented at the 25th Congress of the Latin American Studies Association, Las Vegas, 7–9 October.

Pereira, Luiz Carlos Bresser. 1993. "Economic Reforms and Economic Growth: Efficiency and Politics in Latin America." In *Economic Reforms in New Democracies: A Social-Democratic*

Approach, ed. Luiz Carlos Bresser Pereira, José María Maravall, and Adam Przeworski. Cambridge: Cambridge University Press.

Petras, James. 2002. "Porto Alegre 2002: A Tale of Two Forums." *Monthly Review* 53:11: 56–61.

Phillips, Nicola. 2001. "Regionalist Governance in the New Political Economy of Development: 'Relaunching' the Mercosur." *Third World Quarterly* 22: 565–83.

Pinheiro, Armando Castelar, and Ben Ross Schneider. 1995. "The Fiscal Impact of Privatisation in Latin America." *Journal of Development Studies* 31: 751–85.

Pinheiro, Paulo Sergio. 1997. "Popular Responses to State-Sponsored Violence in Brazil." In *The New Politics of Inequality in Latin America: Rethinking Participation and Representation*, ed. Douglas A. Chalmers, Carlos M. Vilas, Katherine Hite, Scott B. Martin, Kerianne Piester, and Monique Segarra. New York: Oxford University Press.

Pion-Berlin, David. 2000. "Will Soldiers Follow? Economic Integration and Regional Security in the Southern Cone." *Journal of Interamerican Studies and World Affairs* 42:1: 43–69.

Portes, Alejandro, and Kelly Hoffman. 2003. "Latin American Class Structures: Their Composition and Change During the Neoliberal Era." *Latin American Research Review* 38:1: 41–82.

Power, Timothy J. 1998a. "Brazilian Politicians and Neoliberalism: Mapping Support for the Cardoso Reforms, 1995–1997." *Journal of Interamerican Studies and World Affairs* 40:4: 51–72.

——. 1998b. "The Pen is Mightier than the Congress: Presidential Decree Power in Brazil." In *Executive Decree Authority*, ed. John M. Carey and Matthew Soberg Shugart. New York: Cambridge University Press.

——. 2000a. "Political Institutions in Democratic Brazil: Politics as a Permanent Constitutional Convention." In *Democratic Brazil: Actors, Institutions and Processes*, ed. Peter R. Kingstone and Timothy J. Power. Pittsburgh: University of Pittsburgh Press.

——. 2000b. *The Political Right in Postauthoritarian Brazil: Elites, Institutions, and Democratization*. University Park: Pennsylvania State University Press.

Power, Timothy J., and J. Timmons Roberts. 1995. "Compulsory Voting, Invalid Ballots, and Abstention in Brazil." *Political Research Quarterly* 48: 795–826.

Reich, Gary M. 1998. "The 1988 Constitution a Decade Later: Ugly Compromises Reconsidered." *Journal of Interamerican Studies and World Affairs* 40:4: 5–24.

Reis, Elisa P. 2000. "Percepções da Elite sobre Pobreza e Desigualdade." In *Desigualdade e Pobreza no Brasil*, ed. Ricardo Henriques. Rio de Janeiro: Instituto de Pesquisa Econômica Aplicada.

Remmer, Karen L. 1998. "Does Democracy Promote Interstate Cooperation? Lessons from the MERCOSUR Region." *International Studies Quarterly* 42:1: 25–51.

Resende-Santos, João. 2002. "The Origins of Security Cooperation in the Southern Cone." *Latin American Politics and Society* 44:4: 89–126.

Ribeiro, Carlos Antonio Costa, and Maria Celi Scanlon. 2003. "Class Mobility in Brazil from a Comparative Perspective." In *Brazil Since 1985: Politics, Economy and Society*, ed. Maria D'Alva Kinzo and James Dunkerley. London: Institute of Latin American Studies.

Roberts, Kenneth. 2002. "Social Inequalities without Class Cleavages in Latin America's Neoliberal Era." *Studies in Comparative International Development* 36:4: 3–33.

Rodrigues, Maria Guadalupe. 2000. "Environmental Protection Issue Networks in Amazonia." *Latin American Research Review* 35:3: 125–53.

Rosenn, Keith. 1990. "Brazil's New Constitution: An Exercise in Transient Constitutionalism for a Transitional Society." *American Journal of Comparative Law* 38: 773–802.

Sallum Jr., Brasilio. 2003. "The Changing Role of the State: New Patterns of State–Society Relations in Brazil at the End of the Twentieth Century." In *Brazil Since 1985: Politics, Economy and Society*, ed. Maria D'Alva Kinzo and James Dunkerley. London: Institute of Latin American Studies.

Samuels, David J. 2002. "Progressive Ambition, Federalism, and Pork-Barreling in Brazil." In *Legislative Politics in Latin America*, ed. Scott Morgenstern and Benito Nacif. New York: Cambridge University Press.

——. 2003. *Ambassadors of the States: Federalism, Ambition, and Congressional Politics in Brazil*. New York: Cambridge University Press.

——. 2004. "From Socialism to Social Democracy: Party Organization and the Transformation of the Workers' Party in Brazil." *Comparative Political Studies* 37:9: 999–1024.

——. n.d. "Sources of Mass Partisanship in Brazil." Unpublished paper.

Sandoval, Salvador. 2004. "Working-Class Contention." In *Reforming Brazil*, ed. Mauricio A. Font and Anthony Peter Spanakos. Lanham, MD: Lexington Books.

Schneider, Ben Ross. 2004. *Business Politics and the State in Twentieth-Century Latin America*. New York: Cambridge University Press.

Serbin, Kenneth P. 2000. "The Catholic Church, Religious Pluralism, and Democracy in Brazil." In *Democratic Brazil: Actors, Institutions and Processes*, ed. Peter R. Kingstone and Timothy J. Power. Pittsburgh: University of Pittsburgh Press.

Sikkink, Kathryn. 1996. "The Emergence, Evolution, and Effectiveness of the Latin American Human Rights Network." In *Constructing Democracy: Human Rights, Citizenship, and Society in Latin America*, ed. Elizabeth Jelin and Eric Hershberg. Boulder, CO: Westview Press.

Silva, Nelson do Valle. 1999. "Racial Differences in Income: Brazil, 1988." In *From Indifference to Inequality: Race in Contemporary Brazil*, ed. Rebecca Reichmann. University Park: Pennsylvania State University Press.

Silva, Nelson do Valle, and Carlos A. Hasenbalg. 1999. "Race and Educational Opportunity in Brazil." In *From Indifference to Inequality: Race in Contemporary Brazil*, ed. Rebecca Reichmann. University Park: Pennsylvania State University Press.

Skidmore, Thomas E. 1967. *Politics in Brazil 1930–1964: An Experiment in Democracy*. New York: Oxford University Press.

——. 2004. "Brazil's Persistent Income Inequality: Lessons from History." *Latin American Politics and Society* 46:2: 133–50.

Sola, Lourdes. 1995. "Estado, Regime Fiscal, e Ordem Monetária: Qual Estado?" *Revista Brasileira de Ciências Sociais* 10: 29–60.

——. 2004. "Financial Credibility, Legitimacy and Political Discretion: Lula da Silva Government, First Year." Mimeo, PUC-Rio de Janeiro.

Sotomayor Velázquez, Arturo C. 2004. "Civil–Military Affairs and Security Institutions in the Southern Cone: The Sources of Argentine–Brazilian Nuclear Cooperation." *Latin American Politics and Society* 46:4: 29–60.

Souza, Celina. 1997. *Constitutional Engineering in Brazil: The Politics of Federalism and Decentralization*. New York: St Martin's Press.

Souza, Maria do Carmo Campello de. 1976. *Estado e Partidos Políticos no Brasil (1930 a 1964)*. São Paulo: Alfa-Omega.

Stepan, Alfred. 1971. *The Military in Politics: Changing Patterns in Brazil*. Princeton, NJ: Princeton University Press.

——. 1988. *Rethinking Military Politics: Brazil and the Southern Cone*. Princeton, NJ: Princeton University Press.

——. 1999. "Federalism and Democracy: Beyond the US Model." *Journal of Democracy* 10:4: 19–34.

Tarrow, Sidney. 1998. *Power in Movement: Social Movements and Contentious Politics*. 2nd edn, New York: Cambridge University Press.

Tendler, Judith. 1997. *Good Government in the Tropics*. Baltimore: Johns Hopkins University Press.

US Department of State. 2004. *International Narcotics Control Strategy Report (INCSR) 2003*. URL: http://www.state.gov/g/inl/rls/nrcrpt/2003/ (accessed 20 May).

Vázquez, Manuel A. 1999. "Toward a New Agenda for the Study of Religion in the Americas." *Journal of Interamerican Studies and World Affairs* 41:4: 1–20.

Vélez, C., and V. Foster. 2000. "Public Social Expenditures in Brazil: An International Comparison." In *Brazil: Selected Issues in Social Protection*, vol. 2. Washington, DC: World Bank.

Wampler, Brian. 2004. "Expanding Accountability Through Participatory Institutions: Mayors, Citizens, and Budgeting in Three Brazilian Municipalities." *Latin American Politics and Society* 46:2: 73–99.

Weyland, Kurt. 1993. "The Rise and Fall of President Collor and its Impact on Brazilian Democracy." *Journal of Interamerican Studies and World Affairs* 35:1: 1–36.

——. 1996. *Democracy without Equity: Failures of Reform in Brazil*. Pittsburgh: University of Pittsburgh Press.

——. 1998. "From Leviathan to Gulliver: The Decline of the Developmental State in Brazil." *Governance* 11:1: 51–75.

——. 2000. "The Brazilian State in the New Democracy." In *Democratic Brazil: Actors, Institutions and Processes*, ed. Peter R. Kingstone and Timothy J. Power. Pittsburgh: University of Pittsburgh Press.

Wittkoff, E. Peter. 2003. "Brazil's SIVAM: Surveillance against Crime and Terrorism." *International Journal of Intelligence and Counterintelligence* 16: 543–60.

World Bank. 2001. *Brazil: Critical Issues in Social Security*. Washington, DC: World Bank.

——. 2003. *Brazil: Inequality and Economic Development*. Washington, DC: World Bank.

Index